$ õ 95

D1015300

PREACHING
THE
NEW COMMON
LECTIONARY

PREACHING
THE
NEW COMMON LECTIONARY

YEAR A

Lent, Holy Week,
Easter

Commentary by:

Fred B. Craddock
John H. Hayes
Carl R. Holladay
Gene M. Tucker

ABINGDON PRESS
Nashville

Preaching the New Common Lectionary
Year A   Lent, Holy Week, Easter
Copyright © 1986 by Abingdon Press
All rights reserved.

No part of this work may be reproduced or transmitted in any form or by any means, electronic or mechanical, including photocopying and recording, or by any information storage or retrieval system, except as may be expressly permitted by the 1976 Copyright Act or in writing from the publisher. Requests for permission should be addressed in writing to Abingdon Press, 201 Eighth Avenue, South, Nashville, TN 37202.

This book is printed on acid-free paper.

Library of Congress Cataloging in Publication Data
Main entry under title:
   Preaching the new common lectionary. Year A,
   Lent, Holy Week, Easter.
   Includes index.
   1. Bible—Homiletical use. 2. Bible—Liturgical
   lessons, English. I. Craddock, Fred B.
   BS534.5.P7275 1986   251   86-10897
       (pbk.: alk. paper)
   ISBN 0-687-33852-2

Scripture quotations unless otherwise noted are from the Revised Standard Version of the Bible, copyrighted 1946, 1952, © 1971, 1973 by the Division of Christian Education of the National Council of the Churches of Christ in the U.S.A., and used by permission.

Those noted NEB are from The New English Bible. © the Delegates of the Oxford University Press and the Syndics of the Cambridge University Press 1961, 1970. Reprinted by permission.

Those noted JB are from The Jerusalem Bible, copyright © 1966 by Darton, Longman & Todd, Ltd. and Doubleday & Company, Inc. Used by permission of the publisher.

Those noted NJPSV are from *Tanakh: A New Translation of the Holy Scriptures According to the Traditional Hebrew Text*. Copyright © 1985 by the Jewish Publication Society of America.

Those marked NIV are from the Holy Bible, New International Version. Copyright © 1973, 1978, 1984, International Bible Society.

MANUFACTURED BY THE PARTHENON PRESS AT
NASHVILLE, TENNESSEE, UNITED STATES OF AMERICA

Contents

Easter

Special Day

Introduction

It might be helpful to the reader if we make a few remarks about our understanding of our task and what we have sought to accomplish in this volume. The following comments will touch on four topics.

The Scripture in Preaching

There is no substitute for direct exposure to the biblical text, both for the preacher in preparation and for the listener in worship. The Scriptures are therefore not only studied privately but read aloud as an act of worship in and of itself and not solely as prelude to a sermon. The sermon is an interpretation of Scripture in the sense that the preacher seeks to bring the text forward into the present in order to effect a new hearing of the Word. In this sense the text has its future and its fulfillment in preaching. In fact, the Bible itself is the record of the continual rehearing and reinterpreting of its own traditions in new settings and for new generations of believers. New settings and new circumstances are properly as well as inescapably integral to a hearing of God's Word in and through the text.

Whatever else may be said to characterize God's Word, it is always appropriate to the hearers. But the desire to be immediately relevant should not abbreviate study of the text or divorce the sermon from the biblical tradition. Such sermons are orphaned, released without memory into the world. It is the task of the preacher and teacher to see that the principle of fidelity to Scripture is not abandoned in the life and worship of the church. The endeavor to understand a text in its historical, literary, and theological contexts does create, to be sure, a sense of distance between the Bible and the congregation. The preacher may grow impatient during this period of feeling a long way from a sermon. But this time of study can be most fruitful. By holding text and parishioners apart for a while, the preacher can hear each more clearly and exegete each more honestly. Then, when the two intersect in the sermon, neither the text nor the congregation is consumed by the other. Because the Bible is an ancient book, it invites the preacher back into its world in order to understand; because the Bible is the church's Scripture, it moves forward into our world and addresses us here and now.

The Lectionary and Preaching

Ever-increasing numbers of preachers are using a lectionary as a guide for preaching and worship. The intent of lectionaries is to provide for the church over a given period of time (usually three years) large units of Scripture that have been selected because they carry the central message of the Bible and that have been arranged according to the seasons of the Christian Year.

Lectionaries are not designed to limit one's message or restrict the freedom of the pulpit. On the contrary, churches that use a lectionary usually hear more Scripture in worship than those that do not. And ministers who preach from the lectionary find themselves stretched into areas of the canon into which they would not have gone had they kept to the path of personal preference. Other values of the lectionary are well-known: the readings provide a common ground for discussions in ministerial peer groups; family worship can more easily join public worship through shared readings; ministers and worship committees can work with common biblical texts to prepare services that have movement and integrity; and the lectionary encourages more disciplined study and advance preparation. All these and other values are increased if the different churches share a common lectionary. A common lectionary could conceivably generate a community-wide Christian conversation.

This Book and Preaching

This volume is not designed as a substitute for work with the biblical text; on the contrary, its intent is to encourage such work. Nor is it our desire to relieve the preacher of regular visits to concordances, lexicons, and commentaries, but it is our hope that the comments on the texts here will be sufficiently germinal to give direction and purpose to those visits to major reference works. Our commentaries are efforts to be faithful to the text and to begin moving the text toward the pulpit. There are no sermons as such here, nor could there be. No one can preach long distance. Only the one who preaches can do an exegesis of the listeners and mix into sermon preparation enough local soil so as to effect an indigenous hearing of the Word. But we hope we have contributed to that end. The reader will also notice that, while each of us has been aware of the other readings for each service, there has been no attempt to offer a collaborated commentary on all texts or a homogenized interpretation as though there were not four texts but one. We have tried to respect the integrity of each biblical passage and remain within the limits of our own areas of knowledge. It is assumed that the season of the year, the needs of the listeners, the preacher's own abilities, as well as the overall unity of the message of the Scriptures will prompt the preacher to find among the four readings the word for the day.

A final word about our comments. The lections from the Psalter have been treated in the same manner as the other readings even though some Protestant churches often omit the reading of the psalm or replace it with a hymn. We have chosen to regard the psalm as an equal among the texts, primarily for three reasons: (1) there is growing interest in the use of Psalms in public worship and comments on them may help make that use more informed; (2) the Psalms were a major source for worship and preaching in the early church and continue to inspire and inform Christian witness; and (3) comments on the Psalms may make this volume helpful to Roman Catholic preachers who have maintained the long tradition of using the Psalms in Christian services.

This Season and Preaching

Of all the seasons of the Christian's pilgrimage, Lent has probably been most abused. It has in certain times and places become a period of excessive introspection, empty abstinence from tidbits of affluence, and the enjoyment of the gloom of self-denial. Correction of such excesses and distortions does not lie, however, in non-observance of Lent, but rather in the recovery of its rich tradition. The image of forty days as a period of engagement with God, of repentance and prayer is deeply imbedded in Scripture. In the early church, Lent became a time of preparation for baptism, and among the baptized, a time for reflection upon one's baptism and renewal of vows. And in all times and places, Lent looks toward God's act in the resurrection. Sober awareness of sin is appropriate, to be sure, but so is profound joy.

Holy Week is a time of reflection upon the suffering and death of Christ. A major theological task of the early disciples was to understand and accept the death of Jesus as an event transcending tragedy. How did Jesus' passion relate to the purpose of God, to Jesus' own ministry, and to his followers' hopes? In the Passover traditions, in the Suffering Servant of Isaiah, and in the Jewish interpretations of sacrifice, the disciples were able not only to interpret Jesus as "our Passover" (I Cor. 5:7-8) but also to understand in a new way their own sufferings. The preacher will find the Old Testament resources not only enriching during this week but also helpful as a guard against any residue of anti-Semitism which may darken unduly the biblical reports of Jesus' death.

Easter is not one day but a season. It is silence; what does one say when running from an empty tomb? It is a shout, "He is risen!" It is a question, Where do we go from here? When Easter morning fades into late afternoon and some disciples begin to say, "I am going fishing," the church prays and waits for Pentecost.

> *Fred B. Craddock* (Gospels)
> *John H. Hayes* (Psalms)
> *Carl R. Holladay* (Epistles and Acts)
> *Gene M. Tucker* (Old Testament)

Ash Wednesday

*Joel 2:1-2, 12-17a; Psalm 51:1-12; II Corinthians 5:20b–6:2
(3-10); Matthew 6:1-6, 16-21*

Providing guidance for Lent and setting the mood for the season are four texts concerning prayer and piety. The Old Testament reading is a prophetic and priestly summons to a community service of confession and repentance as the day of the Lord approaches. The psalm is an actual prayer of confession and petition by an individual. In many such petitions the psalmist asks for deliverance from illness or disaster, but here he prays for relief from sin and its effects. In the Gospel reading the hearers of the Sermon on the Mount are warned that public piety—including prayer and fasting—for the sake of displaying one's faithfulness is false piety. The epistolary reading points to God's response to the confession of sin, for God "made him to be sin who knew no sin, so that in him we might become the righteousness of God" (II Cor. 5:21).

Joel 2:1-2, 12-17*a*

It is appropriate that verses from the Book of Joel lead the church on a solemn occasion that initiates a season of penitence, fasting, and self-examination, for the book developed and was used in similar liturgical contexts in ancient Israel. The book in general certainly is a prophetic one, and these verses in particular reflect that fact. But there are priestly and liturgical dimensions as well. In fact, many commentators rightly have called Joel a cultic prophet and the book a prophetic liturgy.

The verses before us today contain that merging of prophetic and priestly sensibilities and perspectives on the relationship between God and people. The prophetic

13

dimension, while more detailed in chapter 1 and in 2:3-11, sets the tone at the outset. In Joel 1 and 2:3-11 it is present in the descriptions of the approaching judgment upon the land. In our reading the prophetic perspective is apparent in the announcement that the day of the Lord is coming (verse 1). Thus, while the prophet's explicit message is a call to prayer, fasting, and repentance, that message assumes the announcement of impending divine judgment.

The expectation of the day of the Lord in Joel is almost, but not quite, an apocalyptic expectation. Joel 2:1-2 is closely paralleled by Zephaniah 1:15 and stands in a long prophetic tradition. One of the clearest articulations of that tradition is also one of its oldest, Amos 5:18:

> "Woe to you who desire the day of the Lord!
> Why would you have the day of the Lord?
> It is darkness, and not light."

Clearly, Amos announces the reversal of a contemporary (eighth-century) hope. The tradition behind the hope for the day of the Lord probably was the holy war, the time when Yahweh would act against his enemies. For Amos and other early prophets (cf. Isa. 2:9-11), the people of Israel had become Yahweh's enemies. That is no less true for Joel, who clearly indicates that Yahweh, marching at the head of his army, is ready to destroy his enemies, the people of Israel (verse 11).

Thus the threat of the end, if not of history at least of the covenant people, provides the urgency for Joel's call. The cry is one both of alarm—the trumpet (verse 1) announces the approach of the enemy, "a great and powerful people" (verse 2)—and a summons to assemble for a service of worship. What are the people to do in the shadow of the day of the Lord, before the threat of divine wrath? They must assemble to fast and pray.

The priestly liturgical dimensions of Joel are present in the instructions for the service of worship. Speaking for Yahweh, the prophet calls for the people to "return" (verses 12, 13) to the Lord, instructs them to fast, weep, and mourn, and then spells out the details of the assembly, including the duties of the priests (verses 14-17). The religious ceremony in view here is one that is well known from elsewhere in the Old Testament, especially from the Psalms of lament or complaint. An individual who was ill or otherwise in trouble called for a priest who would gather the person's primary group—family and neighbors—for a service of prayer. At the center of such services were the Psalms of individual lament or complaint. Likewise, when the people were threatened by drought, famine, or enemy invasion, they gathered to plead with God. The prayers they offered (see Pss. 44; 74; 89; Lam. 5) included invocations of the divine name, confessions, affirmations of confidence in God, and, above all, petitions for divine favor. Other texts that reflect such services are Judges 20:26-28; I Kings 8:33-36, 44-45; Jonah 3:5-10; and Isaiah 63:7–64:11.

Joel, like the other texts, emphasizes the corporate, communal dimension of the prayer service. After all, it was the entire community that was in trouble. Thus, everyone is to participate, men and women, from elders to nursing infants. Even the new bride and bridegroom are to join in (verse 16).

The people's public behavior is an important part of the time of prayer. Joel instructs them to fast, weep, and mourn. These actions are known elsewhere in the Old Testament as expressions of grief, as rituals of sorrow following death (I Sam. 31:13; Jth. 16:24). Their purpose here is twofold: to convince God that the people know the seriousness of the threat and to demonstrate the sincerity of their repentance. Contemporary Christians, taking seriously New Testament texts such as our Gospel reading for today, often disparage such outward displays of piety, and rightly so. However, such rituals have their value, for habits of the body may even shape the habits of the heart. One's feelings may be trained by such rituals, even to experience genuine repentance. But lest the point should be missed, Joel enjoins his hearers, "rend your hearts and not your garments" (verse 13).

At the center of the text is the call for the people to return to the Lord their God. This "return" is the directing of their full devotion to the God of Israel, and it is also repentance. Remarkably, there is no mention of the sin or sins for which the community is to repent. The fundamental concern is with orientation in the right direction. On the one hand, the urgency comes from awareness of the impending day of the Lord, the possibility of a judgment that would end the community's life. But on the other hand, the call to repent is based on the conviction that God "is gracious and merciful, slow to anger, and abounding in steadfast love." Indeed, Joel urges all his hearers to repent, for God is one who "repents of evil" (verse 13); that is, the Lord is both able and willing to be affected by the people.

Psalm 51:1-12

This psalm, used on Ash Wednesday in all three years of the cycle as well as on the Fifth Sunday of Lent, Year B, is the penitential psalm par excellence. When Jewish exegetes sought to associate the sentiments of this psalm with the realities of some historical event, they surmised that it must reflect the remorse, contrition, and yearning for forgiveness that David surely felt after being castigated by the prophet Nathan for David's order that led to the death of Uriah so he might possess Uriah's wife (see the superscription or heading of the psalm).

The psalm contains the typical structural features of a lament: an opening address to God (verses 1-2), a description of the predicament, here in the form of a statement confessing sin and wrongdoing (verses 3-5), a plea asking for help, in this case the forgiveness of sin and the rejuvenation of the self (verses 6-12), and a vow committing the supplicant to acts expressive of thanksgiving, in this case, ministry in the form of evangelizing praise (verses 13-17).

This psalm admirably fits with the other readings for today. The Old Testament text from Joel calls for fasting and repentance; the Epistle reading points to Christ as the means of forgiveness from sin; and the Gospel reading offers Jesus' word on the sentiments proper to the practice of piety (or "works of righteousness"), prayer, and fasting.

Psalm 51 may be viewed and preached as theological reflection on the human predicament. As such, the psalm touches on multiple aspects of human guilt and sin as well as the multiform character of human re-creation and the involvement of the divine in both.

In preaching on this psalm, one entry into the text is to focus on what is said about the human predicament, about the human person as sinner.

1. Sin is experienced as a state of being, a condition of the total life. "I was brought forth in iniquity, and in sin did my mother conceive me" (verse 5). Such an assertion comes near not only to the Christian doctrine of original sin but also to the Freudian realization that the parenting generation stamps its image indelibly upon its custodial children. The concept of original sin sees each person sharing, in the act of being human itself, both the state of sin and the consequences of sin. Modern psychology similarly recognizes that children are inevitably, even if not totally, incarcerated in the personality prisons that their parents have inhabited; the scars and festers of the past always mark and contaminate the present.

2. Sin is willful action which ultimately means that human wrong is committed against God. "Against thee, thee only, have I sinned" (verse 4). Wrong and misconduct only become sin when viewed within a context that involves the divine. To speak of sin is to move language beyond the realm of anthropology and into the arena of theology.

3. Sin contaminates, stains, pollutes, and renders unclean. Much of this psalm is concerned with the discoloring and polluting quality of sin and speaks of salvation in "purifying" terminology—wash, cleanse, purge, blot out. The ancient rabbis recognized this dimension in the psalm and taught that "every man who commits a transgression is as unclean as though he had touched a dead body and must be purified." The idea that sin is a pollutant which permeates the whole person means that there is no such thing as an isolated event or action. A sinful act discolors, disrupts, and skews the entire personality like a fading cloth in a family wash.

Over against the psalm's intense sense of sin, presented confessionally, the composition also gives expression to components involved in forgiveness and the renewal of life, expressed in the form of pleas and petitions.

1. There are first of all, the requests that God change the worshiper. In a series of pleas, the psalmist asks to be changed by divine action—teach me, purge me, wash me. There is no striving for divine favor, no effect to achieve divine approval; merely the cascading requests to be the passive recipient of divine action.

2. A second set of pleas focuses on requests for new or renewed experiences—joy, gladness, rejoicing. These may be viewed as concomitant with or the result of the changes in personal status requested.

3. Finally, the psalmist also requests an intimacy with the divine (verses 11-12).

II Corinthians 5:20*b*–6:2 (3-10)

Since this text serves as the epistolary reading for Ash Wednesday for all three years, the reader may wish to consult our remarks in the *Lent, Holy Week, Easter* volumes for Years B and C. Parts of this text also occur elsewhere in the *Common Lectionary:* 5:16-21 in the Fourth Sunday of Lent in Year C and 5:18–6:2 in Proper 7 for Year B. Additional remarks may be found in connection with those readings.

What makes this text suitable for Ash Wednesday is its stress on reconciliation. As Christians, we are called to "be reconciled to God" (verse 20*b*). Naturally this requires a penitent spirit on our part. Being Christian means that we have been forgiven, but it also means that we stand in constant need of forgiveness. This text recognizes above all that our need to be reconciled to God is an ongoing need. We cannot presume that our status before God is ensured. It is rather a relationship that must be constantly nurtured and renewed, and this renewal begins when we acknowledge our need for God's reconciling love.

We should begin by seeing this text as directly confronting Christians—those already in Christ. Living together in community often finds us at odds with one another. This was certainly the context out of which our text emerges—Paul in serious conflict with other Christian teachers. The polemical tone of Second Corinthians is well known, especially chapters 10–13, and the Epistle as a whole unfolds the seriously strained relationship between Paul and the Corinthian church. The place where severe alienation had occurred was in the local congregation, which is often the place where alienation is most sharply felt and reconciliation is most difficult to achieve. What strikes us about today's text is that it rings so true to the life we know in churches. At one level, reconciliation is envisioned on a cosmic scale, as God and the entire world being reconciled to each other (verse 19). At another level, it is envisioned on a local scale, as that which must occur—and recur—among communities of believers.

Verse 21 reminds us that reconciliation is Christo-centric. It is "in him," that is, "in Christ" that we are enabled to become God's righteousness. Christ serves as the locus of reconciliation, the sphere in which our relationship to God and one another is renewed—not only the sphere but the catalyst. It was first the work of Christ, the one who "knew no sin yet became sin" (verse 21*a*), that embodied the paradox of reversal: taking on a status that was not rightfully his—sin—so that we might acquire a character and existence that is not rightfully ours—God's righteousness. The text centers our thoughts on Christ as both agent and sphere of reconciliation—the meeting ground where enemies can become friends, the crucible where pride gives way to penitence.

Another theme presented by today's text is Paul's insistence that we are "God's co-workers" (6:1). The one who has experienced reconciliation becomes a collaborator with God in extending reconciliation into the world. The experience of reconciliation translates into a ministry of reconciliation. The sense of forgiveness becomes expressed in a sense of mission. The God who reconciles us, who forgives us, also commissions us. Here we are reminded that our experience of God's grace, if it has any power at all, compels us to be instruments of that grace in the world. First there is the compelling encounter, then the compelling mission.

We should see clearly this connection between reconciliation and the ministry of reconciliation, between our experience of God and our ministry for God. In his inaugural sermon in the parish of Safenwil, Barth told his congregation,

"I am not speaking to you of God because I am a pastor. I am a pastor because I *must* speak to you of God, if I am to remain true to myself, my better self." The ministry of reconciliation derives from our profound experience of being reconciled.

In a similar vein, Buber wrote, "Meeting with God does not come to man in order that he may concern himself with God, but in order that he may confirm that there is meaning in the world. All revelation is summons and sending . . . . God remains present to you when you have been sent forth; he who goes on a mission has always God before him: the truer the fulfillment the stronger and more constant the nearness."

If we have experienced God's reconciling love this directly, and if it has affected us this profoundly, we can understand the sense of urgency of today's text: "Now is the acceptable time; . . . now is the day of salvation" (6:2). Our ministry can easily become a routine of postponement and accommodation. Ours can became a strategy of gradualism. We may work for change but it may be glacial. There are times when slow change is better than rapid, radical change, but today's text sounds the latter note. It confronts us with God's *now*. God has responded decisively in our behalf (6:2). We are now called to respond as decisively in God's behalf.

Matthew 6:1-6, 16-21

Ash Wednesday begins Lent and the believer's journey to Holy Week and Easter. Over the entrance to that path of repentance and prayer are the words of Matthew 6:1: "Beware of practicing your piety before men in order to be seen by them; for then you will have no reward from your Father who is in heaven." The words are not to frighten but to alert the pilgrim to the seductions that beset the practice of one's faith, seductions that can for the unwary rob piety of its power and appropriateness and turn the sanctuary of devotion into a theater. "Be careful" (NEB, TEV). We will attend later to the dangers pointed out in our lection, but first a few words about the literary structure of Matthew 6:1-6, 16-21.

Today's reading consists of three parts:

First, there is a general warning against a public display of religion (6:1). Having stated at 5:20 that the righteousness of the disciples is to exceed that of the scribes and Pharisees, it is vital that Jesus warn against any distortions of righteousness which might be spawned by that demand. After all, "to exceed" or "to be greater than" could be taken by some as the language of competition which would, of course, disease at the outset the understanding of Kingdom living.

Second, three acts of devotion: alms, prayer, and fasting (6:2-6, 16-18) serve as concrete cases in which the general alert of 6:1 is applied. Verses 7-15 are omitted for two reasons: first, they are of a different literary form, interrupting in a sense the trinity of "when you give alms," "when you pray," and "when you fast." This threefold formula bears all the marks of careful composition, apparently a portion of a catechism for new members. Second, verses 7-15 are omitted because it is clear Matthew used the introduction of the subject of prayer as the occasion to insert the Lord's Prayer. That Luke placed it elsewhere (11:1-4) indicates that the Lord's Prayer owes its specific context to the Gospel writer. Neither it nor verses 1-6, 16-21 are violated by its omission from our lesson here.

The third and final portion of today's reading consists of verses 19-21. Originally verse 21, which is found almost word for word in Luke 12:34, may have existed separately. It is singular in its address (you, your) and in its reference to treasure or riches, whereas verses 19-20 are plural in both cases. The three verses address materialism and fit more easily with what follows than with what precedes. However, materialism is certainly not unrelated to the life of righteousness, especially to the first of the three acts of one's faith, giving alms. In fact, the injunction against laying up treasures on earth (verse 19) could without strain be related to verses 1-6, 16-18, in that piety for public display, which has its reward in human praise, could be a form of collecting earthly treasure.

Clearly, however, the heart of the text before us concerns the giving of alms, prayer, and fasting. These good works of Judaism are to be continued in the Christian community. After all, Jesus has already said that he did not come to abolish the law and the prophets (5:17). Any broad rejection of fundamental ethical behavior or acts of devotion toward

God simply because the synagogue had embraced them was not and is not permitted the church. In fact, the interpreter must beware of easy dichotomies that falsely set an inner Christianity against an outer Judaism. And the warnings against hypocrisy are not given here in some triumphal attack on the synagogue but rather because the church suffers under the very same tendency.

What precisely is the danger about which the reader is being told to be careful? Are these acts of religion intrinsically flawed and hence to be avoided? Of course not. The text says *when* you do acts of charity, *when* you pray, *when* you fast. Who can imagine a life before God that offers no charity, lifts no prayer for self and others, never abstains from food that those without can be fed? Is the warning, then, against doing these things by habit? Of course not. There is no better friend of the good and fruitful life than habit. Jesus went to the synagogue on the Sabbath as was his habit (Luke 4:16). Not every Christian activity need be accompanied every time by emotional investment, nor does visceral authentication function as the criterion by which an act is called genuine or sincere. The danger is in turning the sanctuary of one's devotion to God into a theater, with alms, prayer, and fasting going on stage for applause. The text is laced with the language of a public show: trumpets, masked faces, acting (hypocrisy), and an applauding audience. Perhaps nothing is so attractive, so tempting as public praise. It is meat and bread to the human ego, but it can erode the fundamental posture of the Christian life—before God.

First Sunday of Lent

Genesis 2:4b-9, 15-17, 25–3:7; Psalm 130; Romans 5:12-19;
Matthew 4:1-11

The leading concerns of the texts for the First Sunday of Lent are temptation, sin, and the effects of sin. The Old Testament reading consists of selections from the account of the creation and fall of the first human beings. In the epistolary text Paul presents his interpretation of that Old Testament tradition in the light of the life, death, and resurrection of Jesus. Matthew's account of Jesus in the wilderness, a highly appropriate reading for a season of feasting and prayer, likewise focuses on temptation. The responsorial psalm is a prayer of lament acknowledging human sin while articulating confidence in God's willingness to forgive, in his steadfast love and in his redemption.

Genesis 2:4*b*-9, 15-17, 25–3:7

In each of the years of the lectionary cycle the Old Testament readings for the successive Sundays of Lent present summaries of the history of ancient Israel's relationship with God. For this year the story begins with creation and the fall (Gen. 2–3), moves on to the promise to Abraham (Gen. 12), leads us with the people of Israel out of Egypt and into the wilderness (Exod. 17), shows us the anointing of David as king (I Sam. 16), and then, beyond the Babylonian Exile, leaves us with Ezekiel's vision of the valley of dry bones, bones that the Lord promises to revive.

These verses from Genesis 2 and 3 give a relatively full summary of the total story that begins with 2:4*b* and concludes in 3:24. The two chapters are the Yahwistic writer's account of the creation of human beings (2:4*b*-25), of the first couple's disobedience (3:1-13), and of the results of that

23

disobedience (3:14-24). The Yahwistic source is generally considered to be the oldest written document of the Pentateuch, perhaps as early as the tenth century B.C. In contrast with the creation story in Genesis 1:1–2:4*a*, this one refers to God with the proper name Yahweh ("Lord" in most translations), sees creation as presuming the existence of dry land (2:5-6), and concentrates on the establishment of the conditions of human existence rather than the creation of the cosmos as a whole.

After an aside that gives the time and circumstances (2:4*b*-6), the writer presents—in almost systematic fashion—an account of the establishment of human life as God meant it to be. First, there is life itself, understood as a divine gift (2:7). The human being, according to this understanding, is not a two- or three-part creature, but the unity of physical matter—ordinary dust from the ground—and "the breath of life." This breath is no spirit with an existence apart from the physical stuff. Second, Yahweh gives the creature freedom and limits, leaving him with a choice to make: "You may freely eat of every tree of the garden; but of the tree of the knowledge of good and evil you shall not eat" (2:16-17). Third, Yahweh gives the man work to do, putting him "in the garden of Eden to till it and keep it" (2:15). Work itself is thus not a curse, but one of those factors that makes this creature human.

Another essential element is reported in the verses omitted from our reading for today, the creation of the first woman. One point of this episode is that community, even if only in the presence of the primary family unit, is necessary for this creature to be human. Another purpose is to affirm the goodness of sexuality: the two become "one flesh," that is, unite and produce children. Finally, in a narrative aside, the writer affirms that they were "both naked, and were not ashamed" (2:25). All these factors, however distorted, are seen to be present where full human life exists.

But the direction of the story changes dramatically in chapter 3 with the introduction of a new character, the "serpent." The writer is careful to point out that the serpent was a "wild creature that the Lord God had made" (3:1), but he is "more subtle than any other." The snake is no divine or angelic force against God; he is part of creation. His role is simply to pose the tempting questions, to present the possibility of disobedience to the woman. Note that the serpent draws the woman into a conversation with a question that cannot be answered with a simple yes or no (verse 2), and that when the woman answers she actually makes the prohibition more restrictive than Yahweh had in the first place ("neither shall you touch it," verse 3). The snake's response denies Yahweh's threat of the death penalty and questions his motives: "You will not die. For God knows that when you eat of it your eyes will be opened, and you will be like God, knowing good and evil" (3:4-5).

The woman is convinced to taste the fruit because it was good to eat, was attractive, and—the serpent had told her—would "make one wise" (verse 6). She then offers it to her husband and he accepts. The traditional image of the woman as the temptress who led the man astray is an exaggeration of this account. To be sure, the man himself blames the woman, and in the same breath that he blames Yahweh: "The woman whom *thou* gavest to be with me" (3:12, italics added).

Following in the wake of the simple act of disobedience is a series of effects, none of them good. The man and woman do gain "knowledge," most of it amounting to the loss of innocence. First, they know they were naked; that is, they experience shame. Second, they know fear (3:8), hiding from Yahweh. Third, they experience estrangement, from one another, from the world—represented by the snake—and from God (3:12-13). Then Yahweh pronounces judgments upon each of the three in turn (3:14-19). The purpose of these poetic lines is to account for the pains and contradictions in the world and especially in human life. Work is not a curse for the man—he had been a farmer from the beginning—but his work becomes harder and frustrating because the relationship between effort and results is unpredictable (3:17-19*a*). Moreover, death is not here the curse, for the creature had always been made of dust—here the apostle Paul goes beyond the Old Testament account. Rather, the man is to be reminded of his mortality every time he looks at the earth (3:19), and when God drives the first couple out of the garden, he prevents them from attaining immortality (3:22-24).

Taken as a whole, the purpose of Genesis 2:4b–3:24 is to account for—to explain and interpret—the present circumstances of human life, and in particular its brokenness. The first couple, and all their successors, carry with them the memory or vision of the way life could or should be, but they face the future with ambiguity and tension. A major purpose of the story, then, is to account for human evil and suffering, and it does so mainly in moral terms, by showing the effects of disobedience. It should not be difficult at all for contemporary readers and hearers to identify with the characters in the story, and thereby to better understand themselves, their world, and their God.

Psalm 130

One of the pilgrim psalms (see Pss. 120–134), this psalm nicely complements the other readings for today. The Old Testament reading from Genesis contains one of the Hebrew accounts of the creation of humans. The Epistle lesson builds on the image of the first Adam as sinner. The Gospel lesson describes some aspects of temptation in terms of Jesus' stay in the wilderness. Psalm 130, in this context of readings, may be viewed as reflection on the human predicament and as a pointer to hope and confidence in God.

An initial word about the structure and content of the psalm is in order. Although the psalm may be read as rather straightforward and continuous in content, it is actually rather complex. This can be seen from the different addresses in the psalm. In verses 1-4, God is addressed, in a petitioning, supplicating tone, by an individual worshiper. In verses 5-6, some human audience is addressed in very confessional tones. Finally, in verses 7-8, the community (Israel) is addressed in an admonishing and directive tone.

The address to the Deity (verses 1-4) is fundamentally a description of the human condition although verse 2 appeals to and makes requests for help from God. The human condition is described as "the depths," or at least this is the condition from which prayer is offered. The term "depths" is frequently used to refer to the depths of the seas (see Isa. 51:10; Ezek. 27:34). As such, the expression could be used to symbolize remoteness from God and to characterize the distress of the human predicament (see Jon. 2:2-3). The "depths" may be another way of speaking about Sheol, the world of the dead, the world isolated and estranged from God. At any rate, the "depths" give expression to that experience of life when everything seems askew and out of harmony. It is that point that lies at the outer edge of human control.

A second description of the human condition is found in verse 3. Humans experience life and know themselves as sinners. If God kept a full record, a complete tab on human sin, then no one would warrant being spared (see I Kings 8:46; Ps. 143:2; Prov. 20:9). Other texts, for example Psalms 15 and 24, assume that human beings can measure up to divinely set standards. Here, however, we have a very pessimistic, or realistic, reading of the human situation.

Over against the human experience of being overwhelmed by life (the depths of verse 1) and the realization of the complete misalignment of our existence (the iniquities of verse 3), there stands a theological affirmation about God, an affirmation that relativizes the human predicament—with God there is forgiveness (verse 4). Such an affirmation of forgiveness in spite of the human condition led Martin Luther to speak of the Pauline quality of this psalm.

The second section of the psalms, verses 5-6, is a confessional statement to a human audience. In addressing God, the worshiper in verses 1-4 assumed a position of subordination, perhaps to elicit a favorable response from the divine. In addressing the human audience, the worshiper is allowed to exude confidence and to affirm a hopeful expectation. The speaker describes the waiting as being as intense as that of a watchman—a military sentry—watching for the dawn, when he would be relieved of duty and allowed to relax without the strain and responsibility of staying constantly alert. Perhaps the worshiper has been charged with some crime or been accused of some wrong. If so then "to wait for God" was to wait for a verdict on his case.

The final stanza, a call for the nation to trust in Yahweh (verses 7-8), sounds a bit odd. Does some individual worshiper suddenly address the nation? Or the community assembled in the temple? Or is this perhaps the king speaking? Or maybe a priest addressing worshipers assembled in the sanctuary? Under whatever circumstances, the psalm affirms that with God, there is constancy of love and a plenitude of redemption. Ultimately, the power behind all life is benevolent and beneficent.

Romans 5:12-19

This same text also serves as the epistolary reading for Proper 7 in Year A. The reader may wish to consult our remarks in *After Pentecost, Year A.*

It may be that Christ is the one through whom we are made righteous before God and come to have peace with God, as Paul declares in the preceding verses (5:1-11). But it is not at all obvious how this can be. How is it that one person can affect the destiny of all persons? It is one thing for one person to die in behalf of another person, for one life to be given in exchange for another life, perhaps even for several other lives. It is quite another thing to think of one person's destiny affecting and determining the destiny of every other person—for all time and in every place. How can one person have universal impact, either for good or evil?

These are the questions at the heart of today's passage. They trigger some of Paul's most original thinking about Christ, indeed they help shape his Adam Christology. Today's text is one of two central texts in which he articulates his theological conviction that Christ should be seen as a new Adam (cf. I Cor. 15:20-22). His reflections on Christ as a second Adam should be seen in relation to his theology of the new creation (II Cor. 4:6; 5:16-19). As he saw it, the Christ-event could only be properly understood as a reenactment of Genesis 1. It was a moment of cosmic reordering, the results of which were as dramatically new as was God's original creation.

But the focus of today's text is not so much on the old creation as compared with the new creation, as it is on the *old*

Adam and the *new* Adam. Paul's theological reflections are thoroughly influenced by Genesis 1–3 and its account of how sin and death entered the world through Adam's disobedience (cf. Gen. 2:17; 3:19). From the creation account Paul draws an inevitable conclusion: the effects of one person's actions can extend to many other persons. What Adam did had universal effects. Through his action of disobedience, and thus through him as a representative figure, sin and death entered the scene of world history (verse 12). The whole human race—the children of Adam—was affected by the life and deeds of a single figure—Adam.

The passage is not precisely clear in how the action of Adam relates to the actions of every human being. Read one way, the passage suggests that all of humanity participated in the sin of Adam involuntarily. Read another way, this occurred "because everyone has sinned" (verse 12, JB), that is, because of every individual's sins. In either case, the destiny of all humanity was affected by the work of Adam.

If one takes seriously the Genesis story, as Paul certainly did, it becomes clear that Adam was a representative figure. In him the destiny of the whole human race was prefigured. What he did radically affected what all others did after him.

By analogy, Paul insists that Christ too is a representative figure. Like Adam, his life and work had universal implications that affected the destiny of all humanity. If it is possible to think of one person's actions having universal significance, of the destiny of all humanity resting in a sense on the destiny of the one man Adam, then it is fully conceivable how this can be possible with Christ.

But even though "Adam prefigured the One to come" (verse 14, JB), there is a sharp contrast between the work of Adam and the work of Christ. The one was an instance of disobedience, the other obedience. In one instance, what resulted was judgment and condemnation. In the other instance, there occurred an "act of grace" and a "verdict of acquittal" (verse 16, NEB). One introduced a reign of death into the world, the other a reign of life (verse 17). Both figures were representative, but they represented two radically different orders.

Our text, then, pushes us to see the similarity of Christ and Adam. Theirs was a similarity of role. But it just as forcefully pushes us to place them in sharp contrast, seeing Adam as representative of an old order and Christ as representative of a new order.

Matthew 4:1-11

The Gospel lesson for the First Sunday of Lent is always one of the Synoptic accounts of the temptation of Jesus. In fact, the forty days of Lent (excluding Sundays) as a period of struggle and preparation is a tradition based on the experience of Jesus and of Israel, Moses, and Elijah before him.

That Jesus was tempted or tested has New Testament attestation apart from the Gospels (Heb. 2:18; 4:15). To use the word "tempted" in relation to Jesus is not to state or imply weakness. On the contrary, temptation is a testimony to strength; the greater the strength, the greater the temptation. It is regrettable that temptation has become associated popularly with small morality games. It was not so with the first temptation, the desire to become as God is (Gen. 3:5), or with the testing of Jesus, as we shall see.

Matthew, as does Luke (4:1-13), elaborates and diverges from the very brief account of the temptation of Jesus in Mark 1:12-13. Apart from a difference in the sequence of the three temptations, Matthew and Luke are sufficiently similar to suggest a common source. However, Matthew preserves Mark's order, keeping the temptation closely associated with Jesus' baptism. Luke separates the two with a genealogy (3:23-38). Paul, in warning the Corinthian church about the easy seductions of the world, recalled Israel's "baptism" in the Red Sea and the temptations that followed in the wilderness (I Cor. 10:1-13).

A brief look at the world behind Matthew 4:1-11 will help in our understanding of the writer's portrayal of Jesus' experience in the wilderness. First, in later Judaism the figure of Satan came increasingly to replace God as the source of temptation. For example, compare II Samuel 24:1 and I Chronicles 21:1. However, there was never in later Judaism or in early Christianity the development of Satan into an independent and absolute power of evil over against God.

Only God is absolute; all other powers are subordinate. God, therefore, continued to be associated even with events that tested human beings. Believing in only one absolute divine being makes the problem of sin and evil always a difficult one, but the Scriptures refuse to settle the difficulty by positing a good God and a bad God and putting on the bad God the blame for all that is dark and destructive in the world. Hence the Christian prays to the one God, "Lead us not into temptation" (Matt. 6:13), and Matthew can write of Jesus that he "was led up by the Spirit into the wilderness to be tempted by the devil" (4:1).

A second factor in the background of the text that helps our understanding is the experience of Israel in the wilderness for forty years. That period was described as a time of testing, a time of humbling Israel and letting the people hunger to teach them that one does not live by bread alone (Deut. 8:2-3). Jesus is recapitulating the experience of Israel. Matthew even tells of the flight to Egypt when Jesus was a child and then the return so that Scripture might be fulfilled, "Out of Egypt have I called my son" (2:15; Hos. 11:1). But whereas Israel failed the tests in the wilderness, Jesus did not.

More important for understanding this text are the parallels between Jesus and Moses. Even as a child Jesus was like Moses in that he was in Egypt, was with the rich and powerful, and was saved from the wicked king (Matt. 2:1-23). Here analogies continue: Moses was taken to a high mountain and shown all the land as far as the eye could see (Deut. 34:1-4); Moses was with the Lord for forty days (Exod. 34:28); and during that forty days Moses did not eat or drink. In Jesus, God has raised up one like Moses (Deut. 18:18) and at the same time one who would be a true son of God in complete obedience during the time of trial.

As for the three temptations spelled out by Matthew, the whole issue is the total seriousness with which Deuteronomy 6:4-5 is to be taken: "The Lord our God is one Lord; and you shall love the Lord your God with all your heart, and with all your soul, and with all your might." All Jesus' responses to temptation to waver from this single commitment of life toward political claims, or a ministry of bread to win over the masses, or the use of signs to coerce faith were quotations from Deuteronomy (6:13; 6:16; 8:3). The reader of Matthew is therefore given a non-magician Jesus, one who later would speak sternly about those who would claim, "Did we not prophesy in your name, and cast out demons in your name, and do many mighty works in your name?" (7:22). Later, on the mount of Transfiguration (17:5) and on the mount of Ascension (28:16-18) Jesus would have the authority and power he does not claim in the wilderness, but then that authority will have been given by God.

Matthew's account of Jesus' temptation is to say that the church encountered God in one who did not try to be God or as God (Gen. 3:5) and who did not try to use God to claim something for himself. The church too fond of power, place, and claims would do well to walk in his steps.

Second Sunday of Lent

Genesis 12:1-4a (4b-8); Psalm 33:18-22; Romans 4:1-5 (6-12), 13-17; John 3:1-17 or Matthew 17:1-9

With the texts for the Second Sunday of Lent the church turns to consider human faith and divine faithfulness, God's promises and human responses. The Old Testament and the epistolary readings are linked directly by the figure of Abraham. The first is the account of God's call and promise to the patriarch and Abraham's faithful response. In Romans 4:1-12 Paul lifts up Abraham as one whose faith "was reckoned . . . as righteousness," and stresses that the promise came through grace and not the law. The responsorial psalm, part of a hymn, celebrates the faithfulness of God, his "steadfast love" (Ps. 33:18, 22). Both Gospel readings concern the kingdom of God. The Johannine lesson, the account of Jesus' encounter with Nicodemus, calls for rebirth and emphasizes God's love in sending his only Son, while the passage from Matthew is the report of the Transfiguration.

Genesis 12:1-4a (4b-8)

This report of the call of Abraham is the key transition in the entire book of Genesis. It marks a significant change both in the type of literature and in the theological direction of the story. Genesis 1–11 is the primeval history, the accounts of creation and the establishment of the circumstances of life for all peoples. The stories concern events that happened long ago and far away. Our passage begins the other major unit of the book, Genesis 12–50, the stories of the patriarchs, Abraham, Isaac, Jacob, and the sons of Jacob. Virtually all of these stories focus upon family matters, relationships between husbands and wives, parents and children, and conflicts among siblings.

33

As a theological transition, these verses in Genesis 12 are the pivot on which history turns. Up to this point, most of the stories—particularly those passed on by the Yahwistic writer—add up to a history of human sin. It begins immediately after the creation stories with the disobedience of the first couple (Gen. 3), leads to fratricide (Gen. 4:1-16), reports the flood as divine judgment upon human corruption (Gen. 6–9), and then explains the dispersion of peoples into different nations with different languages as the result of an attempt to storm the heavens (Gen. 11:1-9).

With Genesis 12:1 the story becomes a history of salvation. First and above all, what makes the story such a history is the divine initiative. Quite without explanation, Yahweh calls a particular individual, Abram whose name will become Abraham (Gen. 17:5), and instructs him to leave his homeland and set out to a strange place. The Pauline interpretation is perfectly consistent with the Old Testament understanding: the election of Abraham is an act of grace, of God's freedom, and not in response to the patriarch's obedience to a law that had not yet been given.

Second, this is a history of salvation because it begins with a promise. The promise, reiterated to each successive generation of the ancestors, includes several elements. The meaning of the first element is clear: a "great name," the land (implicit in verse 1 and explicit in verse 7), and progeny. Thus the descendants of Abraham will become a great nation with a territory of their own. But the last part of the promise presents problems of interpretation, as most modern translations indicate. One may read the particular verb form either as reflexive, "by you all the families of the earth shall bless themselves" (RSV; cf. NJPSV), or as passive, "in you all the families of the earth shall be blessed" (RSV footnote). The latter suggests that the purpose of the promise is the good of all peoples, while the former states that all peoples will use Abraham's name in pronouncing blessings. Throughout the book of Genesis, the Priestly writer speaks of covenant where the Yahwist reports a promise. Since the covenant comes at the initiation of God and includes a promissory oath, the two are not fundamentally different.

34

Third, to speak of the accounts that follow this passage as a history of salvation means that history now has a direction, a salvific purpose. Our verses, then, are a foreshadowing of what is to come and point to the events reported in the first six books of the Bible. In particular, they anticipate the Exodus from Egypt, the covenant on Sinai, and the settlement of the land of Canaan in the generation after Moses. The promise to Abraham is reported from the perspective of those who have experienced its fulfillment, who are settled in the land in which he was only a sojourner, and who have become "a great people." Only those who know the rest of the story will recognize just how momentous these words are. The good news actually applies to those descendants more than to the patriarch himself. Moreover, it is worth remembering that Abraham in the book of Genesis is the ancestor not just of the people of Israel, but of others as well.

Note how little is stated explicitly here about the faith of Abraham. We do not hear him speak a word throughout the entire episode, although verse 8 notes that he "called on the name of the Lord." But he is not passive. His faith stands out in understatement, in the simple note that when the Lord sent him, without telling him where he was to go, he went, as the Lord had told him (verse 4). The writer and those who read the text know more than Abraham did. They know that he sets out here on a journey that does not lead to a permanent home, that he and Sarah will live their lives as resident aliens in a land promised, not to them, but to those who come later.

The story does not moralize, although it points gently to Abraham as a model of the faithful servant of the Lord. Above all, it is good news, to be accepted with gratitude: God intends to work salvation in and through history, beginning with a particular individual who is willing to set out to a strange land.

Psalm 33:18-22

Portions of this psalm are used later in Year A (Trinity Sunday and Proper 4) and the entire psalm is used at the

Easter Vigil. This psalm ends as a communal lament in which God is petitioned to bestow his love upon the community (verse 22). Only in this final verse is God addressed directly; elsewhere in the psalm God is spoken about. Verses 1-3 call upon the community to praise God (the verbs are plural imperatives). Verses 4-17 are a hymn of praise to God. Verses 18-19 sound like a priestly response or priestly assurance addressed to the worshiping congregation which responds to the priest in verses 20-21 asserting communal confidence in God.

Verses 18-19 affirm that God's eye, his special care (see Job 36:7; Ezra 5:5; Ps. 34:15), watches over those who fear him and who hope in (or rely upon) his steadfast love. To "fear God" was to show the Deity reverence and obedience rather than to quake in fright. God's eye and care protect his devotees ("their soul") from the dangers of affliction, here represented by death and famine. If God can protect them from these two threats, then he can protect them from any threat.

The confessional affirmation in verses 20-21 serves to place the worshipers within that special context and relationship over which God has concern. Confession of one's trust and hope in God was to place oneself under divine protection.

Romans 4:1-5 (6-12), 13-17

Parts of today's text also occur elsewhere in the *Common Lectionary:* 4:13-18 as the epistolary reading for Proper 5 in Year A and 4:16-25 as the epistolary reading for the Second Sunday of Lent, Year B. The reader may wish to consult our remarks in those settings.

Several features of today's passage, in both its shorter and longer form, make it especially appropriate for the Second Sunday of Lent. At this time of the year, our thoughts focus on our relationship with God, the way our sins and transgressions obstruct that relationship, and penitence as a way of removing these obstructions. In this setting, the words of Psalm 32:1-2, cited in verses 7-8, provide reassurance to the penitent as they offer blessings to those who experience genuine forgiveness from the Lord.

In a similar vein, the concluding verse reassures us, reminding us that God "gives life to the dead and calls into existence the things that do not exist" (verse 17). With reference to Abraham, this recalls the God who was able to create life in a lifeless womb and bring into existence the son of promise, Isaac, and thus make good on the divine promise. With reference to the penitent, this offers hope in a God who creates and re-creates, who renews, who makes possible what we otherwise think impossible (cf. Isa. 48:13; I Cor. 1:28).

These are direct assurances to the penitent, but there is more. The central focus, of course, is on Abraham, the one Old Testament figure Paul regarded as the paradigm of faith. His main prooftext was Genesis 15:6, "Abraham put his faith in God, and this faith was considered as justifying him" (verse 3, JB; cf. Gal. 3:6; also James 2:23). The example of Abraham became crucial for Paul in his understanding of salvation and the way humans experience salvation.

Paul's theology of salvation is well known: we are saved by grace through faith in Christ not by works of the law (verses 4-5; cf. 3:28; 5:1; 11:6; Gal. 2:16; 3:2, 8, 24; Phil. 3:9; also Eph. 2:8-9). The essential question that he addresses in Romans 4 is how we are justified before God, how we experience salvation, how we come to participate in God's promise. For Paul, there were essentially two options: by works or by faith.

The way of works was most clearly embodied in the law of Moses, and circumcision was the most visible symbol. It was the initiation rite that sealed the relationship with God (verses 9-12). In this way of construing the religious life, the way to God is through what we do. It is assumed that God rewards us for what we do. On this showing, God's acceptance of us is seen as a response to our good deeds. Salvation comes to be seen as a *quid pro quo*—something we receive from God in exchange for our good works. To paraphrase a modern commercial, we receive salvation the old-fashioned way—we earn it!

One of Paul's main difficulties with this approach is that it wrongly conceives the essential nature of God's saving act. Seen this way, salvation is a matter of earning wages, of being justly rewarded (verse 4). If we do good works, we may have reason to be rewarded, but not from God (verse 2). Salvation conceived this way is no longer a gift freely bestowed. It is a wage paid for something earned.

The other way is the way of faith. It is the polar opposite of the way of works because it construes God, and consequently our relationship with God, in a fundamentally different way. It is essentially a way of trust. But what makes it different is the nature of the God in whom our trust is placed. It is a God "who justifies the ungodly" (verse 5). This way requires us to see God not as one whose actions are calculated, who rewards good deeds with good wages, who responds in kind to our efforts. It is rather a God whose actions are uncalculated, a God who does the unexpected—forgives rather than condemns the sinner.

For Paul, the true paradigm of this second way—the way of faith—was Abraham. In the first place, Scripture assures that God reckoned him as righteous because of his faith (verses 3, 9). It was his capacity to trust in God's promise, to believe in a God who could do the impossible, who could act out of character, as it were, and extend grace to a childless, aging couple with no hope of fulfilling God's promise on their own. In the second place, this display of implicit trust preceded circumcision (verses 10-12). He behaved this way before his formal initiation into the people of God.

The true children of Abraham, the legitimate heirs of the promise that God made through him (cf. Gen. 18:18; 22:17-18) are those who construe God, and their relationship to God, this way. The God who extends righteousness to us is the God who "counts [us] as just, apart from any specific acts of justice" (verse 6, NEB). It is the God who, instead of responding in kind to sinners, forgives by extending grace. God is finally an uncalculating God who bestows salvation as free gift and not as wages earned.

John 3:1-17

The lectionary offers an alternative Gospel reading today, but the preacher is not to attempt to see any relationship between the two. The second lesson, Matthew 17:1-9, honors

a long tradition in some churches to consider the Transfiguration of Jesus on the Second Sunday of Lent. If such a tradition
seems unusual for Lent, it must be remembered that actually
all Sundays of Lent are non-Lenten in the sense that Sundays
partake of Easter and are not fast days. In John 3:1-17 the
church overhears Jesus tell a religious leader that the life
abundant and eternal is a gift from above and is not attained
by achievement, claim, or proof. Nothing could be more
appropriate for Lent than a reminder that prayer and fasting
do not earn anything.

John 3:1-7 consists of a conversation between two religious
leaders, a conversation that gradually phases into a
theological summary. Precisely at what point the conversation ends is uncertain (verse 12? 15? 16? 21?). For our
discussion, verses 1-15 will be treated as the conversation
and verses 16-17 as a portion of the theological summary
ending at verse 21. Such summaries are common in John
(3:31-36; 5:19-29). The conversation may be taken as set in the
context of 2:23-25; that is, in Jerusalem at Passover, but time
and place settings often appear more symbolic than
historical. However, 3:1-17 does appear to be a particular
instance of that which is generally stated in 2:23-25.
Nicodemus represents a faith, unclear and seeking more
proofs, which is based on signs, and to him and through him
Jesus declares that God loves and gives life to the world.

The subject of the text from beginning to end is God. The
issue is, How do God and human beings relate so as to please
God and redeem the world? Jesus and Nicodemus meet "at
night," an expression designating kind of time, not point in
time. What follows, says the writer, will contain mystery and
misunderstanding. By means of the Johannine device of
double meanings (for example, bread, light, water, temple,
and other terms carry two meanings in this Gospel), Jesus
says life in the kingdom comes by birth "from above" (verse
3), but Nicodemus translates "from above" as "again," and is
confused. How can an old man be born again (verse 4)? It is
striking that the popularization of this expression has
accepted Nicodemus' misunderstanding (born again) rather
than Jesus' word.

At verse 7, the "you" of Jesus' address to Nicodemus

becomes plural, indicating that we cease to have a private conversation and have a sermon to all. That this is a post-Easter sermon is further indicated by additional uses of plural "you" (verses 11, 12), "we" (verse 11), references to baptism and the Holy Spirit, which in John is a post-Easter gift (7:39), and the reference to Christ's ascension as a past not future event (verse 13).

And so a conversation becomes a sermon to all who need to hear that life in God's realm is not achieved, calculated, or safely fixed on a faith that has been proven by signs. Rather, life is given of God, as free from our control as the whence and whither of the wind (verse 8). But this is not a truth about God that begins with Jesus. God has always offered life, as the serpent story in Numbers 21:4-9 (verses 14-15) illustrates. There is no B.C. or A.D. on the love of God; John 3:16-17 announces what has always been true of God.

Matthew 17:1-9

The preacher may not wish to return so soon to the Transfiguration since the Last Sunday After Epiphany (two weeks ago) always centers on this event and this year Matthew 17:1-9 was the text. If the Transfiguration is customarily treated today, the preacher may wish to review the comments on this text provided earlier. However, seasons affect interpretations of texts, and Matthew 17:1-9 does not say the same thing during Lent as it does following Epiphany. Therefore, the following comments on this lection are offered with Lent in mind.

Matthew 17:1-9 follows closely Mark 9:2-9, with Luke's account (9:28-37) departing more noticeably from the common source. All agree in placing the Transfiguration immediately after the confession of Peter, the first prediction of the passion, and Jesus' teaching on cross-bearing. The Transfiguration does not, however, rob those passages of their stern teaching and demand as though to say, "Do not take the cross seriously; Jesus is really the divine Son with eternal glory." On the contrary, the Transfiguration confirms the truth of the passion and the cross by assuring the disciples that the crucified one is not a victim of history but as

Son of God is carrying out the divine will. The passion prediction is thus underscored not erased, just as Easter interprets rather than removes Good Friday.

The background to this text is to be found in Exodus 24:16 and 34:29-35. Moses was six days on the mountain, God spoke out of a cloud, and afterward Moses' face shone. In the middle of a long and difficult wilderness experience, Moses and the people experienced God. If Lent is a journey to Easter involving prayer and fasting, then the people of God are blessed by the revelation of the Transfiguration. The unveiling of Jesus' eternal nature, the dramatic demonstration of his messianic glory, give reason to go on when murmuring about turning back begins.

Moses and Elijah talk with Jesus (only Luke indicates the subject matter, 9:31), a clear indication of the unity of God's activity and purpose in the law, the prophets, and Jesus. Preachers want to avoid giving the impression that God tried with the law and failed, tried with prophets and failed, and so, finally, decided on a new plan in Jesus.

However, when the clouds lifted, Jesus stood alone and alone was to be heard. Jesus is not the abolition but the fulfillment of the law and the prophets (5:17-18). God's purposes have been long in unfolding, and God's servants have been many, but all have their center in Jesus Christ. It is no small matter to be a follower of Jesus (Heb. 1:1-3).

Luke says Peter, James, and John told no one about this in those days (9:36); Matthew and Mark say Jesus told them to be quiet until after the resurrection (Matt. 17:9; Mark 9:9). In either case, the silence was appropriate and perhaps necessary. Truth too soon is neither believable nor meaningful; both the speaker and the listener appear to be engaged in interesting rumors. But with Easter's help, both can say, "Now I see."

Third Sunday of Lent

Exodus 17:3-7; Psalm 95; Romans 5:1-11; John 4:5-26 (27-42)

Water is the dominant motif of the texts for the Third Sunday of Lent, leading in various ways to reflection upon human need and divine grace. The Old Testament lesson is one of the many accounts of the people of Israel complaining in the wilderness, in this case because of thirst. The Lord's response is to tell Moses how to bring water from the rock. The psalm, a liturgy of praise, responds directly to Exodus 17, celebrating God's care for his people and admonishing them with the example of the complainers in the wilderness. In Romans 5 Paul presents a picture of endurance in suffering that contrasts with that of Israel in the wilderness and celebrates God's love in Jesus Christ as the foundation for rejoicing. The Gospel lesson is the account of Jesus at the well in Samaria, offering living water to the Samaritan woman.

Exodus 17:3-7

Exodus 17 finds the people of Israel on the way in the wilderness, between the Exodus from Egypt and entrance into the Promised Land. The wilderness stories frame a long account of the covenant and the giving of the law on Mount Sinai (Exod. 19:1–Num. 10:10). In its immediate context, our passage is found between the story of the manna and quails in Exodus 16 and the account of the war with Amalek in Exodus 17:8-16. Exodus 18 then reports the visit of Jethro, priest of Midian and father-in-law of Moses, to the Israelite camp, and the establishment of means to resolve legal disputes among the people.

Although there are repetitions and tensions that suggest the presence of different sources or—more likely—a complex oral prehistory, most of our reading comes from the hand of the Yahwistic writer. However, the location of the events had been established by the Priestly source, with its concern for geographical detail, as in the wilderness of Sin at a place called Rephidim (17:1), where there was no water.

What transpires is an all-too-familiar pattern throughout the period of the wandering in the wilderness. First, the people find themselves in need. In this case they are thirsty (verses 1*b*, 3*a*). Then they complain or murmur "against Moses." Their complaint becomes a standardized accusation: "Why did you bring us up out of Egypt, to kill us?" (verse 3*b*). Second, Moses prays to the Lord. Often in such instances he intercedes for the people (cf. Num. 20:6), but here the petition itself contains a note of complaint, emphasizing Moses' concern with the seriousness of the situation: "What shall I do with this people? They are almost ready to stone me." (verse 4). Third, the Lord gives instructions for actions that lead to meeting the people's need through miraculous means. Moses, with some of the elders as witnesses, is to take his staff and strike the rock on which the Lord stands (verses 5-6). When he does so, water springs from the rock.

The conclusion of the episode gives an account of the place named Massah and Meribah. Remarkably, the names do not memorialize the miracle of the water, but the people's contentiousness and lack of faith. "Meribah" means contention or quarrel and "Massah" means trial, test, or proof. Both names occur independently in the wilderness narratives (Deut. 6:16; 9:22; 32:51; Num. 20:13); their combination here is probably a relatively late stage of the tradition.

Noteworthy are the references to Moses' rod, to Horeb, and to Yahweh's standing on the rock. The writer reminds us that Moses' rod is the one he used to strike the Nile (verse 5), recalling the miraculous plagues against Egypt. The power for such actions resides not in the rod, but in the word of the Lord. It, like Moses, is an instrument of the divine power. The reference to "Horeb" (verse 6) is out of place, for the people are not at the sacred mountain. The allusion is one of those tensions that show a complex oral tradition behind the story. The reference to Yahweh's standing on the rock (verse 6) is difficult to understand, but likely indicates simply the presence of the Lord as Moses carries out his instructions.

Two major themes predominate in the accounts of Israel in the wilderness, and both of them are present here. The first is the murmuring and rebellion of the people of God. Old Testament tradition is hard on the wilderness generation. Having been rescued from slavery, and either on their way to or from Sinai where God made them his covenant people, they find every occasion to find fault, or even to worship other gods. For these reasons they were not allowed to enter the Promised Land. Psalm 95 continues the criticism of these people, holding them up as bad examples. But are all their complaints illegitimate? After all, at Rephidim they found themselves without water. Small wonder that they should fear death by thirst and wish they were back in Egypt. However, the tradition takes their complaints as more than a prayer for water, for in complaining "against Moses" they are questioning the presence of the Lord among them (verse 7). Would not the one who chose them and rescued them also care for their physical needs? Such an understanding is conveyed in the typical divine response to the complaints: the Lord patiently gives them what they need.

The second leading theme of the wilderness traditions is thus the gracious care of the Lord for the people wandering in the desert. The promise first given to Abraham (Gen. 12:1-4) will be fulfilled, the people will be sustained so that their descendants can become a great nation and receive the land. Thus the story so full of contention is a tale of the grace of God, grace in the form of such a simple but essential gift as water to drink.

Psalm 95

This psalm may be divided into the following components: verses 1-2 are a communal call to offer praise to God. Verses 3-5 stipulate, in hymnic fashion, the reasons why God should be praised. Verse 6 reissues the call to praise with verse 7a offering the reason for praise. Verse 7b calls on the people to listen to God's address while verses 8-11 are an oracle delivered as a speech of God.

The opening call to praise (verses 1-2) speaks of four sentiments or actions that manifest devotion to God: sing (or "shout for joy"), make a joyful noise (or perhaps "pay homage"), come into his presence with thanksgiving (or "greet him" or "approach his presence [enter the temple] with thanksgiving"), and acclaim him with songs. In these verses, only one metaphor is used to describe God—he is the rock of salvation, a rather common description in the Old Testament (see Pss. 18:2, 31, 46; 19:14; Isa. 44:8) that denotes God's reliability and stability.

The reasons offered for praising God focus on his status as Lord over the world and the status of the world as his creation (verses 3-5). God is *the* great God (see Ps. 77:13) who rules as king over the other gods. Verse 3 thus clearly presupposes a polytheistic background. God is not the only god but he is the greatest of the gods. The whole of creation belongs to him. The concept of the totality of creation is expressed in the employment of opposites—the depths of the earth and the heights of the mountains and the sea and the dry land. The world is his because he made it (verse 5) and because he controls it (verse 4).

The second call to praise (verse 6) is actually a call to worship, employing three synonymous expressions—worship, bow down, kneel. The image of God as creator is carried over in the expression, the Lord, our Maker, in verse 6. In verse 7, the emphasis is not so much on God as creator as much as caretaker; he is the shepherd and the people are the sheep.

The divine oracle (verses 8-11), similar to a prophetic address, is introduced by the last line of verse 7. In the oracle, the people are admonished not to repeat the disobedience and obstinacy of the past.

In their midrash on this psalm, the ancient rabbis understood the disobedience at Meribah and Massah as one of the ten rebellions in the wilderness. "You will find that the children of Israel put the Holy One, blessed be He, to proof ten times, as is said *All those men that have seen My glory, and My miracles which I wrought in Egypt and in the wilderness . . . have put Me to proof these ten times (Num. 14:22)*: twice at the Red Sea, as is said *Our fathers understood not the wonder in Egypt; they remembered not the multitude of Thy mercies; but provoked Him at the sea, even at the Red Sea (Ps. 106:7)*; twice with the quail (Exod. 16:13; Num. 11:31-32); once with the manna (Exod. 16:20); once with the golden calf (Exod. 32); once at Paran (Num. 13:26) this one being the most provoking. You say ten proofs, but you instance only seven. What are the other three? The other three are mentioned in the verse *At Taberah, and at Massah, and at Kibroth-hattaavah, ye provoked the Lord to wrath* (Deut. 9:22). And why does not Scripture instance these with the others? Because these three were more provoking than the seven preceding ones."

Romans 5:1-11

The two halves of this passage are employed elsewhere in the *Common Lectionary:* 5:1-5 as the epistolary lection for Trinity Sunday in Year C and 5:6-11 as the epistolary lection for Proper 6 in Year A. The reader may wish to consult our remarks in connection with the passage in those settings.

In the context of Lent, this passage both challenges and reassures us. It speaks straight, without flinching, as it exposes our humanness for what it is and reveals what we know ourselves to be: helpless, "ungodly" (verse 6), "sinners" (verse 8). It also squarely confronts us with the reality of suffering (verse 3). Rather than blinking at this reality of life, it acknowledges what we all know and experience: suffering is part and parcel of the human condition and being Christian does not exempt us. In fact, suffering may be the price we pay for being Christian. At one level, then, our text is coldly honest with us, leaving us with no illusions about ourselves and the life we are called to lead. It is a level of honesty that commends itself in periods of penitence and thoughtful examination. It sees life as we know it and live it.

At another level, however, the text reassures us, for with its honest assessment of the human condition there is the bold declaration of God's saving act. It begins with the premise that "we are justified by faith" (verse 1), the principle Paul has argued and established in the preceding chapters. Like Abraham, we are justified by God on the basis of our willingness to trust. But the locus of our trust is in Christ, the one through whom our new relationship is made possible. The work of Christ has resulted in several benefits.

First, peace with God (verse 1). In a sense, we find here the fulfillment of Isaiah's hope that "the effect of righteousness will be peace" (Isa. 32:17). Elsewhere, Christ is seen to be the locus of God's peace (John 16:33), the one enabling us to have confidence before God (I John 3:21).

Second, access to divine grace (verse 2). Christ becomes, as it were, a sphere of divine grace, the space in which "we stand" (cf. I Pet. 5:12). Finding our footing in Christ grants us proximity to God that provides genuine access that otherwise does not exist (Eph. 3:12; Heb. 4:16).

Third, hope in sharing God's glory (verse 2). The emphasis here is eschatological. Paul looks to the future when God's glory will finally and fully be revealed (Rom. 8:18, 30; cf. Titus 2:13). But it cannot be thought of apart from Christ (cf. Col. 1:27).

Fourth, the capacity to transcend suffering (verses 3-4). What is envisioned here is not a stoic endurance of suffering, a steeling of the will against pain. It is rather the capacity to experience suffering but at the same time be transformed by it into someone different and better. There is first the recognition that it is real. It should neither be denied nor avoided (cf. James 1:2-4; I Pet. 1:6-7; II Cor. 12:9; also II Cor. 4:17). Yet properly experienced and interpreted, it can be transforming; it can teach us endurance and in doing so refine our character as it directs us to God's future, which we confront in hope.

Fifth, the Holy Spirit as God's gift (verse 5). The sure sign that God's love has been poured out among us is the Spirit (cf. Acts 2:17, 33; 10:45; Titus 3:6; I John 4:13). It is a lavish inundation of God's own presence (cf. Sir. 18:11).

Sixth, God's love manifested in Christ (verses 5-8). As Paul states in the preceding chapter, our faith is in a God who "justifies the ungodly" (4:5). It is precisely in our helplessness as sinners that God responds in love (cf. John 3:16; I John 4:10; I Pet. 3:18). Specifically, the act of Christ was in our behalf (verse 8; 3:25; Eph. 1:7; cf. I Cor. 11:25).

Seventh, salvation from God's wrath (verse 9). One of the stark realities of salvation history is that God's wrath is unleashed on all forms of human iniquity (Rom. 1:18; 4:5; cf. Matt. 3:7; I Thess. 1:10; 2:16).

Eighth, reconciliation (verses 10-11). Formerly, we were enemies of God (verse 10), with a mind-set hostile to the nature of God (Rom. 8:7; James 4:4). But through Christ reconciliation enables us to participate in his saving life (cf. II Cor. 4:10-11; 5:18; Col. 1:21-22). In this sense, Christ himself is our reconciliation (cf. I Cor. 1:31; II Cor. 10:17; Gal. 6:14; Phil. 3:3).

The passage thus presents us with reality and possibility: an honest assessment of who we are without God and apart from Christ but an honest assessment of what life with God can entail. But at the same time it speaks of God's saving work through Christ that creates new realities, and with them new possibilities as we face both present and future.

John 4:5-26 (27-42)

John 4:5-42 is a story of unusual dramatic force as well as theological insight. The writer offers us the story in several clear movements. First, Jesus and the Samaritan woman are alone on stage, the disciples being removed by a trip into town for food (verse 8). Following the conversation between Jesus and the woman, the longest recorded in the New Testament between Jesus and anyone, the disciples return (verse 27) and the woman leaves (verse 28). Following the conversation between Jesus and his disciples, the Samaritan villagers come to Jesus because of the woman (verse 39). Jesus abides (a key word in John indicating the strongest and deepest level of faith) two days at their request (verse 40), and the Samaritans arrive at profound faith: "We know that this is indeed the Savior of the world" (verse 42).

A second way to view the text is in terms of geographical movement. John 4 is in many ways a missionary text. In Acts 1:8 it is reported that the gospel was to move from Jerusalem to Judea to Samaria, and to the world. In John 4, Jesus moves from Jerusalem into Judea and then into Samaria. At the close of John 4 Jesus is declared "the Savior of the world" (verse 42). Whether there is any literary or historical connection between this text and the Samaritan mission of Acts 8:5-25 is unclear, but John 4 certainly gives Jesus' authorization to the proclamation of the gospel in Samaria.

A third perspective on this text available to the preacher is that of noting the stages in the movement of the woman's faith. At first the conversation seems to hold no promise, the two being distanced by race, sex, and religion. Again the Johannine double meanings appear: Jesus says "water" and she says "water" but the subjects are not the same. However, the conversation moves to a deeper level as this man is compared to Jacob who had drawn water from this well without having to draw. According to legend, living or bubbling water rose to the surface for Jacob. Now the woman is asking Jesus for the water he can give (verse 15). The conversation deepens further as the woman recognizes Jesus as a prophet (verse 19). Her faith in him as prophet is based on his having supernatural knowledge, as in the case of Nathaniel (1:47-49). But in the Johannine church, believing Jesus has special powers is not sufficient for she has not yet "beheld his glory"; that is, seen him as the revelation of God. At this point, the woman, apparently uncomfortable, tries to be evasive by introducing the tensions between Jewish and Samaritan religions (verses 20-24). It is an old ploy: when on the spot, begin an argument. The maneuver failed, the woman expresses a hope in a coming Messiah and Jesus responds, "I am" (verses 25-26).

It is a question whether Jesus' response, "I am," should be translated, "I am he"; that is, "I am the Messiah you have been looking for." After all, in this Gospel, Jesus is not simply the Messiah; he is that and more. Jesus is God's presence among people looking for a Messiah. The messianic expectation had become so corrupted and distorted by social, cultural, and political definitions of Messiah that to say Jesus was the Messiah was true but also in a measure false. At any rate, there is no clear indication of the degree or shape of the woman's faith. She witnessed to others with a question, "Can this be the Christ?" (verse 29), and her characterization of Jesus was of a man "who told me all that I ever did" (verses 29, 39). However, a word needs to be said about her as a witness. She may not have arrived at a full faith in Jesus as son of God but she witnessed to the extent of her faith. Others were invited to affirm what for her remained an uncertainty: "Can this be the Christ?" And the point is, her word about Jesus initiated a relationship between others and Jesus, the fruit of which was a faith beyond her own. They said, "We know that this is indeed the Savior of the world" (verse 42). Had she waited until her own faith was full grown, that remarkable conclusion to this story would have been aborted.

In this Gospel, there are various kinds and qualities of faith. Growth is possible if the believers "abide," but no faith is so new, so partial, so unclear that witnessing to Jesus Christ out of that faith is inappropriate.

Fourth Sunday of Lent

I Samuel 16:1-13; Psalm 23; Ephesians 5:8-14; John 9:1-41

The Old Testament reading continues the Lenten recital of ancient Israel's history. With the report of the election and anointing of David to be king, I Samuel 16 takes us from the wandering in the wilderness beyond the settlement in the land and to the next decisive turning point, the establishment of the monarchy. Psalm 23 expresses the deepest possible trust in the Lord. Both New Testament readings contrast light and darkness. Ephesians 5 is a call for the faithful to forsake the "works of darkness," for they are now "children of light" (verse 8). John 9 contains the account of Jesus' healing of the man born blind, including the debate with the Pharisees over the blind man's guilt and the authority of Jesus.

I Samuel 16:1-13

In ancient Israel's memory, the establishment of the monarchy ranks in importance only with the Exodus from Egypt, the Exile, and the return from Babylon. The promise to Abraham (Gen. 12:1-3) was seen to have set into motion a history of salvation that reached its fulfillment with the settlement of the people in the land. But the Lord's care for Israel does not end there. New problems and needs arise, and God responds, eventually with new promises.

One of Israel's major problems led to theological controversy. What would be the form of government for the people of God? Specifically, would they have a king or not? After all, Yahweh was their king. Samuel presided over that debate, which seemed to have been resolved with the anointing of Saul as king. Yes, as long as the people of God are in the world, they will need a human government. However, the kingship of Saul failed. That failure is reported in the chapter that immediately precedes the reading for today. Although Saul will continue to rule for many years, the matter has already been settled, for "the Lord repented that he had made Saul king over Israel" (I Sam. 15:35). After David was anointed, "the Spirit of the Lord departed from Saul" (I Sam. 16:14).

The text before us is the first of the stories of David, and it marks the final public appearance of Samuel. David will become king, establish an empire, and leave the throne to his son Solomon. The climax of the David stories is found in II Samuel 7, the account of the Lord's promise that one of his descendants would always sit on the throne in Jerusalem. It is that promise that subsequently became the basis for messianic expectations and for the early Christian emphasis on Jesus as a son of David. The foundation for it is already laid in the chapter before us with the anointing of David. From the Hebrew word for "anoint" *(mashah)* comes the designation "Messiah."

On the surface, the central character in I Samuel 16:1-13 is the old prophet Samuel, serving as a bridge between the period of the judges and that of the monarchy. The contrast between the old and the new is heightened in the contrast between the aged prophet, who has seen so much, and the youngest son of Jesse. Samuel, however, is only the instrument of the word of Yahweh. Except for his initial objection to the Lord's command, he does only what he is instructed to do. David, too, is a passive participant in the drama, speaking not a word. Thus, the central actor is Yahweh, who is setting his will into motion through Samuel and David.

The episode has both priestly and prophetic dimensions, but the latter predominate. The setting is a liturgical one, and Samuel performs some liturgical acts: the sacrifice of the heifer and the consecration of the participants (verse 5). It seems, the sequence of events suggests ritual designation by lot. When Yahweh instructs Samuel to go to Bethlehem and anoint one of the sons of Jesse—note that his name is not revealed until the end—the prophet objects that Saul will get word of the plan and kill him (verse 2). Yahweh instructs

Samuel to take an animal and perform a sacrifice. Such a ruse would not be effective if Samuel were not known to do such things.

One may even take the anointing of David to be a more-or-less priestly act. There are many reports of anointing in the Old Testament. Some have to do with sacred objects connected with places of worship (Gen. 28:18; Exod. 29:36; 30:26; Lev. 8:12; Ezek. 28:14), but frequently the reports concern the designation of a king (Judg. 9:8, 15; I Sam. 10:1; 15:1; II Sam. 5:3, 17; I Kings 1:39; II Kings 9:3, 6, 12). Often the king is described as "the Lord's anointed" (I Sam. 24:6, 10; 26:11, 16, 23). Anointing was a simple but solemn ritual involving the pouring or smearing of oil. The ritual sanctified the object or person (Exod. 29:36; Lev. 8:12) by transferring the sacredness of the deity. One who was anointed thus was holy, set apart from the profane or ordinary, and given divine authority.

However, the Samuel of this story is mainly a prophetic figure who receives his instructions at each step through the word of Yahweh. Even his objection (verse 2) is similar to that of prophets at their call (Jer. 1:6; Isa. 6:5; cf. Exod. 3:13–4:17). Above all, the prophetic perspective concerns the "Spirit of the Lord" (verse 13). Once the youngest son has been brought out, and Yahweh reveals to Samuel that this is the one, Samuel anoints him, and "the Spirit of the Lord came mightily upon David from that day forward" (verse 13). This sentence is the heading for the entire story of David that is to follow. He is the divinely designated ruler of Israel.

At this stage of the narrative as a whole, the Lord's choice is quite unexpected. The one chosen is the youngest son of Jesse, who belongs to the smallest clan of the smallest tribe of Israel. David was not even allowed to come to the sacrifice, but was left to keep his father's sheep (verse 11). The oldest son Eliab, obviously because of his size, seemed to be the right one, but while human beings look on the outward appearances, "the Lord looks on the heart" (verse 7). Despite this observation, the narrator cannot avoid commenting on the physical beauty of David when he appears (verse 12).

After this episode, the story of Saul will continue, and David will appear on the public scene. There are two quite different accounts of that appearance, one in which David is recommended to Saul as an attractive and skilled musician and soldier (I Sam. 16:14-23) and another in which the unknown but courageous shepherd boy turns up on the battlefield to defeat the Philistine giant (I Sam. 17:1-58). But in both accounts we are to understand David's remarkable abilities as manifestations of his divine designation, the presence of the Spirit of the Lord.

Psalm 23

This, the best known of all the Psalms and frequently used in Year A (Easter 4 and Proper 29), has been selected to accompany the reading of the account of David's anointment in I Samuel 16:1-13. The imagery of sheep and shepherd are common to both.

If we analyze Psalm 23 in terms of speaker and addressee, we find the following pattern: the worshiper confesses confidence in God apparently speaking to some human audience (verses 1-3); the worshiper addresses the Deity, stressing what God has done (verses 4-5); and finally, the worshiper again addresses the audience summarizing the person's assurance of divine favor (verse 5).

It is possible to understand the images of God in this psalm in two different ways. In one, God is the skillful and compassionate shepherd who leads the worshiper like a good shepherd who cares for his sheep, a widespread view of both gods and kings in the Near East (verses 1-3). If the shepherd imagery in verses 2-4 is applied to verse 5, it can be said that the shepherd looks after the feeding and care of the sheep. Shepherds in the Middle East (Lebanon and Syria) used the expression, "to set the table," when referring to preparing fields for grazing. Such activities included uprooting poisonous weeds and thorns and clearing the area of the sheep's enemies such as snakes and scorpion's nests. In the evening as the sheep were corralled, the injured or sickly ones were separated from the others and treated with oil and a curative drink made of fermented material and herbs sweetened with honey. If one follows this line of interpretation, then the imagery of the shepherd runs throughout the psalm.

It is also possible to look at the psalm as presenting a double image of God, that of shepherd for the sheep (verses 1-3) and that of a human host for a guest (verses 4-5). (Note that this breaks the text between the section spoken to a human audience, verses 1-3, and that spoken to God directly, verses 4-5.) The image of God as host emphasizes not only the sufficiency of the Divine to feed but also the care that he takes to meet the other needs of the guest—anointing oil for the head and soothing cup for the psyche.

To decide between these two alternative interpretations is almost a matter of taste, although the latter is certainly found more widely in literature on the Psalms.

If the psalm compares the experience of God and his care to that of a shepherd and/or a human host, then what does the imagery of the person's distresses refer to? That is, what happened to the worshiper? From what straits has he or she been saved? Some possibilities are: (1) one could see that imagery to be that of sheep changing or entering new pastures, thus the psalmist could be describing one of life's points of transition; (2) another view is to see the prayer as one offered by a wandering traveler who has safely returned to Jerusalem; (3) the entire imagery may be simply that of a worshiper who eats a sacrificial meal in the sanctuary; (4) a further alternative is to see all the imagery as merely verbal images without any exact frames of reference; and (5) a final interpretation suggests that this psalm may have been used by a fugitive guilty of manslaughter or accidental killing who took refuge and sought asylum in the temple and lives beyond the reach of the family of the deceased. (See Exod. 21:12-14; Deut. 19:1-13; I Kings 1:49-53; 2:28-35 for this practice.) Dwelling in the temple or house of God would thus be taken literally. There the fugitive could eat in the temple in the presence of his/her enemies.

Regardless of how one interprets the psalm, the general picture of what is stressed is quite clear. One who has known trouble or experienced life-threatening situations has also experienced the protection of the Divine. The psalm exudes confidence that God protects so that whatever life brings to his people, they will not be overwhelmed.

Preaching on this text, one could focus on the diverse

expressions of human experience found in the psalm. One set emphasizes the troubles that threaten to overwhelm human life: valley of the shadow of death (or darkness or total darkness), evil, and enemies. Another set stresses the positive instruments and acts of God's care: green pastures, still waters, reviving of the soul, reliable paths, rod and staff, table, oil, and cup. Human life, of course, experiences both the negative and the positive. At times, even the Shepherd must use the rod and staff against his own sheep for their best interests.

This psalm presents the human predicament without any illusion about persons being superhumans and above pain, loneliness, and lostness; yet the symbol of God as protector and even corrector affirms the potential of a tranquil life lived amid adversaries and the harsh realities that are the ingredients of every life.

The closing verse affirms that goodness and mercy, not tribulation or ravenous enemies, shall be a constant companion. To dwell (or to return) to the house of Yahweh in this verse did not refer to immortality but to either residence in the temple (by a priest or a fugitive) or, if read as return, to a visit to the temple.

Ephesians 5:8-14

From earliest times Lent served as the time when catechumenates prepared intensively for their baptism at the Easter Vigil. Over the centuries this explicit connection with baptism diminished as Lent came to be viewed as a time of preparation generally for all Christians who moved toward the celebration of Easter. Vatican II served to reemphasize the baptismal features of the Lenten liturgy.

Certainly these baptismal allusions are dominant in today's epistolary text. The opening contrast "once you were . . . but now you are" is widely regarded as formulaic instruction for Christian initiates to set their former way of life in contrast to the new life they have embarked on. It is easy to see how this could have provided a basic form of early Christian teaching, perhaps connected with the "two ways" scheme (cf. Eph. 2:11, 13).

There is also the dominance of the contrast between light and darkness. In fact, these two themes are interwoven throughout today's passage. So universal are these images that they are frequently found in a variety of ancient religions and are used to typify two contrasting ways of life. The common assumption is that light is identified with the good and true, while darkness betokens what is sinister and evil (cf. I Thess. 5:5; also Luke 16:8; John 12:36). Accordingly, conversion is typically viewed as the transition from darkness to light (I Pet. 2:9).

One striking feature of today's passage is that the readers are actually identified with darkness and light. It is not the usual "you were living *in* darkness, but are now living *in* the light." It is rather "once you were darkness, but now you are light" (verse 8). Such direct identification reminds us of Jesus' injunction, "you are the light of the world" (Matt. 5:14). It was thoroughly in character with this emphasis when early Christian initiates were referred to as "the enlightened ones."

It is at this point that today's epistolary text converges with the Gospel reading, the story of the man born blind (John 9). This highly ironical account, which is typical of the Johannine narrative, unfolds for us the story of a blind man who becomes enlightened, and as such provides a counterpoint to those around him who presumably have 20/20 vision, but who fail to "see." It is John's way of portraying faith in Christ as an illumination, an enlightenment, a coming to the light.

Along with the transition of status comes the appropriate behavior. We are thus enjoined to "walk as children of light" (cf. I John 1:7). Positively, this means learning what "is pleasing to the Lord" (verse 10; cf. Rom. 12:2; 14:18; II Cor. 5:9; Heb. 13:21). Negatively, it means casting off the unfruitful "works of darkness" (Rom. 13:12), indeed turning against them in order to expose them. We now become aggressive foes of darkness, bent on exposing evil in all its forms. This is a hard saying, but there are numerous sharp-edged injunctions that call us to be active in censure and rebuke (I Tim. 5:20; II Tim. 4:2; Titus 1:9, 13; also Gal. 2:14).

What is called for here is a form of life that is out in the open, transparent as it were before God. There is a hint in verse 12 at things done in secret too shameful to be mentioned. We are reminded elsewhere that the gospel has no truck with secret, underhanded methods (II Cor. 4:2).

The final verse appears to be a fragment of an early Christian hymn, sung perhaps in a baptismal liturgy. As such, it would have been addressed to the initiate, who is invited to awake to the new life in Christ and be enlightened by Christ himself (verse 14; cf. Rom. 13:11; I Thess. 5:6).

All of these motifs are fitting reminders during the Lenten Season that our baptism marks a transition from an old way of life to a new, enlightened existence. They also serve as ethical imperatives, enjoining us to conform our lives to the nature of true existence in Christ.

John 9:1-41

The Gospel lesson for today is one lengthy narrative and the preacher would do well not only to study the text as a whole but to try to preserve the dramatic narrative quality of the text in the sermon itself. Above all, it is important to keep in mind that this is not simply a story of Jesus healing a blind man but Jesus healing a blind man *according to John's Gospel.* In Mark 8:22-26, Jesus heals the blind, but one has only to read the two stories to see the difference.

John 9:1-41 and John 5:1-17 are healing stories which resemble each other and bear the marks of Johannine theology. Both are healings on the Sabbath, both are signs revealing God and are not presented as acts in response to need, both portray Jesus taking the initiative rather than healing persons who come to him in faith, both involve persons who suffer hardship because Jesus healed them, and both accounts are followed by theological discourses. The two most unusual features of both stories are that two lives are changed by divine initiative and not because of anything said or done by the one in need, and much of the action of both stories occurs in Jesus' absence. In John 9 Jesus comes and heals and then is gone. He returns at the end of the story to encourage and vindicate the one healed. In other words, our text records what life is like for those whom Jesus has blessed but who are living in the world between the first and second appearances of Jesus. John's church was suffering a great deal (15:20–16:4) and most likely identified closely with the healed man who received abuse from family, neighbors, and religious leaders.

If we may think of John 9:1-4 as a drama, then the action can be followed most easily by focusing on the six scenes presented by the story. Scene one (verses 1-7) is introductory. Jesus and his disciples see a man blind from birth. The disciples want to discuss the man's malady theologically, but Jesus will have none of it. Rather, Jesus sees the occasion as one in which the works of God can be revealed. With a procedure very much the same as used by other healers in that day, Jesus restores the man's sight. In scene one, Jesus disappears from the story. In scene two (verses 8-12) we find the healed man back in his old neighborhood, but not comfortable. Friends and neighbors are disturbed that he is no longer blind. They bombard him with questions: Who did it? How? Where is the healer now? Arguments break out among those who believe the man is healed and those who do not; there is no joy, no praise, no thanking God, no encouragement, only quarreling.

In scene three (verses 13-17) the poor fellow is hauled before the religious authorities. After all, this healing was perpetrated on the Sabbath, and therefore, the healer, if there was one, is a criminal to be punished. The clergy are divided, and so the healed man is asked to testify. He calls Jesus a prophet of God, his testimony is rejected, and further evidence is sought. In scene four (verses 18-23) the authorities quiz the parents. Intimidated and afraid of punishment by reason of association or consent, they ask not to be involved. A house has been divided over Jesus and his power to help the needy, and the healed man is feeling very much alone.

Scene five (verses 24-34) returns to scene three: the authorities again interrogate the healed man. Pressure builds and tempers flare. The man answers with personal testimony ("I was blind, now I see") and with reason (Jesus must be of God to have the power to heal). The authorities are in a bind; they must accept the man as healed and accept the healer as a person of God or they must hold to their view of the law concerning the Sabbath and reject the healed and the healer. The healed man is excommunicated. And he never asked to be healed in the first place! Those who are blessed by Jesus soon run into trouble in the world because good news has enemies.

In the final scene (verses 35-41) Jesus returns. The healed man meets and confesses faith in Jesus while the oppressors come under the judgment of the revelation of who they really are. And this is the judgment, that "the light has come into the world, and men loved darkness rather than light" (3:19). The healing has made it clear: light comes to those who recognize that life is blindness without Christ; darkness comes to those who without Christ claim to see.

Fifth Sunday of Lent

Ezekiel 37:1-14; Psalm 116:1-9; Romans 8:6-11; John 11:(1-16),
17-45

In their contrasts between life and death, the texts for today anticipate Easter. However, all of them focus more upon the life of the people of God this side of the grave than upon the resurrection. Ezekiel's vision of the valley of dry bones is a prophecy that the people of Israel, dead in exile, will live again on their land. The responsorial psalm is an individual's song of thanksgiving for being delivered from a fatal illness. In the epistolary reading Paul compares the spirit with life and the flesh with death, for "to set the mind on the Spirit is life and peace" (Rom. 8:6). John 11 is the account of Jesus raising Lazarus from the dead.

Ezekiel 37:1-14

With this season's summary of Israel's history from the Old Testament we are left to supply a major event between last Sunday's reading and the one for today. The anointing of David introduced the period of the monarchy and Ezekiel 37 announces the revival of Israel. What occurs between these two is the Exile. The end of Israel's history through military defeat and exile had been anticipated in prophetic announcements as early as the eighth century B.C., as judgment upon the sinful people. First the Northern Kingdom was defeated by the Assyrians and the population dispersed throughout the empire (722/21 B.C.). Then the Babylonian king, Nebuchadnezzar, captured Judah, destroyed Jerusalem with its temple, and carried off the population to Babylon (597, 587 B.C.).

The prophet Ezekiel must have been one of the leading citizens of Jerusalem, for he was taken with the first wave of captives in 597. Although the captives had some autonomy, were allowed to gather, and could continue some of their religious practices, it is difficult to exaggerate the seriousness of the Exile as a national disaster and a crisis of faith. The Judeans had lost the land promised to the ancestors and granted in the time of Joshua. The last of the Davidic kings was a captive, first in prison and then at the court of the Babylonian monarch (II Kings 25:27-30). The temple, where the Lord made his name to dwell, and where his glory was known, lay in ruins. Ezekiel envisioned defeat as the departure of the glory of the Lord from the temple (Ezek. 10–11). Small wonder that the exiles asked if the history of Yahweh with his people had come to an end.

Ezekiel 37:1-14, the vision of the valley of dry bones, is the prophetic answer to that question. It is one of the most memorable scenes of the Bible. The prophet reports that he was taken by the Spirit of the Lord and set down in the middle of a great plain covered with bones, dry bones— human bones. As is so often the case in prophetic vision reports, a dialogue transpires within the vision itself between the prophet and Yahweh. This stresses an important fact: what is heard is essential, for it is the word of the Lord, a message for the people. Thus the vision moves from a description of what was seen to an interpretation of its meaning.

The dialogue within this vision concerns life and death, opening with Yahweh's question, "Can these bones live?" The prophet's answer is not an evasion, but an acknowledgment of the source of life, "O Lord God, thou knowest" (verse 3). It then becomes clear how the Lord intends to work his will, for he commands Ezekiel to prophesy to the bones. He does so, and they come to life. When the bones have come together and have flesh on them, they still do not live, so through the prophet Yahweh calls for the breath from the four winds, and when it breathes upon them they live (verses 9-10).

The interpretation of the vision follows (verses 11-14). The vision is an announcement, a promise of life, not of the general resurrection, but of the revival of the people beyond the Exile. The vision stresses that this revival is corporate; it is the restoration of the people of God. It is accomplished by word and spirit; the word of God through the prophet, the life-giving spirit as a divine gift.

Ezekiel is not, of course, to keep this vision to himself, but to report it to the people. It then becomes unqualified good news to those who consider themselves dead. It is the good news that people can live, can be enlivened by the spirit of God this side of the grave. It is a promise of release to exiles who have been oppressed by military powers, by the overwhelming political forces that control their existence. It is good news to the oppressed exiles who have been beaten down by their own sins and are suffering under the weight of the sins of their ancestors. To all those, the spirit of God can and will give life. To such people this vision brings hope, beginning with release from bondage to the hopelessness of the situation.

Psalm 116:1-9

This psalm, portions of which are a lection for Holy Thursday in all three years, like Ezekiel 37, gives expression to the theme of "escape from death." Although frequently interpreted as expressing a belief in the resurrection (so similarly Ps. 16; see Acts 2:25-31), the psalm was originally composed to be utilized in a thanksgiving ritual following recovery from sickness.

Thanksgiving rituals, in ancient Israel, as in most cultures, were intent on two goals: (1) celebration of the new or renewed status of the person/group/community and (2) offering testimony to the one who had granted the status being celebrated. Both of these goals focus more on the human situation than on gaining the attention of the divine. (This is unlike the lamenting situation where exactly the opposite is the case.)

Thus in this psalm, the addressee is fundamentally the human audience. (God is addressed only in verses 16-17 and possibly in verse 8. In verse 7, the worshiper engages in self-address and self-assurance.)

The condition of trouble or the state of distress from which the worshiper has been saved is depicted in various ways throughout the psalm: snares of death, pangs of Sheol, distress and anguish, brought low, death, tears, stumbling. All of these illustrate the marginal state of existence into which sickness had thrown the person.

The worshiper's actions, in taking to God the predicament of illness, is noted in verse 4 as calling "on the name of the Lord" or simply praying for help. The recovered or assured worshiper even provides a summary of the prayer spoken on that earlier occasion (see verse 4*b*).

The divine aid granted by God is also described in various ways: he has heard, he inclined his ear, he saved me, he delivered my soul, my eyes, my feet.

Verse 7, in which the worshiper's own soul is addressed, could suggest that the person's illness or disease is still present and that the worshiper has only been assured of recovery rather than actually having recovered.

Verse 9 in which the worshiper rejoices and is once again walking in the land of the living may be seen as fitting hand in glove with the "resurrection" narrative in Ezekiel 37.

Romans 8:6-11

The part of today's epistolary text that resonates with the readings from the Old Testament and the Gospel is the final verse, with its emphasis on resurrection. Here we are told that God's Spirit who raised Jesus from the dead lives within us, and by virtue of this indwelling our mortal existence will eventually be enlivened (verse 11).

It was a cardinal element of early Christian faith that it was God who raised Christ from the dead (Rom. 4:24; I Cor. 15:15, 20; Gal. 1:1; cf. II Cor. 13:4). Equally central was the conviction that God would raise those "in Christ" (I Cor. 6:14; II Cor. 4:14). In the Christ-event God unleashed the dynamic force that Paul calls "resurrection life." To be incorporated into Christ is to be introduced to this new force, to share in the resurrection. Even though resurrection existence begins now, it is not fully realized or consummated until the eschaton.

What is striking about today's text is the role of the Spirit in this process. The Spirit becomes the mediating locus of this force. The Spirit who dwells within us is the carrier of God's resurrection power. Indeed, the Spirit is so closely identified with this power that the two are indistinguishable. The means, the energizing force, through which God brings about resurrection life within us is the Spirit.

Here we can see how the Christ-event inaugurates a new era that is defined by the Spirit. Since the Spirit is the earmark of the new aeon, the sign that God has bestowed marking the beginning of the new age, hence the eschatological gift (Rom. 1:4; II Cor. 1:22; 3:3, 6, 7-18; cf. Acts 2), it becomes the defining norm for existence. Accordingly, Paul envisions two realms, or two spheres of existence: that of the flesh and that of the spirit (8:4-5). The two are antithetical. They represent two ways of construing reality that are fundamentally opposed. They form reference points for our minds (verse 5), or as the NEB suggests, they constitute two essentially different "outlooks"—"the spiritual outlook" and the "outlook of the lower nature" (verses 6-7; cf. John 3:6).

These two opposing outlooks bring fundamentally opposite results. They bring us to radically different destinations. The "outlook of the flesh" eventually leads to death, while the "outlook of the spirit" eventuates in "life and peace" (verse 6; cf. Rom. 6:21; Gal. 6:8). "As the kingdom of Christ the community stands in conflict with the flesh as the sphere of subjection to the world" (Kasemann). What distinguishes them is their orientation toward God. The one is essentially "hostile to God" (verse 7; cf. 5:10; John 4:4), and for this reason does not, because it cannot, yield itself to the divine will, spoken of here as "God's law" (verse 7; cf. John 5:44; 6:60; 8:43; 12:39). It goes without saying that it brings about God's displeasure (verse 8).

The other is dynamically intertwined with God's own Spirit, so much so that the relationship is reciprocal. We both "dwell in the Spirit" as the domain of our existence (verse 9), but the Spirit also dwells within us as the concrete form in which God's presence exists within the world (verse 11). It is in this sense that the Spirit serves as the sign of possession. The true mark of Christian identity is whether we possess the Spirit. Nor is this a possession of spiritual enthusiasts alone, those who claim special, visible measures of the Spirit that distinguish them from the ordinary believer. It is rather the characteristic feature of existence *en Christo* and as such marks off Christian existence from other forms of existence. It takes shape within ordinary forms of life and service.

The presence of the indwelling Christ acknowledges, on the one hand, the existence of our mortal bodies, which are "dead because of sin" (verse 10). They reflect the old order that is on the way out, even though they provide the form in which we experience the world. Yet, on the other hand, our inner selves, our "spirits," have already begun to feel the impact of acquired righteousness and hence are "alive" (verse 10). As difficult as this verse is, it points to the inner transformation at work within us as the result of God's indwelling Spirit. It is a process that will eventually be finished in the final resurrection.

In many senses, today's text, with its strong emphasis on the Spirit, takes us ahead to Pentecost. It certainly points us toward Easter as we are directed to think of both Christ's resurrection as well as our own. Yet within the context of Lent, it speaks a direct message, urging us to see clearly the contours of two antithetical forms of existence that continue to pose options for us, even though we have taken up the "outlook of the Spirit." What rings true is the moral tension of the text. This is what Lent forces us to confront before we celebrate Easter.

John 11:(1-16), 17-45

Next Sunday is Passion Sunday. It is appropriate that we come to it with a Gospel text that prompts in the reader the thought of Jesus' approaching death. John 11 does just that, for the raising of Lazarus recorded in this chapter is the event in this Gospel that precipitates the plot against Jesus' life (11:45-53). In fact, as we shall see, the story seems to be about the death and raising of Lazarus, but just beneath the surface the careful reader discerns the deeper subject: the death and resurrection of Jesus. But first a word of warning to the preacher: John 11 is filled with one-liners, phrases and sentences that easily seduce the reader into focusing on them for catchy messages rather than for the whole story. Even if one begins at verse 17 the message needs several clues from verses 1-16.

The raising of Lazarus is a sign story. This is to say about it two things: first, Jesus will act on his own, or more precisely, "from above" rather than responding to the urging of others or the contingencies of the situation. Hence, he does not go running to Bethany upon news of his friend's illness; he stays two days longer where he is (verse 6). Second, as a sign story, the primary function of the event is to reveal God. What is about to occur, says Jesus "is for the glory of God" (verse 4). However, this sign has another purpose: "that the Son of God may be glorified by means of it" (verse 4). The purpose of what Jesus does for Lazarus is to glorify the Son which, in this Gospel, refers to the Son's return to God (12:23). The means of this return to God would be the cross. "When I am lifted up from the earth" (12:32) carried a double meaning: the cross and the ascension. The reader is told at the outset, then, that the story to follow is not about a family crisis in Bethany so much as it is about the crisis of the world caught in death and sin, not so much about resuscitating a corpse as it is about giving life to the world. So understood, the text is relieved of having to answer nagging questions, such as: Why did Jesus not rush to Bethany when he heard of Lazarus' illness? Or, does being a friend of Jesus mean that private miracles will give back your deceased loved ones? Or, does the raising of Lazarus mean Martha and Mary will now have to experience two bereavements and pay for two funerals?

Of course, problems remain because we want always to know historical facts. But the story of Lazarus becomes unclear on one level because bleeding through the page from beneath is the deeper truth of which the death and resurrection of Lazarus is but a sign: apart from trust in God, the world is a cemetery, but into that world God sends Jesus Christ as the offer of resurrection. "I am the resurrection and the life" (verse 25). In chapter 6, the crowds wanted bread and Jesus gave them that but offered also the bread of life; here the sisters want a brother and Jesus gives them that but offers also life to the world through his own death and resurrection.

To see the many clues that point to Jesus' own death and resurrection, one has but to read carefully the story. At verse 4 we are told that the end of this story will be the glorifying (death) of the Son. At verse 16 Thomas says, "Let us also go, that we may die with him." And verses 28-44 can best be understood in the light of Jesus' having said that his own death would be effected by what takes place. So much here is reminiscent of Gethsemane, Golgotha, and Easter. Notice: Jesus is deeply moved and troubled (verses 33, 38); Jesus weeps (verse 35); the tomb is near Jerusalem; the tomb is a cave with a large stone covering it; the stone is rolled away; Jesus cries with a loud voice; the grave cloths are removed from the one dead but now alive. One can hardly read the account and continue to think of Lazarus; one thinks of Jesus.

Lazarus left the tomb but the price was that Jesus had to enter it (verses 45-53). Jesus himself said it: one cannot give life unless one dies (12:24). Jesus made no exception in his own case. "Now is my soul troubled. And what shall I say? 'Father, save me from this hour'? No, for this purpose I have come to this hour." This willingness to submit to the giving of life which he had asked of his disciples is dramatically stated in verse 34. When Jesus asked where Lazarus had been laid, they said to him, "Come and see." This expression, "come and see" is in this Gospel as an invitation to discipleship (1:39; 1:46; 4:29). Here the word is turned upon Jesus himself. The hour has come for the Son of man to be glorified. Perhaps this realization interprets the next verse: "Jesus wept."

Passion/Palm Sunday

Matthew 21:1-11; Psalm 118:19-29; Isaiah 50:4-9a; Psalm 31:9-16; Philippians 2:5-11; Matthew 26:14–27:66 or Matthew 27:11-54

The final Sunday of Lent is either Palm Sunday, Passion Sunday, or both. The Palm Sunday Gospel reading is Matthew's account of Jesus' triumphal entry into Jerusalem. The response for the Palm Sunday celebration from Psalm 118 is part of a liturgy for entrance into the temple, including the blessing pronounced on the one who enters in the name of the Lord. The same Old Testament and epistolary readings serve for both Palm and Passion Sunday. The Old Testament lesson stresses the latter, emphasizing the suffering of the Lord's servant. The Epistle takes us through the suffering to the exaltation of Jesus. The long form of the Passion Sunday Gospel is Matthew's full account of the passion and death of Jesus, from before the Last Supper to the sealing of the tomb. The shorter version recounts the trial and crucifixion of Jesus, concluding with the centurion's affirmation of faith.

Matthew 21:1-11

To observe this Sunday as Palm Sunday is to create an entirely different mood from that of Passion Sunday, one of praise and shouts of hosanna; it is to recall Jesus' entry into Jerusalem. Only John's account mentions palm branches (12:13), but all report an occasion of great acclamation. Matthew and Luke (19:28-38) follow Mark (11:1-10), but Matthew cites explicitly what lies only implicitly in Mark, the oracle in Zechariah 9:9. Matthew prefaces it with a line from Isaiah 62:11, "Tell the daughter of Zion." In quoting the Greek translation (Septuagint) of Zechariah 9:9, which gives the impression of two animals, an ass and a colt, Matthew builds his story around two animals (verses 2, 5, 7). By so doing he creates a circus effect: "they put their garments on *them* and he sat thereon" (literally, "on *them*," verse 7). But even with this unusual element in the story, Matthew's account makes a declaration important to the church's understanding of Jesus.

First, the story itself. Following the expression, "And as Jesus was going up to Jerusalem" (20:17), Matthew records three events prior to our lection: the third prediction of the passion (20:17-19), the incident involving the request by the mother of the sons of Zebedee for chief places for James and John (20:20-28), and the healing of two blind men as Jesus was leaving Jericho (20:29-34). This route would mean that Jesus and those with him now travel the steep fifteen-mile road up from Jericho to Jerusalem. Any trip up to Jerusalem revived national hopes fanned by good memories of grand days, but for Jesus it was clearly a move to his death. Near Jerusalem Jesus sends two disciples for the animals (21:1-2). That the owner released them probably is not intended to indicate prearranged plans, but the divine foreknowledge and authority of Jesus (verse 3). Thus the messianic king approached the city "humble, and mounted on an ass" (verse 5), the garments of his disciples serving as a saddle and the garments of the pilgrims along with tree branches serving as a carpet along the road (verses 7-8).

According to Matthew, great crowds followed Jesus as he entered Judea (19:2; 20:29) and as he made his way toward Jerusalem. Here a great crowd both preceded and followed him (verse 9). Luke identifies the participants in the event as "the whole multitude of the disciples" (19:37), while for John they are persons already in Jerusalem for the feast who come out to meet Jesus (12:12-13). The shout of the crowd: "Hosanna" ("save us") and "Blessed be he who comes in the name of the Lord" (verse 9) are lines from Psalm 118:25-26, a processional psalm. "The Son of David," meaning not only one of David's line but one like David, indicates the nature of the expectation of some of the people. The other Evangelists have other titles on the lips of the shouting crowds.

Mark closes the story with Jesus entering the city, making a quiet visit to the temple, and then going out to Bethany

(11:11). However, in Matthew, Jesus entering the city creates quite a stir (a tumult, a form of the word translated "earthquake"), with all the city asking, "Who is this?" (verse 10). The answer is not "Son of David" as one would expect from verse 9 but "the prophet Jesus from Nazareth of Galilee" (verse 11). Whether this is a specific reference to the prophet like Moses whom God would raise up (Deut. 18:18) is not clear. What is clear is that all Jerusalem is affected by the presence of Jesus. Matthew had said this earlier (2:3) when the Magi came seeking the king of the Jews. That disturbance of the city initiated a plot on the life of Jesus while he was yet a child. Now he comes again, and again he is childlike. He is humble, riding a donkey (21:5); he is "gentle and lowly in heart" (11:29); he is the suffering servant of Isaiah 42:1-4 who "will not wrangle or cry aloud, nor will any one hear his voice in the streets; he will not break a bruised reed or quench a smoldering wick" (12:19-20).

We know, of course, what happened to him in the city. But let us not pick on Jerusalem. What city is there today with its values, its centers of power, its established institutions, that would not resist strongly the radical realignment of values and relationships, of priorities and commitments, that Jesus teaches and models in his own life?

Psalm 118:19-29

Psalm 118 is appropriate for Palm Sunday reading for three reasons: (1) it is a psalm originally used by a leader (probably a king) entering the city and sanctuary triumphantly; (2) it is a psalm deeply rooted in the Jewish celebration of Passover, a festival around which much of the Christian passion narrative revolves; and (3) according to the gospel tradition (Mark 11:9-10; Matt. 21:1-10; Luke 19:37-38), the psalm was sung by pilgrims accompanying Jesus as they entered Jerusalem on Palm Sunday. Before looking at verses 19-29, let us note some factors associated with the first two points just mentioned.

1. The depiction of the distress undergone by the worshiper indicates a major battle as the background to the psalm. Nations surrounded and assailed the person (verse

10). Songs of victory were sung in soldiers' tents on the field of battle (verse 15). All Israel is called upon to participate in the services of thanksgiving (verses 2-4).

2. Psalms 113–118, called the Egyptian-Hallel psalms, were sung in Passover celebrations. On the afternoon of Passover, when the lambs were being slaughtered in the temple, these psalms were sung by the Levites in the temple precincts as part of the worship services. Again, in the evening, when the Passover meal was being eaten in the homes, the diners sang Psalms 113–118 as part of the Passover Seder. The ending of Psalm 118, from verse 22 on, could be understood as a messianic text anticipating the coming of one who had been rejected by men but who would be God's chosen. Thus the Passover celebration, which always commemorated the national birth of Israel, also looked forward to coming redemption.

With verse 19, the psalm becomes complicated in terms of the speakers and addressees. The following represents one possible way of looking at the psalm in terms of an entry ritual:

verse 19	the victorious king requests entry to the temple
verse 20	priests or others respond to the request
verses 21-22	the king offers thanksgiving addressed directly to God
verses 23-24	worshipers or a choir proclaim the celebration as a consequence of God's intervention
verse 25	people, choir, or priests offer a prayer to God
verses 26-27	the king is blessed as he enters the sacred precincts of the temple and reference is made to part of the festal celebrations
verse 28	the king offers thanksgiving
verse 29	a general summons to offer thanks

Several aspects of Psalm 118:19-29 are worthy of special note: (1) the celebration that is reflected in the psalm is one of triumph, success, and victory; (2) the royal features of the ritual, that is, their connection with a ruler or king seem clearly evident; (3) the celebration is one in which a key emphasis is God's action and intervention on behalf of the triumphal figure; and (4) the triumphal figure describes himself as one who has been rejected but who has now become victorious. In verse 22, we have what was apparently a common proverb: "The stone which the builders rejected has become the head of the corner." Such a saying implies that someone or something has moved from a state of rejection to a position of prominence, in fact, to a position that is irreplaceable. "The head of the corner" would suggest either a corner of the foundation stone or perhaps the keystone in an arch. The first part of the psalm refers to how the figure was threatened, challenged, and nearly defeated on the field of battle before God granted him triumph.

The numerous parallels between this psalm and Jesus' career and triumphal entry into Jerusalem, the Holy City, should be obvious although Psalm 118 should not be read as a prophetic prediction of Jesus. The analogy between the psalm and Jesus' activity is to be found in the fact that in both God worked to elevate and exalt the lowly to a place of prominence. Though in each case the lowly had to move through oppression and opposition, they were not overtaken by death, literal or otherwise (see verse 18).

Isaiah 50:4-9*a*

With the exception of Holy Thursday, the Servant Songs of Second Isaiah provide all of the Old Testament readings for Passion/Palm Sunday through Good Friday. Commentators have long recognized that these four poems (Isa. 42:1-4; 49:1-6; 50:4-11; 52:13–53:12) are distinctive units both in terms of form and contents. In fact, they stand out so much that some have attributed them to a different author. However, we concur with the majority of modern commentators in attributing them to the same prophetic poet responsible for Isaiah 40–55, Second Isaiah.

While we know virtually nothing about Second Isaiah, we have no difficulty identifying his date and historical circumstances. His work contains allusions to historical circumstances that can be dated with precision on the basis of external evidence. More than once (Isa. 44:28; 45:1-7) he mentions the campaigns of Cyrus the Mede, who is on the march toward his eventual capture of the city of Babylon and then the establishment of the Persian Empire. The new king is on the scene, but he has not yet arrived in Babylon. Since Cyrus took Babylon in 538 B.C. the work of Second Isaiah is confidently dated ca. 539 B.C. The prophet speaks so strongly of Cyrus as the Lord's "anointed," the one chosen by God to accomplish his will, that some commentators have argued that he is the servant of the songs.

Second Isaiah lived and worked in Babylon, among the Israelite captives who had been taken there some fifty or sixty years earlier. One of his favorite themes is to ridicule the religious practices he must have observed there, including the worship of idols and the Babylonian liturgies. But his leading message is the announcement of release from exile and return to Judah. Like most of his prophetic predecessors, his message comes with divine authority and it is contrary to the expectations of his audience. When the people of Israel expected peace and prosperity, earlier prophets, such as Amos and Hosea, announced judgment in the form of military defeat and exile. Now, to a people who have lost hope, Second Isaiah announces unqualified—and unmerited—salvation. Basing his proclamation on the ancient traditions of Israel's election, of God's creation of the world, and the promises to the ancestors, the prophet announces a "new thing," but one like the old salvation event, an exodus out of Babylon, a glorious return through the wilderness, and reestablishment of Jerusalem. The Servant Songs must be read in the context of that message as a whole.

Opinions differ considerably on the question of the identity of the servant. Some of the evidence, especially in the context that surrounds the songs, argues for a collective interpretation, in which case the servant is the people of Israel. But much of the language of the songs themselves is highly personal and individualistic. Some interpreters have identified the servant with specific individuals, such as the prophet himself (since some of the language is autobiographical), earlier figures such as Jeremiah, or even Cyrus. However, it is not even clear what traditional role the servant filled. Was he a royal, messianic figure, or a prophetic figure? It is even possible that the concept of the servant is fluid and that the different passages have different figures or roles in view. In the second of the songs, the passage before us today, form and style are autobiographical—that is, the servant himself speaks—and the emphasis is upon the servant's prophetic functions.

Both the structure and contents of the passage suggest three themes for our consideration on this occasion. The first, expressed in verse 4, concerns the prophetic word. The servant affirms that the Lord God has given him the power of speech and the knowledge of what to say. This is consistent with the deep prophetic tradition in Israel in which prophets understood themselves to be called by God and given specific messages to deliver. The servant has listened to God's voice like a student listens to a teacher. Moreover, like all true prophetic words, the message of the servant has been powerful and effective. He does not tell us what that word was, but since its purpose was "to sustain with a word him that is weary" we may conclude that it was a message of encouragement and salvation, good news to those—such as the Babylonian exiles—who were discouraged.

The second theme is the servant's obedience to the divine call in spite of serious opposition (verses 5-6). He suffered because of his particular message and that suffering included physical abuse, ridicule, and shame. We are not told who handed out such harsh treatment. It could even have been those same ones whom he sought to sustain with a word. He was not the first bearer of God's word to receive such treatment—consider Jeremiah 15:10-21; 26; 36:11-21—nor was he the last. The servant's reaction was courageous and persistent obedience to the God who called him to speak, and it was nonviolent. He turned the other cheek.

Third, the servant was able to endure opposition because of his trust in God's support and confirmation (verses 7-9). Acts of personal courage were possible for the servant not because of his own strength of character but because of his confidence in the justice of God. The confession of confidence, common in individual lament or complaint psalms, includes a general affirmation of God as helper (7a, 9a) and a more specific assertion that God vindicates (8a) the servant. Such vindication calls up images of both the law court and the practice of worship. Metaphorically, God is like the judge or jury that determines a charge, and declares one party not guilty (cf. 9a). Likewise the priest, either before a worshiper was allowed to enter the sanctuary or with the offering of a sacrifice, could declare the one before him to be innocent.

Heard in its original context, this passage was the servant of God's self-defense and argument for the validity of his message of good news. It was to evoke a response of affirmation from an audience of Judean exiles. Heard in Christian worship in this season, the lines interpret the life and death of Jesus for the church. Certainly Christians will hear in the obedience of the servant parallels to the life of Jesus. In addition, one of the specific contributions this text can make is to call attention to the prophetic dimensions of the life and death of Jesus.

Psalm 31:9-16

This lament, perhaps written for use by persons suffering some form of illness, contains all the features of this particular genre. Most of the psalm is speech directly addressed to the Deity. Verse 21, a bit of praise and proclamation, and verses 23-24, admonition in the form of a sermonette, are addressed by the worshiper to a human audience.

The overall structure of the psalm is as follows: (1) a general opening address to God which already contains the initial plea for help (verses 1-2); (2) a statement of confidence and trust in God (verses 3-6); (3) a future-oriented statement of confidence (verses 7-8); (4) a description of the trouble and distress (verses 9-13); (5) a third statement of confidence (verses 14-15a); (6) a second plea for help (verses 15b-18); (7) a third assertion of confidence (verses 19-20); (8) proclamation (verse 21); (9) thanksgiving (verse 22); and (10) admonition (verses 23-24).

The imagery of verses 6-19 clearly suggests the employ-ment of this psalm by one suffering from some form of illness. The author of Ecclesiasticus (or Sirach) in the Apocrypha outlines four steps to be taken when sick:

> My son, when you are sick do not be negligent,
> > but [1] pray to the Lord, and he will heal you.
> [2] Give up your faults and direct your hands aright,
> > and cleanse your heart from all sin.
> [3] Offer a sweet-smelling sacrifice,
> > > and a memorial portion of fine flour,
> > and pour oil on your offering,
> > > as much as you can afford.
> [4] And give the physician his place,
> > > for the Lord created him;
> > let him not leave you, for there is need of him.
> > > > > (38:9-12)

The four steps therefore were (1) prayer (perhaps the recitation of a psalm such as Ps. 31), (2) repentance, (3) the offering of a sacrifice (perhaps in conjunction with step number 1), and (4) a visit to the physician. (This, by the way, is the first "biblical" text that has a good word to say about doctors.)

The description of the distressful situation in verses 9-13 presents the person as one decimated by physical suffering (verses 9-10) and as a social outcast forced to endure life at the periphery of society without the benefit of friends or close acquaintances (verses 11-13).

Few psalms use as graphic descriptions to depict human misery and affliction as does Psalm 31. The descriptions are very graphic although reasonably nonspecific. Thus, when persons used this psalm in worship to describe their state of being, they could vent true feelings yet do so in highly stylized terms. Praying this psalm allowed persons to verbalize and express the deep-seated sense of alienation and hurt that they were feeling. The language appears to be highly metaphorical, probably using stereotypical and formulaic expressions that were highly graphic in content and emotional in nature. The labeling of one's troubles in such graphic fashion was probably therapeutic in and of itself since it allowed one to express sorrow and grief.

The expressions drawn from the arena of illness, in verses 9-10, if taken literally, suggest that the person was near death and had suffered miserably for years. The common words of suffering and affliction appear throughout these verses: distress, grief, sorrow, sighing, misery, wasting away.

In verses 11-13, the depiction of the distress uses the language of social ostracism. The descriptions here seek to present the worshiper's distress in the severest form possible. Adversaries, neighbors, acquaintances, and even the persons encountered in casual street meetings are all depicted as standing in terror and expressing disdain at the person's appearance (verse 11). Perhaps the supplicant was a person with some physical malady which rendered him or her unclean and required special isolation from general society (see Lev. 13:45-46). Job's description of his predicament, in Job 19:13-22, sounds very much like the cries of the outcast in verse 11.

The psalmist declares that he/she is like one already dead: passed out of life and even out of memory, cast aside like the shattered pieces of a broken pot—unwanted, useless, fit only for the garbage heap of the city dump (verse 12).

In fact, the psalmist describes the many out there who not only dislike him/her but who even scheme and plot to take his life (verse 13). Such language as this may sound like the ravings of a paranoid but should be seen as therapeutic language that allowed distressed persons to objectify their suffering to its most graphic, even exaggerated, level.

This psalm is not simply a recitation or a vale of sorrows. Throughout the text, there are frequent statements of a calm confidence in the Deity. Such is to be found in verses 14-15 in which the worshiper confesses trust in God and affirms that come what may the times of one's life are in the hand of God who can deliver one from the hand of enemies and persecutors.

Confidence in the Deity fades naturally into plea and petition for salvation (verses 15b-16). In spite of the description of the supplicant's condition in such sorrow-drawn and affliction-etched contours, confidence and calm flow through the psalm like a soothing stream. In this way it may parallel the composure of Jesus as he rode into Jerusalem—the man of sorrows but one confident of being in the hands of God.

Philippians 2:5-11

Since this text serves as the epistolary reading for Passion/Palm Sunday in all three years, the reader may wish to consult our remarks in *Lent, Holy Week, Easter* for Years B and C. Part of this passage (2:9-13) also supplies one of the options for the epistolary lesson for Holy Name of Jesus, Solemnity of Mary, observed on January 1. Our remarks can be found in the *Advent, Christmas, Epiphany* volumes for all three years. The longer form of today's text (2:1-13) supplies the epistolary reading for Proper 21 in Year A. In fact, the Epistle to the Philippians provides the semicontinuous readings for Propers 20–23 in Year A. Additional remarks can be found in *After Pentecost, Year A.*

Because this text is so extensively used in the *Common Lectionary*, we have treated certain of its features in other settings. As to its form, the preacher should note first that it is widely regarded as an early Christian hymn in which the work of Christ is unfolded as a cosmic drama: the heavenly Christ voluntarily relinquishes his exalted position, takes on human form, and lives as an obedient slave even to the point of humiliating death, but is returned to his heavenly status as the exalted Lord. The saving story is told in wide sweep. It is all there, and if we let our imaginations work, we can see small clusters of early Christians gathered for worship at house churches and hear them sing the story of their new faith.

Another angle of vision on the passage is provided by its history of interpretation. It has played a crucial role in kenosis Christology. The term is derived from *kenao* (verse 7), which means "to empty." At issue, of course, is what it meant for Christ to empty "himself, taking the form of a servant" (verse 7). We are quickly introduced to prickly questions of Christology with which the church has struggled historically. Does this mean that Christ emptied himself of his divinity when he became incarnate in human form? If so, did he do so entirely or partially, or even at all?

It is also a crucial passage for preexistence Christologies. It was not obvious to every early Christian that the Jesus who was confessed as Messiah necessarily existed prior to the time of his birth, much less that he had existed with God from the beginning, or even before the beginning of time. The Gospel of Mark, for example, unfolds a richly textured portrait of Christ without ever developing the notion of his preexistence. But in other circles, Christians drew this conclusion (cf. John 1:1-18), and today's text is one of the boldest assertions of this. It also suggests that this was an element of Christian faith and worship quite early on.

It should be noted, however, that today's text does not necessarily place the preexistent Christ with God *at the beginning of time*, as does the prologue to John's Gospel. Conceivably, Christ is simply envisioned as having existed in the "form of God" prior to his incarnation. But, if so, what does it mean that he did not regard equality with God as something to be clutched, snatched, or held on to (verse 6)?

Such christological questions abound and will continue to abound, and they deserve to be given serious attention because they introduce us to the way the church has struggled with the mystery of the Incarnation. But in the context of Passion/Palm Sunday and the celebration of Holy Week, several major themes emerge from the passage that we cannot easily ignore.

First, there is the clear insistence on the humanity of Christ (verses 6-8). The language used graphically underscores his full identification with and participation in earthly existence as we know it: "slave," "human likeness," "human form" (verse 7). Serious observance of Lent reminds each of us of the limitations of human existence and our need for God to complement this existence with divine possibilities by extending forgiveness to us. We cannot begin to celebrate this Christ-drama unless we understand fully that it occurred within the crucible of human history. No heavenly, cosmic drama, this. It is rather earth's story.

Second, there is the centrality of the death of Christ. In one sense, the center of this Christ-hymn occurs in verse

8—becoming "obedient unto death." It has been plausibly suggested that the following phrase, "even death on a cross," or more literally, "indeed a cross death," is Paul's editorial addition to the hymn. The language is surely his (cf. I Cor. 1:18–2:5; Gal. 6:14). If this is the case, it would suggest that, for him, "death" needed to be rendered more specifically, that the real scandal lay not in the death of Christ, but in the death of Christ *this way*. Herein was the curse (Gal. 3:13), the stark fact with which Good Friday annually confronts us.

Third, there is his vindication (verses 9-11). As surely as there is the humiliation, there follows exaltation. Perhaps the most striking feature of the second half of the hymn is God as subject. What we see here is the dramatic work of God bringing about the vindication of the obedient Son.

Matthew 26:14–27:66 *or* Matthew 27:11-54

The lectionary respects the two traditions about this Sunday, offering readings for its observance both as Passion and as Palm Sunday. For Passion Sunday the reading is the passion narrative of the appropriate Gospel or an alternate briefer reading from within the longer narrative, usually focusing on the crucifixion itself. As we shall see in the next lesson, the Palm Sunday reading is the record of Jesus entering Jerusalem.

First, a few words about the passion narrative itself (in Matt. 26:1–27:66). The apparently disproportionate amount of space given to this material by all the Evangelists testifies to its central place in the church's recollection of Jesus and in its preaching. And the fact that all four Gospels present basically the same sequence of events indicates that this tradition became fixed quite early and writers did not deal with it in the same freedom as with the remainder of the sources about Jesus' life. Matthew follows Mark closely, perhaps more closely than elsewhere. Except for variations in wording here and there, Matthew alters Mark primarily with four insertions: the death of Judas (27:3-8); the disturbing dream of Pilate's wife (27:19); Pilate washes his hands and all the people accept the guilt of Jesus' blood (27:24-25); and the placing of the guard at Jesus' tomb (27:62-66). One notices in this material the disappearance of the Pharisees as Jesus' opposition and the emergence of the chief priests and elders of the people as the primary force in effecting Jesus' death (26:3, 14, 47; 27:1). As a final introductory comment, notice how few are the sayings of Jesus in the passion narrative. Except at the table during the Last Supper, Jesus is relatively silent and is more the recipient of the actions of others than the one acting.

But how shall the preacher handle this extensive body of material in the sermon? Of course, the alternate reading is much briefer and the message could confine itself to that. In fact, the preacher could restrict the sermon's focus even further, leaving the remainder of the narrative to be carried by the liturgy. In some traditions the entire passion narrative is read with appropriate songs and prayers. It is here urged that whether through readings without comment, or with running comments interspersed, or with summary comments at noticeable breaks in the story, the entire passion narrative be shared in the service. This is the foundational tradition of the Christian community, providing its identity, its basic definition, and its message to the world. So seldom does the congregation get a continuous story, a sense of historical movement of cause and effect in its exposure to Scripture, that opportunities such as this should not be sacrificed in favor of a smaller and more manageable sermon text.

One way to divide the text for reading and comment is as follows:

The treachery of Judas (26:14-16)
The Last Supper (26:17-29), involving
    preparation for the Passover (verses 17-20),
    Jesus foretelling his betrayal (verses 21-25), and
    the institution of the eucharist (verses 26-29)
The arrest in the garden (26:30-56), involving
    Jesus' prediction of Peter's denial (verses 30-35),
    the hours of prayer (verses 36-46),
    betrayal and arrest (verses 47-55), and
    the disciples abandoning Jesus (verse 56)

The trials of Jesus (26:57–27:26), involving
  his appearance before the Sanhedrin (verses 57-68),
  Peter's denials in the courtyard (verses 69-75),
  the appearance before Pilate (27:1-23), and
  Pilate washing his hands of the affair (verses 24-26)
The crucifixion, death, and burial (27-66), involving
  the mockery of Jesus (verses 27-31),
  the crucifixion (verses 32-44),
  the death (verses 45-56), and
  the burial (verses 57-66)

On this particular Sunday the minister will want to resist the temptation to moralize, to exhort, or to grow sentimental. The text will create its own world in the minds and hearts of the listeners.

Monday in Holy Week

Isaiah 42:1-9; Psalm 36:5-10; Hebrews 9:11-15; John 12:1-11

All of the texts for the day evoke christological reflection and more in the mood of Palm Sunday than Passion Sunday. Their tone is hopeful, pointing beyond the crucifixion and even the resurrection of Jesus to the meaning of these events not only for the faithful but also for all peoples. Thus both the Old Testament and the epistolary lections look to a covenant for the people. The responsorial psalm is a hymn of praise to God for his steadfast love. One hears in the Gospel reading foreshadowings of all that will take place in Holy Week, from meals together with friends, to betrayal, to death, and even to resurrection.

Isaiah 42:1-9

This passage consists of the first of the Servant Songs (verses 1-4) plus the beginning (verses 5-9) of a unit (42:5-17) announcing and praising God's triumph in nature and history. For a general introduction to the Servant Songs and their literary and historical context, see the commentary on Isaiah 50:4-9*a* for Passion/Palm Sunday in this volume.

In the song itself, God is the speaker throughout, and he speaks to introduce the servant, whom he does not address but refers to in the third person. While the audience is not identified, it most likely is the same as the audience for most of the remainder of the book, that is, the people of Israel in exile. In view of the role of the servant to the nations as a whole, it is important to keep that perspective in mind.

Three points are of particular importance in the song, any one of which—or all three—call for proclamation in Christian worship. First, the servant has been chosen—and therefore authorized and empowered—by God (verse 1*a*). Forms of the

Hebrew word translated here "chosen" express the divine election of the people of Israel (Deut. 7:7; Isa. 14:1), of individuals such as Abraham (Neh. 9:7), of groups such as the Levites (Deut. 18:5; I Chron. 15:2), of David as king (I Sam. 10:24), and of the city of Jerusalem (II Chron. 6:6). Here the Lord expresses his warmth and pleasure in choosing this one ("in whom my soul delights"), and confirms that election with the gift of the divine spirit.

Second, in terms of demeanor and behavior, the servant is gentle, strong, and persistent. At this point we encounter some of the more difficult exegetical problems of the passage. Verse 2 probably means that he will speak quietly, not shouting in the street. It is the metaphors in verse 3*a* that are not clear. The "bruised reed" and "dimly burning wick" probably refer to the weak and downtrodden, those who have virtually lost hope if not life, whose fire is about to die. That would be consistent with the prophetic concern with the weak and oppressed.

Third, the role of the servant is to establish justice in the entire earth. This is the same justice that Amos (Amos 5:24) and Isaiah of Jerusalem (Isa. 1:17; 5:7) called for. It includes fair and equitable procedures, especially in the law courts, and equitable distribution of resources, particularly in its concern for the weak. Above all, its substance is based upon divine justice. Here that is expressed in the parallel between justice and "law" (verse 4). The law in view here probably is not the Torah or the law of Moses itself, but the servant's instructions and the application of the divine will for particular circumstances. The prophet envisages a world in which justice prevails because all live under the same law, the divine will.

The other part of today's reading (verses 5-9) gives a summary of the message of Second Isaiah as a whole, and in this context suggests a particular interpretation of the servant. First, in a series of subordinate clauses, the prophet states his understanding of God. God is the one who created the world and gave life to all its inhabitants (verse 5); he is not to be compared with any other, especially with "graven images" (verse 8). Second, this same God has called and chosen his people Israel, and kept them as his own (verse 6*a*).

Third, Israel has been called for a particular purpose, quite consistent with the role of the servant to establish justice in the earth. Israel is "a covenant to the people, a light to the nations" (verse 6*b*). It is their role to set prisoners free and to open the eyes of the blind. Doubtless this language is both literal and metaphorical. It includes actual release from prison or captivity and the enlightenment of those who do not see that God is doing "new things" (verse 9).

Thus verses 5-9 suggest a national but not a nationalistic interpretation of the servant as the people of Israel. They are the ones to bring justice to the nations, through the law of the Lord. If the church understands itself to be the chosen people of God, then it will assume that role as its own. But the passage contains more good news than law, more announcement of the saving will of God than obligation. It is, after all, God who intends to establish justice in the earth, both through his servant as an individual and his servant as the people.

Psalm 36:5-10

These verses of hymnic praise appear almost as a counter to verses 1-4 of the psalm. The latter describe the self-sufficiency, the self-flattery, the deceitful action, and the mischief-plotting of the wicked. One would anticipate such a depiction to be followed by a similar, contrasting portrait of the righteous (as in Ps. 1). This however is not the case since with verse 5 the focus shifts to affirmations about God, to descriptions of his righteousness and qualities. Humans again enter the horizon of the psalm with verse 7*b* but here the focus is on the benefits humanity derives from God. Verses 7*b*-9 may thus be seen as the contrast to verses 1-4. The description of the wicked (verses 1-4) in speaking of such people presents a picture of isolated individuals, living without any sense of fear before God, taking actions based on their own plans, constantly plotting and continuously being obsessed with their doings. On the other hand, the benefits described in verses 7*b*-9 speak of humans as a class sharing unstrivingly in what the Divine gives. In speaking of evil, the psalm speaks of the lone, isolated, self-occupied individual;

in speaking of the good, it speaks first of God and then of the people enjoying the blessings under the divine umbrella.

The ancient rabbis exegeted this text (at least verse 6) in terms of punishment for the wicked and reward for the righteous. In the midrash on the psalm, one rabbi put it this way: "Even as there can be no numbering of the mountains, so there can be no numbering of the rewards for the righteous. Like the deep which has no bounds, so the punishment for the wicked has no bounds. Like the mountains which are high and lofty, so the rewards for the righteous are high and lofty. And just as the waters of the deep are not all alike, some salty, some bitter, and some sweet, so the punishment for the wicked is not all alike."

In verses 5-6, God's love and faithfulness are extolled in terms of their immeasurable quality. In height, they extend to the heavens and up to the clouds. In constancy, they are like the mountains and the great deep beneath the earth. In breadth, God's concern to save is not limited by the boundaries of human existence but extends even to the beasts of the earth.

In verses 7-9, the poet focuses attention on the human benefits that accrue from the Divine or on what might be called the delights of enjoying God and his love. In verse 7, the neutral inclusive term "children of men" is used instead of the more customary "children of Israel." One could suppose that the psalmist here made a deliberate choice so as to universalize those included under divine favor. The image for protection in the verse—"in the shadow of thy wings"—may draw upon the protective role of the parent fowl in caring for its young. Such imagery, however, could be based on the fact that the ark, the representative symbol of God, rested in the Holy of Holies beneath the outstretched wings of the cherubim (see I Kings 8:7).

Just as verse 7 emphasizes the nature of protection offered by the Divine so verse 8 emphasizes the divine provision of food and drink. Some uncertainty exists about what "thy house" refers to. Is it reference to the earth or the world as a whole? (See Ps. 93:5 where this appears to be the case.) Or is it a reference to the temple as the house of God? In the former, "feast on the abundance of thy house" would refer to eating the fruits and products of the earth. In the latter case, the expression would refer to the sacrificial meals consumed in the temple precincts where eating and drinking were common (see I Sam. 1:3-8). In any case, the psalm emphasizes the value and worth of the more sensual aspects of life—eating and drinking—which are seldom viewed and enjoyed in relationship to the Divine.

Two images characterize the statement in verse 9—life and light; God is seen as the source of all life and divine light as the source of human light.

Lest the blessings of God prove to be temporary, the psalmist prays that God will continue his love and salvation (verse 10). Here the request is hemmed in somewhat when compared with verse 7b. In verse 10, those who know God and the upright of heart are the expected recipients of God's favor.

The association of this psalm with Holy Week can be made through its emphasis on God's loving-kindness and on the divine blessings bestowed upon humanity.

Hebrews 9:11-15

Some of the exegetical difficulties presented by this epistolary text, as well as its place and function within the Epistle to the Hebrews as a whole, are treated in our remarks in *Lent, Holy Week, Easter* in Years B and C. Today's remarks will be more broadly focused.

One of the real difficulties for modern readers of this text, clergy and laity alike, is its foreignness. It speaks of priests, animal sacrifices, and sanctuaries. We find this language of Israelite cult both ancient and mystifying. To complicate things further, our text envisions the cult at two levels— earthly and heavenly. Most of us find it difficult enough to understand the complexities and nuances of primitive religious cultic practices as they were actually practiced, or described, in historical settings, much less how they might have been envisioned as taking place in some supraterrestrial universe. To break through this barrier of unfamiliarity, the minister is well advised to consult commentaries on Hebrews as well as relevant dictionary or encyclopedia articles on topics such as "worship," "cult," and "sacrifice." In short, to understand this text and the conceptual framework it presupposes will require homework.

Having said this, however, we can make several observations. First, this text, like the Epistle to the Hebrews in general, is a critique of the cult. We are told earlier that the Levitical "offerings and sacrifices . . . cannot give the worshipper inward perfection" (verse 9, NEB). The Levitical sacrificial system is repeatedly criticized as being deficient: it consists of "outward ordinances" (verse 10).

As sharp and unqualified as this critique is, it is by no means the first or final polemic against the cult. The Old Testament consistently recognized the way in which cult could sidetrack religious devotion. Offering sacrifices and being truly obedient need not be the same. In fact, the one may be done as a poor substitute for the other. Samuel chides Saul for divorcing the two, reminding him that at the heart of meaningful sacrifice must lie obedient service (I Sam. 15:22-23). It is a theme that the prophets hammer home: "Loyalty is my desire, not sacrifice, not whole-offerings but the knowledge of God" (Hos. 6:6, NEB; Amos 4:4-5; 5:21-24; Mic. 6:6-8).

As long as sacrificial forms of religion have existed, the limitations of the cult have been recognized. Perceptive observers have seen the inadequacy of religious rites and the ease with which worshipers substitute form for meaning. We properly view our text when we see it as a critique of the cult standing within a long critical tradition.

Second, we should observe that the critique is distinctively christological. What was deficient about the Levitical system is now remedied by Christ. At the heart of our text is the conviction that Christ's death was sacrificial. It is compared with animal sacrifices and found to be eminently superior. For one thing, it was a *human*, as opposed to an *animal*, sacrifice. For another, it was no ordinary human, but the Son of God whose life was one of unblemished perfection (verses 14; 4:15; 5:9). Moreover, it was a death that ushered Christ into the very presence of God, the "heavenly sanctuary." What is implicit here, of course, is the conviction that Christ's resurrection elevated him to God's eternal presence (4:14;

8:1). Christ's role is thus seen as that of an extraordinary high priest, one who has gained access to the heavenly "Holy of Holies" in the most paradoxical fashion imaginable: by offering himself as a sacrifice.

What we find here is a critique thoroughly informed by Christian confession: Christ the perfect, unblemished high priest offering himself for the sins of the people.

Third, we should note the central emphasis on inward transformation. The sacrificial death of Christ somehow broke through a barrier and enabled a form of inner purification, a cleansing of the human conscience, which was not possible previously (verse 14). It enabled a form of genuine "service of the living God" (NEB).

We do well to ask how this was done, since it is a remarkable claim and one not altogether obvious from the text. There appear to be two aspects to the answer, both of which are functions of the work of Christ: (1) Christ as the paradigm of obedience, and (2) Christ's death as effecting moral purification.

At one level, the death of Christ is seen as an act of quintessential obedience in which the Son yields to the will of the Father (5:8-9). In this respect, he proves obedient and confirms Samuel's insistence that loyalty to God's will surpasses sacrificial offerings. What Christ offers us is a clear example of the superiority of obedience to sacrifice.

At another level, the death of Christ is seen as the event in which the effect of human sin is canceled. It is not simply a matter of sacrificial transfer, as if the moral purity of Christ is somehow transferred to those on behalf of whom he died. It is rather that the shedding of his blood actually serves as the effective cleansing of human impurity. It becomes a rite of purification in which the blood of Christ shed on the cross serves as a sacrificial offering through which God forgives those on behalf of whom the offering was made—in this case, those in Christ.

John 12:1-11

We have had many occasions to observe how a Gospel writer's location of a particular story within the narrative affects the meaning of the story. It is also true that the lectionary's location of a particular text in the Christian year affects the interpretation of that text. John 12:1-11 is a case in point. In John's Gospel the anointing of Jesus precedes his entry into Jerusalem (12:12-19), and in this same order the lectionary placed this text for the Sunday preceding Passion/Palm Sunday for Year C. Here, however, this lesson follows Passion/Palm Sunday, alerting the preacher that the text is to move the listeners even closer to Good Friday and the cross. By placing this story between Palm Sunday and Good Friday the lectionary is using the chronology of Matthew (26:6-13) and Mark (14:3-9). However, even though John has the anointing precede Passion/Palm Sunday, the story is most certainly a Holy Week event theologically, for this Evangelist fills the story with many pointers to Jesus' death.

First, let us separate the account from those of Matthew and Mark. (Luke has, at 7:36-50, the record of an anointing of Jesus by an unnamed sinful woman, in Galilee, in the house of Simon a Pharisee, and the message of the event is unrelated to Jesus' death.) For both Matthew and Mark, the anointing occurs in Bethany near Jerusalem, in the house of Simon the leper, is performed by "a woman," and is interpreted by Jesus as an anointing for his burial. John also locates the event in Bethany, and Jesus says of the anointing, "Let her keep it for the day of my burial" (verse 7). However, it occurs in the house of Lazarus and it is Lazarus' sister Mary who performs it. All the accounts have enough common elements to suggest they are derived from one occurrence, but the text before us has its own special accents.

The anointing in Bethany, like the event of the raising of Lazarus (11:1-44) which precedes it, has as its primary focus the prophecy of Jesus' death. This is stated explicitly in verses 9-11 which elaborate on 11:45-53 to the effect that the raising of Lazarus not only precipitated the plot to kill Jesus but also tied the fate of Lazarus to that of Jesus. However, prophecies of Jesus' death also fill the small drama of verses 1-8. The scene is Bethany where a cave tomb waits for a new occupant; the time is six days before Passover, the festival that in this Gospel prompts death talk as easily as 2:13-22 and 6:4-59; the house is that of Lazarus whose life will cost Jesus his (11:4); the anointing itself points to Jesus' burial (verse 7); and at the table is Judas who will betray Jesus (verse 4).

It will be important for the preacher of this text to distinguish between what the reader knows and what those present knew. The gloom and sorrow of Golgotha should not hang over that table. Out of love and gratitude for a brother restored, Martha and Mary provide a supper for Jesus. Mary enlarges that act of hospitality into a drama of devotion, submission, and beauty. It is the reader and not Mary who knows that the raising of Lazarus will effect Jesus' death, that Passover will be death time, that Judas will be chief accessory in Jesus' death, that the sweet aroma of the room prophesies the odor of burial spices. This is, or will soon be, a time of both grief and joy for Mary: grief that within a few days of preparing her brother's corpse she now anoints her friend's body for burial; joy that she was permitted to have a small role in the drama of Christ's redeeming passion. Mark adds to the story these words of Jesus: "And truly, I say to you, wherever the gospel is preached in the whole world, what she has done will be told in memory of her" (14:9; Matt. 26:13).

That Mary anointed Jesus for burial unwittingly does not rob the event of its meaning. In fact, that she did so unwittingly may even deepen the significance of her act. It is God's gift added to our simple acts that often elevates them to a place in the grander purposes that God has in mind. What we do and say is not limited in scope or effect to what we intended at the time.

Tuesday in Holy Week

Isaiah 49:1-7; Psalm 71:1-12; I Corinthians 1:18-31; John 12:20-36

The Gospel lections for Holy Week take the church at worship through the last days of Jesus and provide the framework for the other readings. John 12:20-36 gives us scenes of Jesus teaching the disciples and the crowd concerning the nature and meaning of his death. Isaiah 49:1-7 recounts the life, suffering, and exaltation of the servant of God. The psalm is a prayer for deliverance from enemies, the kind of petition that Jesus considered but decided not to make (John 12:27). The epistolary reading is Paul's meditation on the meaning of the cross as folly and the power of God.

Isaiah 49:1-7

Today's reading includes the second Servant Song in Deutero-Isaiah (verses 1-6), plus one additional verse. For information on the songs in general and on their historical and literary setting, see the commentary on Isaiah 50:4-9*a* for Passion/Palm Sunday in this volume.

In the first of the Servant Songs (Isa. 42:1-4; see the commentary for Monday in Holy Week), the Lord introduced the servant to the people of Israel. In this poem the servant himself is the speaker, addressing the peoples of the world as a whole, "you peoples from afar" (verse 1). The prophetic aspects of the servant's role, mentioned in the first song, are central in our passage. He speaks in a prophetic tone and style, opening the address with a typical call to attention (cf. Isa. 1:10; Amos 3:1; 4:1; 5:1) and speaking in the name of the Lord. Like many other prophets, the servant reports that he was called by God. His call "from the womb" (verses 1*b*, 5*a*) is a direct parallel to Jeremiah 1:5. Moreover, his frustration with his mission (verse 4*a*) is similar to that of other prophetic figures, especially Jeremiah. In the first song, the Lord insisted that he had called the servant; in this one the servant himself confirms and accepts that call (verses 5*b*, 6*a*), despite the difficulties he has encountered.

The passage is rich in themes and issues for reflection. Among these are the stress on the power of the divine word, the naming of the servant, and the role of the servant to the nations.

1. Since the prophetic dimensions of the servant's role are central, it is not surprising that his preparations for his task concern speaking. As in prophetic vocation accounts (Isa. 6; Jer. 1:10-17; Ezek. 1–3), attention is called to the mouth of the prophet (verse 2). Strong metaphors ("sharp sword," "polished arrow") emphasize the power and effectiveness of the servant's mouth. It is assumed as well that the authority of the servant's words, like that of a true prophet, stems from the fact that they are not his own but the Lord's. It is clear that in ancient Israel the word of God was creative (Gen. 1:3, 6) and that such creative power was unleashed through the speeches of prophets:

"See, I have set you this day over nations and over kingdoms,
to pluck up and to break down,
to destroy and to overthrow,
to build and to plant."
            (Jer. 1:10; cf. Amos 1:2)

It is clear, then, that the servant is to accomplish his call (bring Israel back, restore Israel, and extend God's salvation, verses 5-6) by means of the word of God which he is given to speak.

2. The servant knows who he is because the Lord has told him so: "You are my servant" (verse 3). Notice how much is said about the identity of the servant of God. God, he says, "named my name" (verse 1) and gave him as "a light to the nations" (verse 6), and he is confident that his "right" and "recompense" are with God. Such words convey far more than information. Such designation communicates identifi-

cation, but it also establishes identity. The servant knows who he is because God has declared him to be that one.

3. That the servant has a role toward Israel is clear: he is to bring the people back and to restore them. That return and restoration are not simply "spiritual," e.g., to revive their morale, but are concrete and political, that is, the servant is to be an agent in Yahweh's plan to return them to their land. But the servant has a task as well to the whole world. The meaning of that task is not so obvious, especially in view of the numerous passages in Second Isaiah that condemn, criticize, or even ridicule foreigners and their religious practices in particular (41:11-13; 49:7, 22-23; 43:3-4). But here, God says, the servant is a "light to the nations, that my salvation may reach to the end of the earth" (verse 6). It seems unlikely that the prophet anticipates explicit missionary activities to bring all peoples to acknowledge that Yahweh is God, and he certainly considers Israel to be a special, chosen people. However, since he knows that there is but one true God, whose will is justice, the prophet's vision cannot in the last analysis be contained. Finally, God will establish "salvation" to the ends of the earth, and that salvation will include justice and peace.

Psalm 71:1-12

This psalm, sharing features and wording with Psalm 31, is a lament as are all the psalms in Holy Week except for Psalm 116 used on Holy Thursday. Psalm 71 begins with a statement of trouble and a plea for help, that is, with a lamenting situation, but concludes with a strong sense of confidence and assurance that matters will be rectified. A sense of trust and a feeling of comfort and encouragement run throughout the psalm.

The following elements go to make up the psalm's content: description of trouble (verses 7-11), appeals for help (verses 2-4, 12-13, 17-18), statements of trust and confidence (1, 16, 19-21), and vows to perform certain actions in the future (verses 14-15, 22-24).

We can examine the salient features of this psalm in terms of (1) the nature of the distress, (2) the worshiper's statements of confidence, and (3) the nature of the help requested from God.

1. The troubles undergone by the worshiper are related primarily to his enemies. The gallery of opponents are described as "the wicked," "the unjust and cruel man," and "enemies" who seek the worshiper's life. (Reference is made to "accusers" in verse 13.) The bitterest opponents appear to be those enemies who consider the person forsaken by God and thus without help and support (verses 10-11). One might assume that the malady or problem the person had was taken as a sign that God has forsaken or is no longer supporting the one praying.

2. This psalm is permeated by a strong sense of trust and confidence. As the person looks back to the past, he or she affirms that God has been his/her trust from youth. God is even seen as the one who like a midwife took him/her from the mother's womb (verse 6). Looking to the future, the psalmist prays that the trust in and association with God, which was begun as a child, will continue into "old age and gray hairs" (verses 9, 18). A common theme throughout the psalm is that God is a refuge. The worshiper confesses that God is a refuge and at the same time prays that God will be a refuge (compare verses 1 and 7 with verse 3). The concept of a refuge is further explicated with reference to God as a strong fortress and a rock—all expressive of both stability and protection.

An interesting feature of the psalm's statements of confidence is the reference to the special role the person has for making known or proclaiming God not only to the contemporaries of the day but also to generations yet to come (verses 7-8, 18). This would suggest that the psalm was not originally composed for an ordinary Israelite but was probably written for the king who had a special responsibility for proclaiming the nation's God.

3. The petitions and appeals made to God for help focus primarily on the requests that God not forsake the worshiper (verses 9-10) or let the person be put to shame (verse 1). Shame plays both a positive and a negative function in the psalm. The worshiper asks to be preserved from shame (verse 1) and at the same time prays that the accusers be put

to shame and consumed (verse 13). Shame, of course, meant being put in a humiliating situation and at the same time having to accept the identity that the situation imposed.

This psalm can be exegeted and preached in the context of Holy Week since it expresses many of the factors that we think of in terms of Jesus' suffering: the opposition of enemies who do not believe God is his supporter, the trust and confidence of the worshiper, and a message to be proclaimed and made known to generations yet to come.

I Corinthians 1:18-31

This text figures prominently in the *Common Lectionary*. It is the fixed epistolary text for Tuesday in Holy Week and thus treated in *Lent, Holy Week, Easter* for Years B and C. The same text is also used as the second reading for the Fourth Sunday After Epiphany in Year A. Part of this text (1:18-24) provides the epistolary reading for Holy Cross (September 14) and is treated in *After Pentecost* in Years A, B, and C. Another portion (1:22-25) serves as the epistolary text for the Third Sunday of Lent in Year B.

Naturally, a text so popular and so historically influential within the church has many facets and can be explored in numerous directions.

First, we should note the polarizing effects of the message of the cross. It forces options among those it addresses, dividing "those who are perishing" from those "who are being saved" (verse 18). This is a common distinction in Paul, who recognizes that his gospel of the cross is veiled to outsiders (cf. verses 23-24; II Cor. 2:15; 4:3; also II Thess. 2:10). They fail to see because their eyes are blinded by "the god of this world" (II Cor. 4:4). To see the cross as a display of God's power, as a moment of illumination, requires special discernment (I Cor. 2:14).

Seen at one level, the cross represents a tragedy played out as a human drama: political forces at work against an unfortunate messianic pretender. But to see it at this level alone, Paul insists, is to see it with blinded eyes. Much more is at work: in this event cosmic forces struggle against the divine will (I Cor. 2:8-10). It is not a moment of human darkness but an event through which God's light shines (II Cor. 4:4). In a word, it is a revelatory event. In it, we learn something fundamental about God and the way God works in the world.

Paul knows full well that seeing the cross in this way is more than a matter of objective perception: it requires us to stand inside the cross, indeed to be transformed by the cross. It involves a special calling (verse 24). Some look at the cross and feel repelled, others are summoned. Seeing and experiencing the cross this way becomes a saving event. It creates a community of believers, those "who are being saved" (verse 18; cf. Acts 2:47; Luke 13:23).

This transformed vision of the cross sees in it a unique display of divine power (verse 18). If the crucified death became a moment of weakness, the resurrection became a display of divine power (II Cor. 13:4). This is the same gospel through which God's saving power is mediated to the believer (Rom. 1:16). What happened in the Christ-event also becomes normative for Christian existence. Human weakness, or human existence in all its limitations, serves as the focal center through which God's power is experienced (II Cor. 12:9). Christ is "God's power" (verse 24) since he serves as the focal event through which divine power transformed human weakness.

Second, the cross highlights the difference between human and divine wisdom. Human ways are sharply contrasted with God's ways. Here Paul launches a sustained critique of human wisdom and its limitations. In doing so, he is informed by a long and rich set of Old Testament traditions. There are passages he quotes explicitly (verse 19; Isa. 29:14; Ps. 33:10), but there are also various other echoes. The threefold: "Where is the wise . . . ? Where is the scribe? Where is the debater?" (verse 20), recalls prophetic critiques that question the limits and capacity of human wisdom (Isa. 19:11-12; 33:18; 44:25). We hear similar echoes in the Wisdom tradition (Job 12:13, 17). Just as Israel was reminded that God has no need of human consultants, so we are reminded in our text that God's way of confronting us through the cross need not conform to our expectations, much less require our approval.

This is an ironic thread woven throughout our text: what appears wise to us is foolish to God. Human systems of thought at their best are inadequate to contain or express God's wisdom. If we try to build intellectual towers of Babel to God's presence, they are bound to collapse (Rom. 1:21). Consequently, God takes the drastic action of reversing "the wisdom of the world" (verse 20). God turns our wisdom on its head. The mysteries of God become hidden to the "wise and understanding" and are revealed instead to babes (Matt. 11:25; cf. Rom. 11:33).

The prime example of human misguidedness is our fixation on the wrong indicators of God's divine presence: signs and wisdom. One way to look for evidence of God's power in the world is to look for signs and wonders, graphic displays of divine intervention (Matt. 12:38; Luke 11:16, 29-32; Matt. 16:1-4; Luke 23:8; John 2:18; 4:48; 6:30; 9:16; 11:47). For Paul, this is a sure way of being misguided. The paradox of the cross is that it appears to be a sign of divine impotence and absence when in fact it is precisely the opposite. We turn our heads away from the cross because it does not square with our expectations of divine presence, nor does it present us with grand, visible displays of the divine.

As such, the cross becomes a "scandal." It is a stumbling block to Jews, something on which the mind trips (cf. Matt. 16:23; also Isa. 8:14; I Pet. 2:8; Rom. 9:32-33).

The other way is through human wisdom: "Greeks seek wisdom" (cf. Acts 17:18). This is the way of the intellect. God stands at the end of a syllogism. But Paul also eschews reason as the avenue to God. One cannot look at the cross and see reasonableness. When we measure the cross by the canons of human reason, we conclude that it is folly (verse 23). Since this is the inevitable assessment, the cross calls our rational faculties into question. It forces us out of our categories of reason and it requires us to reconsider our universe of meaning.

The cross becomes a third option. It breaks the horns of the dilemma posed by signs and wisdom. It provides us a radically different lens through which to see God. As such, it becomes a testimony to God's power and wisdom (verse 24; cf. Rom. 1:16; Col. 2:3; Wisd. of Sol. 7:24-25; Hab. 3:19; Job 12:13).

What Paul is calling for here is an epistemological transformation. For him, the cross forces us to construe God and God's ways in a radically different fashion. It calls us to look for God's presence in unexpected places: in the cross rather than in signs, wonders, and reason. It undercuts our own tendency toward human presumption and excludes boasting (verses 30-31; cf. Jer. 9:22-23; II Cor. 10:17; Rom. 5:11; Gal. 6:14; Phil. 3:3). It teaches us that "all things are of God" (verse 30; II Cor. 5:18, 21; Phil. 3:9). The cross is the constant reminder that we stand before God and that God does not stand before us. We live subject to God, under and not over God. It is a reminder of the transcendent God.

John 12:20-36

We continue throughout Holy Week with texts from the fourth Gospel. Today's lesson follows John's account of Jesus' entry into Jerusalem (verses 12-19), a unit replaced this year with Matthew's record of the same event (21:1-11), the Gospel lection for last Sunday. The preacher may wish to reread John 11:45–12:19, not only to locate our text in Jerusalem at Passover time but also to capture the atmosphere of death and betrayal that surrounds the festivities of the high sabbath of Passover. The reader will also be reminded that in the midst of the celebrating and plotting, Jesus stands clear and firm as to "the hour" of God's purpose for his life.

"The hour has come for the Son of man to be glorified" (verse 23). This statement of Jesus was prompted by the coming of Greeks to see Jesus (verse 20), which in turn was prompted by a statement of the Pharisees, "Look, the world has gone after him" (verse 19). In other words, the unwitting comment by some Pharisees that the whole world was drawn to Jesus is a prophecy fulfilled in preview by the coming of Greeks. Who these Greeks are, what their origin is, and what happens to them are not primary concerns of the Evangelist. One would guess them to be Greeks who practice Judaism. Some commentators understand them symbolically as representing through Philip and Andrew (verse 22) a subsequent mission to Gentiles. For the writer they serve to prompt from Jesus a series of statements about his death, his return to God, and the meaning of that glorification (John's word for Jesus' death and exaltation) for the life of the world. Once Jesus' comments begin, the Greeks vanish from the story.

Apparently, the line of thought prompted by the request of the Greeks to see Jesus is as follows: in order to be available to the Greeks, that is, to the world, Jesus must die and be exalted to God's presence. The earthly career of the historical Jesus must now continue in the ministry of the dead and risen Christ who will be present and available to the church everywhere. The presence and availability of the living Christ will be the primary subject matter of the farewell discourses of chapters 14–16. The extensive and repeated treatment of this theme testifies to its importance for the Johannine church, and for us. Whether stated in terms of the living Christ or the Holy Spirit, the divine presence is essential for the life of the church.

The line of thought continues: Jesus reflects upon death in a threefold soliloquy: (1) there is a law of nature that death is a necessary precondition for the increase of more life (verse 24); (2) there is a law of discipleship that demands hating, or releasing, or giving one's life in order to have life (verse 25); and (3) the question arises immediately, But is the lord of nature and the master of disciples exempt from the law of death as essential for life? (verse 27). The answer is clearly a no. Instead of the Synoptics' "let this cup pass" Jesus says, "Father, save me from this hour? No, for this purpose I have come to this hour" (verse 27). Instead of the cry of dereliction from the cross (Mark 15:34), Jesus here receives heaven's confirmation (verse 28). Even though Jesus' soul is troubled (verse 27), very little of Gethsemane's painful struggle appears in John's Gospel. In fact, Jesus did not actually need the confirming voice of heaven; it was, he said, for the benefit of those nearby (verse 30). Not all heard the voice, of course (verse 29); Scripture and experience teach us that events which are for some people occasions of God's self-disclosure are for others natural occurrences.

The time has come; Jesus will be lifted up, both in the sense of being put on a cross and of being elevated to God (verse

32). From this point through verse 36 Jesus speaks of his death in two ways. His death is judgment in that light is judgment upon those who prefer darkness and in that life is judgment upon those who prefer death. And Jesus' death is victory over the ruler of this world (verse 31), for in Christ's presence in word and in the Holy Spirit persons of all nations and of all times will be drawn again to God (verse 32).

But even the clear word of judgment is softened a bit. "The light is with you for a little longer" (verse 35). For the sake of those of Jesus' time, of John's time, and of ours, the grace of God has stayed the end of all things.

Wednesday in Holy Week

Isaiah 50:4-9a; Psalm 70; Hebrews 12:1-3; John 13:21-30

The Old Testament lesson contains an address of the servant of Yahweh to a human audience. In this speech the servant confesses a serene confidence in God, in the instruction given by the divine, and in an ultimately successful vindication against charges hurled against and oppression carried out against the servant. The psalm is a prayer replete with pleas for help in a time of trouble. The Epistle text calls upon the Christian to endure suffering and hostility as did the Christ and a host of earlier Christians who in their trials bear witness to the faith. In the Gospel passage, the future course of suffering is set for Jesus by his dialogue with the disciples over the betrayal and the departure of Judas into the night to perform his act of darkness.

Isaiah 50:4-9*a*

This passage, the third of the Servant Songs in Second Isaiah, is the Old Testament reading for Passion/Palm Sunday, and has been discussed at that point in this volume.

Psalm 70

An almost identical doublet of Psalm 40:13-17, Psalm 70 is composed totally of speech directed to God (prayer). Except for verse 5, the psalm is all pleas and requests for God to act on behalf of the supplicant. Verse 5*a* may be said to describe the condition of distress ("poor and needy") while 5*c* is a statement of faith and trust in God ("Thou art my help and my deliverer").

The psalm could be interpreted in terms of four persons or groups spoken about in the psalm.

1. There is first of all the supplicant who is speaking. This supplicant says two things in self-description. (a) "My life is lived under threat and persecution." Various expressions give vent to this sense of living under the gun—others seek my life, desire my hurt, and already say, "Aha, Aha," as if my guilt and humiliation were already evident and clearly deserved. (b) In the self-description, the supplicant is said to be poor and needy. Such a depiction may be taken as mercy-seeking through pathetic appeal, as enticement to get God to act, or as a human response to anxiety. Perhaps all three factors underlie the expression.

2. A second group consists of the enemies/opponents of the supplicant. They are characterized in two fashions. (a) On the one hand, they are vicious, destructive, and anxious to witness the downfall of the worshiper. Remembering that such descriptions may be stereotypical and stylized rather than actual and historical, we are unable to produce a composite drawing of culprits. Was the worshiper a king? Then the enemies may have been conceived as foreigners. If the worshiper were a normal, average Israelite, then the enemies may have been fellow citizens or the imaginative product of the worshiper, and thus only symbolically real. (b) Other comments on the enemies are pleas for their embarrassment and failure. Note the strong terms expressive of harsh emotions—shame, confusion, turned back, brought to dishonor, appalled.

3. A third group spoken about are those "who seek thee" and "those who love thy salvation." This group, among which the supplicant would have been counted, could be called the faithful or righteous. The supplicant intercedes on their behalf asking that they be made to rejoice and be glad and allowed to affirm continuously that "God is great."

4. The final figure in the psalm is God. Two nouns describe the Deity (help and deliverer), two verbs ask for divine intervention (help and deliver), and one adjective characterizes God (great).

These four were also part of the scenario of the last week of Jesus' ministry, and thus this psalm manifests and reflects frequently encountered universal human situations.

Hebrews 12:1-3

Besides serving as the epistolary text for Wednesday in Holy Week in Years A, B, and C, this text also supplies part of the epistolary lection for Proper 15 in Year C. The reader may wish to consult our remarks in *Lent, Holy Week, Easter* in Years B and C as well as those in *After Pentecost, Year C*.

For Holy Week it is a fitting passage because of its singular focus on Jesus as the one "who leads us in our faith and brings it to perfection" (verse 2, JB). We are reminded of his willingness to "endure the cross," while "disregarding the shamefulness of it" (verse 2, JB). This is an illuminating remark concerning Jesus' own inner perspective. It suggests that he was fully aware of the scandal of the cross. Its curse he knew as he faced and experienced it, even as Christians recognized it in retrospect (Gal. 3:13-14).

We are told not only that he "endured the cross," but did so "for the joy that was set before him" (verse 2). The preacher will do well to pause at this phrase, because it jars us. If we read it too glibly, it looks as if Jesus headed to the cross with a sadomasochistic smile, as if the endurance of such pain could be motivated by some twisted quest for joy and blessedness. The Greek is not altogether clear, and the NEB provides an alternative rendering: "Who, in place of the joy that was open to him." This would be in keeping with the sentiment of the Christ-hymn in Philippians 2:5-11, where Christ lays aside his elevated status in order to become flesh (cf. II Cor. 8:9). To read it this way, the pain of the cross is a clear alternative to the joy of staying alive. If, however, we retain a reading that sees the joy as something lying in the future, we should see it as the *future* joy that would be his eventually in his exalted position as God's Son (cf. Acts 2:33; Ps. 110:1).

In either case, we should note that Jesus' endurance is not mitigated by his eventual exaltation. His was still a decision made in faith. In this respect, he was not unlike the host of faithful witnesses described in Hebrews 11. He looked to the future in hope and endured the cross. He did not endure the cross because the future was somehow already his. It is in this sense that he is "pioneer and perfecter of our faith" (verse 2). In faith he forged his way ahead, committing himself fully to the God of promise. Even though looking back, we know that humiliation gave way to exaltation, our text insists that Jesus had no clue of this as he looked ahead. His joy still lay *in the future* (so verse 2, JB), and the future lay beyond the cross, not before it.

Now Jesus has been fully exalted (verse 2), and for this reason he is the "perfecter of our faith." The witnesses mentioned earlier "did not receive what was promised" (11:39, JB). Their faith, like ours, is still to be vindicated. But unlike everyone else, Jesus has already been vindicated by God. His example is singular.

The point of this exposition is clear: it is to keep us from losing heart and growing weary (verse 3; cf. Gal. 6:9). The author is genuinely concerned that his readers might lapse into unbelief. He is already aware that some have turned back (6:1-8). What is desperately needed is a strong, compelling incentive for his readers.

This is how the athletic metaphor is intended to function. The Christian is envisioned as the runner who lays aside every weight and prepares to join the race that others have run (cf. I Cor. 9:24-27; Phil. 3:14). Surrounding us is the "cloud of witnesses," those who have run before us. This gallery is populated by those mentioned in chapter 11, and they are to serve as reminders and examples. The author realizes how powerful an incentive are those who have gone before us in faith. The deeds of our predecessors are well worth rehearsing even though we tend to idealize them. In retrospect, their flaws tend to fade. They should not for that reason be forgotten.

The preacher may wish to compare today's text with the extended list of Israel's notable predecessors in Sirach 44–50. It is much lengthier than Hebrews 11. The list of figures runs from Enoch to Simon, son of Onias, that is, from the patriarchal period to the Maccabean period. Unlike Hebrews 11, the various figures are not portrayed in terms of a single virtue such as faith, but they are praised nevertheless.

In this connection, we do well to note the way in which figures from the past provide both examples and incentives: Abraham (Rom. 4; James 2:21-24), Rahab (James 2:25-26), Job

(James 5:11), Elijah (James 5:17-18). But like Sirach, we can extend the list into our own time, so that our immediate ancestors are placed in the great succession of God's witnesses. This is precisely the move the author of the Epistle to the Hebrews makes. For him, the list that begins with Abel ends with Jesus. It is brought from the remote past into the recent past, and his readers are expected to link themselves with this story of faithful witness that has preceded them for centuries.

In the midst of Holy Week, our text provides us with a powerful incentive to be faithful. In one sense, the example of Jesus is singular and stands out from all the rest. He is, after all, the center of faith in a way no one else is. And yet, we stand surrounded with a gallery of faithful witnesses who, like us, committed themselves to the future of God's promise and leaned into it in hope. Theirs is an example of expectant faith even as Jesus is an example of realized faith.

John 13:21-30

The Gospel lessons for today and tomorrow are drawn from John 13. Verses 21-30, which record the exchange between Jesus and Judas at the last meal, are treated today so that verses 1-15, the account of the last meal itself, may direct our thoughts for tomorrow, Holy Thursday. Chapters 13–17 of John's Gospel are devoted to Jesus' preparation of his disciples for his farewell. Luke is the only other Evangelist to deal extensively with Jesus' departure, and he does so in two ways: (1) the risen Christ remains with his disciples forty days, teaching and preparing (Acts 1:1-5); and (2) Luke follows his Gospel with a second volume (Acts), which narrates how the disciples continue Christ's work in the world. John has no forty days or a second volume. Rather, he compresses into what seems to be one night prior to Jesus' arrest Jesus' preparation of the Twelve through exemplary act, discourse, and prayer.

In John 13:1-30 the crowds are not present and neither are the opponents; only Jesus and his followers are in view. Clearly the message here is for the church and not for outsiders. And the message is a strong one, warning the church against arrogance and triumphalism. As we will see in tomorrow's lection, the warning is first given in Christ's example of washing the disciples' feet, but it also occurs in the fact of treachery in the inner circle: "He who ate my bread has lifted his heel against me" (verse 18; Ps. 41:9). The act of Judas served as a painful reminder to the church of the ever-present possibility of disloyalty and betrayal within the community of faith. But Judas was a problem for the church, not only as a reminder that believers should never cease asking, "Lord, is it I?" but also as a burden upon the church's efforts to understand the death of Jesus. How else would one explain the fact that next to Jesus it is Judas whose presence is most determinative in the conversation and action of the three paragraphs in 13:1-30?

In verses 21-30, the action unfolds quite simply: Jesus predicts his betrayal, the disciples seek to learn who it is, Jesus reveals the betrayer by giving to Judas the morsel of bread, Jesus commands Judas to move quickly to his ugly deed, the disciples do not understand what Jesus meant, and Judas leaves. For the preacher to paint Judas in the obvious colors of a villain would be to miss the point of the text. Were he clearly the epitome of undisguised evil, then Jesus would not have had to point him out and the disciples would not have missed the meaning of the interchange between Jesus and Judas (verses 28-29). In fact, were Judas the very picture of evil, then his act would not have been so ugly. The stabbing truth is, Judas was chosen by Jesus to be a disciple, he had participated in all the benefits of working with Jesus and belonging to the inner circle, and he had been selected as treasurer of the group. Verses 21-30 give absolutely no indication that Judas had created in the other disciples any cause for suspicion. They simply do not see or hear betrayal in Jesus' words to Judas or Judas' early departure from the table. Of course, the Evangelist has been alerting the reader to Judas' treason since 6:71, but those are statements of hindsight and retrospection. John is not alone in the New Testament or in subsequent church history in the effort to understand the motives for Judas' behavior. Perhaps the quest has continued so long because the church has known that to understand Judas is to understand a darker side of itself.

Two details in verses 21-30 deserve brief attention. The first is the reference to "one of his disciples, whom Jesus loved" (verse 23). This unnamed disciple appears in six scenes in chapters 13–21, and except for the one at the cross with Jesus' mother (19:25-27), all will be in the company of Simon Peter (13:21-26; 18:15-18; 20:1-9; 21:4-7; 21:20-24). Commentaries will provide all the speculation about this disciple's identity. Suffice it here to say that this disciple was especially close to Jesus and gave to the Johannine church its authoritative continuity with Jesus. And since this disciple is presented as always preceding Peter in knowledge, faith, and relation to Jesus, we can assume that the Johannine circle of Christianity regarded itself as closer than the Petrine circle to the heart and truth of the Jesus tradition.

The second detail drawing our attention is the expression "and it was night" (verse 30). One suspects that the Evangelist is here, as in 3:2, using night symbolically to convey the nature of the activity being described. However, it is not without its literal reference to the time. The earliest known tradition related to the Last Supper preserves the time of that supper by referring to Judas' act: "The Lord Jesus on the night when he was betrayed took bread" (I Cor. 11:23).

Holy Thursday

Exodus 12:1-14; Psalm 116:12-19; I Corinthians 11:23-26;
John 13:1-15

The remembrance of Holy Thursday is awash in rich and multifaceted imagery. The visions ignited by the sparks of that imagery bring to mind the holy eating, drinking, and storytelling that memorialized the Passover celebration of the Exodus from Egypt (recalled in the Old Testament reading). Psalm 116 was one of the traditional psalms sung in conjunction with Passover, first in the temple as the paschal lambs were being slaughtered and then in the evening when the Passover meal was eaten in the homes. Christian celebrations bring to memory not only the imagery of the Passover but also, as in the Epistle lesson, they recall Jesus' last meal with the disciples and his words instituting the Eucharist celebration. Foot washing (the Pedilavium) has long been a component in celebration of Maundy (Holy) Thursday recalling the episode reported in the Gospel reading.

Exodus 12:1-14

The account of the institution of the Passover, the most appropriate Old Testament lesson for Holy Thursday, stands very close to the heart of the Old Testament story and ancient Israel's faith. Nothing was more central to that faith than the confession that Yahweh brought Israel out of Egypt. The Passover, believed to have been instituted on the very night that Israel was set free from Egypt, takes its meaning from the connection with the Exodus. Thus, each time the Passover was celebrated, including in the time of Jesus, the people of God remembered that they were slaves set free by their God.

While the section before us is relatively straightforward, it is part of a very complex section in the book of Exodus. Since it is the climax of the Exodus traditions, it has attracted a great many diverse elements. The unit, which reports the events immediately surrounding the departure from Egypt, begins in Exodus 11:1 and does not end until Exodus 13:16. One can identify four distinct motifs within this section. The most important is, of course, the departure from Egypt itself. Although this is noted quite briefly (12:37-39), it is the focal point of all other motifs. Second is the report of the final plague, the killing of the firstborn children of the Egyptians. This plague is quite distinct from those that preceded it, both in the fact that it was effective and in the extensive preparations for it. The third and fourth motifs are the religious ceremonies connected with the Exodus, the celebration of Passover and the Feast of Unleavened Bread. Passover is linked to the final plague because it entailed a procedure for ensuring that the Israelite firstborn would not be killed, and it is connected in very direct ways with the immediate departure from Egypt. The final plague is what motivated Pharaoh to release Israel, and the Passover was to have taken place just before they left.

Within this section of the book of Exodus there are duplicates, repetitions, and inconsistencies that reveal the presence of at least two sources, the Priestly Writer and the Yahwist. The style and technical terminology of Exodus 12:1-13 reveal that it comes from the Priestly Writer, and thus would date from the postexilic period, ca. 500 B.C. Exodus 12:14 begins a section that probably comes from the J source, perhaps as early as 900 B.C.

It is important to keep in mind that this passage is part of a narrative, a story more of divine actions than human events. Its setting is the history of salvation, the account of Yahweh's intervention to set his people free. In that context, Exodus 12:1-14 is a report of divine instructions to Moses and Aaron concerning the celebration of the Passover. Thus, everything except verse 1 is in the form of a speech of Yahweh, a direct address to Moses and Aaron. These instructions have the tone and contents of rules established for perpetuity, and thus reflect the perspective of Israelites centuries after the events.

The instructions are precise and detailed with regard to both time and actions. The month in which the Exodus takes place is to become the first month of the year, and the preparations for the Passover begin on the tenth day of the month (verses 2-3*a*). It is a family ceremony, with a lamb chosen for each household—that is, unless the household is too small for a lamb, in which case neighboring families are to join together to make up the right number to consume the lamb (verses 3*b*-4). A lamb without blemish is to be selected and then killed on the fourteenth day of the month (verses 5-6). Blood is to be smeared on the lintels and doorposts of the houses, and the meat is to be roasted and eaten with unleavened bread and bitter herbs (verses 7-9). The meal is to be eaten in haste, and anything not consumed by morning is to be burned (verses 10-11).

An explanation of the meaning of the meal and of the practices associated with it follows the instructions. The Lord will pass through the land of Egypt to destroy the firstborn, but will see the blood and "pass over" the Israelites (verses 12-13). Verse 14, which comes from another writer, stresses that the day is a "memorial day," and forever later generations will remember the Exodus.

In both the present text and later practice, Passover was combined with the Feast of Unleavened Bread. The former was a one-night communal meal and the latter was a seven-day festival. The combination was quite ancient, but the two originally were distinct. It seems likely that the Feast of Unleavened Bread was a pre-Israelite festival related to the agricultural year in Canaan. Passover, on the other hand, probably originated among seminomadic groups such as the Israelites, as a festival related to the movement of their flocks from winter to summer pasture. The feast certainly was a family ceremony during the early history of Israel. In later generations, Passover was one of the three major annual pilgrimage festivals, for which the people were to come to Jerusalem (Deut. 16:2-7).

The word "passover" (Hebrew *pesach*) is explained in this passage by connecting it with a verb for "to skip" or "hop over," but the actual etymology of the word is uncertain. Throughout the Old Testament it refers either to the festival described here or to the animal that is killed and eaten. Many passages use the word in both senses (e.g., II Chron. 35:1-19). The ceremony had both sacrificial and communal dimensions, in that the animal was ceremonially slaughtered but then consumed as a family meal.

No ceremony was more important in ancient Israel or early Judaism than Passover. It was the festival in which the people acknowledged and celebrated who they were and who their God was. In remembering the day as the memorial day for the Exodus (Exod. 12:14), they acknowledged that God is the one who sets people free and makes them his own. They knew thereby that they were God's people. Moreover, in the gathering of family and friends for a communal meal in which the story of release from slavery was told, they bound themselves together and to the God who acted to make them who they were.

Psalm 116:12-19

The first nine verses of this psalm were the psalm selection for Lent 5, Year A (see pages 63-64). This particular reading for Holy Thursday has been selected on the basis of the reference to the cup in verse 13 and thus its connection with the imagery of the Last Supper.

Psalm 116 was composed as a thanksgiving psalm to be offered by someone who had escaped the clutches of death, who had stood at the doors of Sheol, but who had recovered from sickness and could again worship and celebrate in thanksgiving at the temple.

In early Judaism, at the time of Jesus, this psalm along with Psalms 113–115 and 117–118 was sung in the temple by the Levites at the time of the slaughter of the Passover lambs and again at dinner when the Passover meal was eaten in a family celebration.

Verses 12-19 of this psalm are concerned with the fulfillment of vows made earlier, probably at the time when the worshiper petitioned God for deliverance from trouble, most likely a debilitating illness. In rendering the vows, which would certainly have included offering the sacrifice, the worshiper addresses a human audience (verses 12-15,

18-19) as well as the Deity (verses 16-17). We should think of such thanksgiving rituals as times of great happiness and jubilant celebration. A person whose life has been threatened, disoriented, and removed from the normal course of activity had been restored to wholeness. The life that had fallen into the grip of hell itself and had been invaded by the power of death was now free of both the illness and the anguished turmoil that the sickness brought. Now the worshiper can look back and speak of the sorrowful plight of the past which now is only a life transforming memory. There certainly must be "scars" from such a past, but they are signs of past triumphs and the residues of God's grace, to be cherished and celebrated, not embarrassingly hidden. At such a celebration, friends and family of the formerly ill person would have attended worship with the redeemed. Such worship would have included not only thanksgiving in word but also feasting, drinking, and dancing. These festive symbols marked the end of a former state and the beginning of a new state of living. They were enjoyed as the sacramental signs of God's concern and care.

In verses 12-15, the worshiper addresses a human audience of friends and family. The elements of the thanksgiving spoken of included the offering of a cup of salvation, the worship of God, and the fulfillment of vows. The cup mentioned is best understood as the drink offering made as part of the thanksgiving sacrificial ritual (see Num. 28:7) or perhaps the cup of wine drunk in the thanksgiving meal (Ps. 23:5). Such a cup symbolized God's deliverance, the opposite of the cup of God's wrath (see Isa. 51:17; Jer. 25:15). The worshiper reminds the listeners that God does not wish the death of one of his faithful worshipers because for God such a death is a serious, weighty matter (verse 15).

The place of the thanksgiving celebration was the temple in Jerusalem where sacrifices would be made (verses 18-19). In such thanksgiving services, most of the animal sacrificed would have reverted to the worshiper to be cooked and eaten in the temple precincts before the next day had passed (see Lev. 6:11-18). Thus the sacrifice of thanksgiving imposed lavish and extravagant eating and communal sharing.

Verses 16-17 would have been prayed directly to God in

conjunction with offering the thanksgiving sacrifice. The worshiper thus declared his/her status before God, "I am thy servant," a status dependent upon the redemptive work of God, "Thou hast loosed my bonds."

I Corinthians 11:23-26

Here we have Paul's account of the institution of the Lord's Supper (cf. Matt. 26:26-28; Mark 14:22-24; Luke 22:14-23). It is especially remarkable in being the earliest Christian account of the institution of Eucharist. Since Paul's first epistle to the Corinthians was written in the early 50s, this account precedes the written Gospel accounts by some fifteen to twenty years at least.

It is, of course, even earlier than this. When Paul speaks of "receiving" and "delivering" this tradition, he is using the technical language used in both Jewish and non-Jewish writers to describe the transmission of sacred teachings or tradition. He uses similar language to introduce summaries of early Christian preaching (I Cor. 15:3). What we have here, then, is a tradition that is older than Paul, one that he had received "from the Lord" (verse 23). This is his way of underscoring its divine authority (cf. I Cor. 7:10, 12, 25, 40; 9:14; 14:37; 15:3; I Thess. 4:5). Rather than signifying that he had received it in a moment of inspired ecstasy, the language suggests that this tradition is ultimately traceable to the Lord (cf. Gal. 1:12). It was a tradition begun by Jesus and transmitted through successive witnesses who faithfully preserved it in tact. Paul stands in this succession as a faithful tradent.

The tradition is cited here in response to certain abuses within the Corinthian church (11:17-22). Their celebration of the sacred meal had become an occasion for accentuating the social differences within the church. The rich were being distinguished from the poor (verse 22). Rather than serving as an occasion for reinforcing a sense of community, the sacred meal was becoming a divisive force (verse 18). In addition, it had become an occasion for overindulgence (verse 21). In a word, it had ceased to be the "Lord's Supper" (verse 21). It had lost its sacred function as it served their own ends.

This helps explain some of the distinctive features of the Pauline version of the eucharistic tradition. We notice first that the bread is celebrated as the "body which is for you" (verse 24). The stress is on an act performed in behalf of others. In the Matthean and Markan accounts, we find a similar interpretation of the cup which is "poured out for many" (Matt. 26:28; Mark 14:24; cf. Luke 22:20). In one version of the Lukan account, the bread is similarly interpreted. But in the context of I Corinthians 11, where Christians are observing the sacred meal with "robust individualism," Paul's words serve as an important corrective. The bread serves as a reminder that the death of Christ should solidify the church as a community of believers—all believers, rich and poor alike. It is not the sole possession of any one person, much less an event observed by indulging the self.

Another remarkable feature, which is shared with the Lukan account (Luke 22:19), is the injunction: "Do this as a memorial of me" (NEB). The Greek word for memorial *(anamnesis)* has a long and rich history and seems to imply both recollection and reenactment. If so, it invites us to recall the event as a past event, but in doing so to appropriate the event to our own present by making that historical moment part of our own history. The text clearly envisions that the meal would be celebrated subsequently as Christians gathered for worship. Thus "as often as" Christians ate the bread and drank the cup (verse 26), they would celebrate the death of Christ in expectation of his return.

We should also note the stress on the cup as the "new covenant" (verse 25), another feature the Pauline account shares with Luke (22:20). What was envisioned by Jeremiah (Jer. 31:31; 32:40; cf. Zech. 24:8) is now seen to be fulfilled in the death of Christ. The fuller implications are explored by Paul in the second epistle to the Corinthians (II Cor. 3:6; cf. Heb. 7:22).

The preacher will do well to note these distinctive features of the Pauline tradition of the Eucharist. Its similarities with the Lukan version may suggest dependence or common origin. But the Synoptic accounts are one with Paul in their insistence that the Eucharist celebrates a sacred moment in the Christ story. It serves as a reminder that the breaking of Christ's body and the shedding of his blood are central elements of Christian belief and practice.

John 13:1-15

"Now before the feast of the Passover" (13:1), says this Evangelist, alerting the reader that the account that follows will be different from the Synoptic records of the last meal. In the Synoptics, Jesus eats the Passover meal with the Twelve (Matt. 26:17-19; Mark 14:12-16; Luke 22:7-13, and especially Luke 22:15) and, following the meal, institutes the Lord's Supper (Matt. 26:26-29; Mark 14:22-25; Luke 22:15-20). In John, the last meal is before Passover and there is no account here of the institution of the Eucharist. For this Evangelist, Jesus does not *eat* the Passover; he *is* the Passover, bleeding and dying as the Passover lamb (19:31-37). In chapter 6, John presents the feeding of the five thousand as a Passover meal with a eucharistic interpretation. The commentaries will discuss whether John is to be taken as a correction of the Synoptics, as exhibiting evidence of a different source, or as the writer's willingness to sacrifice chronology for theology.

For this Evangelist, therefore, the last meal is the occasion, the setting for particular words and acts of Jesus. The central act of Jesus in this text is the washing of the disciples' feet (verses 2-5). The act is not understood (verse 7), even though it is followed by two interpretations (verses 6-11, 12-20). It is very important, however, for the reader to understand that Jesus knows exactly what he is doing and what it means. Notice: "Jesus, knowing that the Father had given all things into his hands" (verse 3); "for he knew who was to betray him" (verse 11); and, "I know whom I have chosen" (verse 18). This portrayal of Jesus is consistent with the way John presents him from the prologue through the entire Gospel. Whatever clashes with other portraits of Jesus this may create for the reader, it should be appreciated that John is giving confidence and engendering faith (verse 19) in Christians who might otherwise look upon the events of betrayal, arrest, and death as defeat. After all, John's readers were experiencing betrayal, arrest, and death (15:20–16:3), and to understand these events in Jesus' life as part of a divine plan of redemption would help them interpret their own experiences as having purpose. In other words, Jesus was not really a victim, and, even in death, neither are they victims.

The scene, then, is a powerful and moving one. Jesus is fully aware of his origin in glory; he is fully aware that he is soon to return to that glory; he is further aware that while on earth, all authority from God is his (verses 1-3). The stage is set by verses 1-3 for Jesus to act in a dazzling way. Will he be transfigured before their eyes? Will he command the disciples to bow in adoration? No; instead he rose from the table, replaced his robe with a towel, poured water in a basin, washed the disciples' feet, and dried them with the towel (verses 4-5).

Following the foot washing, two interpretations of the act are offered. Whether the fact that there are two represents two traditions about the meaning of Jesus' act or whether both were from the beginning associated with the event is a matter debated in the commentaries. As we shall see, the two interpretations are not unrelated. The first (verses 6-11) insists that the church is in the posture of recipient, having its identity and character in the self-giving act of the servant Jesus. The church exists by the cleansing act of Jesus. (Some ecclesiastical traditions therefore associate the washing with baptism.) It is this understanding that Simon Peter resists (verses 6-9). The church in the person of Simon Peter does not want its Lord and Savior to wash its feet.

The second interpretation (verses 12-15, but it actually extends through verse 20) understands Jesus' act as a model of humility and service which the church is to emulate. This has been the more widely embraced interpretation, both by the few churches that have accorded foot washing sacramental status and the many that have not. The lesson is not lost even among those who do not continue the practice of foot washing. Perhaps one reason this second interpretation is more widely embraced than the first is that giving service is easier for the ego than receiving it. However, the two interpretations are not necessarily independent of each other. In fact, the church in a state of spiritual health and with a clear sense of its own nature and calling would practice the second because it had embraced the first.

Good Friday

Isaiah 52:13–53:12; Psalm 22:1-18; Hebrews 4:14-16; 5:7-9;
John 18:1–19:42 or John 19:17-30

Good Friday services tend to focus on the suffering of Jesus as the servant of God. This is a correct and proper theme for the day. Good Friday also, however, looks forward, beyond itself, beyond suffering and humiliation, to exaltation, triumph, and Easter. Suffering is a theme in all of today's texts but the texts also point beyond suffering. The so-called fourth servant song in Isaiah ends on a note of triumph as does the psalm reading. The Epistle exhorts Christians to meditate on the sufferings of Christ, sufferings that reflect his identity with humans but sufferings over which he was triumphant. The Gospel lesson speaks of the suffering and death of God's elect but the narrative it tells is not the final word of the gospel.

Isaiah 52:13–53:12

Second Isaiah's fourth Servant Song is the obvious Old Testament reading for Good Friday. As early as the first century, Christians have seen in these lines a prophecy of the suffering and death of Jesus (cf. Acts 8:34), but clearly the passage served as far more than proof that Jesus was the one sent by God. It helped the earliest church both to understand the meaning of the death of Jesus and to communicate that understanding to others. Furthermore, in addition to seeing Jesus through these verses, Christians through the centuries have recognized themselves here as well, letting many of the words spoken by the crowd about the servant express their own responses to the death of Jesus.

Such inclinations to hear a Christian meaning in this text certainly are strengthened on Good Friday, one of the most important days in the church year, and in the last analysis they should not be resisted. However, if the Old Testament reading is to make its particular contribution to worship and understanding on this occasion, it is important to remind ourselves that it comes from a different religion than the Christian faith, and from an age distant not only from ours but from the early church as well. The poem was originally written about 539 B.C., and its audience was the Judean exiles in Babylon. (For a general introduction to the Servant Songs of Second Isaiah in their literary and historical context, see the commentary on Isa. 50:4-9*a* for Passion/Palm Sunday in this volume.)

The poem evokes theological reflection on matters essential to faith, including vicarious suffering, redemption from sin, and the will of God. Certainly this text lends support to a Christology that sees the power of God revealed in weakness. Far more important than deriving dogma from the text, however, is allowing its narrative and dramatic features to be heard, seen, and felt.

The dramatic aspects include the shifts in speakers. At the beginning (52:12-15) and the end (53:11*b*-12) the Lord is the speaker. The addressees are not indicated, but probably are the people of Israel. Nevertheless, the content of the divine speeches concerns the whole world. God presents the servant as his chosen one and indicates that he intends to exalt him through and beyond his suffering, because he has faithfully fulfilled his vocation (52:13, 15; 53:12). In the central part of the poem (52:1-11*a*) the words are spoken by a corporate body, doubtless the members of the servant's community. They speak to and among themselves, recounting the life and suffering of the servant and their own reaction to him and meditating on the meaning of his life and death. It amounts to dramatic understatement that the servant himself speaks not a word in the poem. His life and death are the subject of the entire passage, but, as in his trial (53:7), he is silent. Everything here concerns the reaction of others—both divine and human—to the servant's faithfulness.

Dramatic also are the numerous reversals of roles and expectations. God exalts the lowly one (52:13-15), so that those who were astonished at his horrible appearance will be amazed at his elevation. The one who was considered guilty is the one who carries away the guilt of others (53:11-12). Those who rejected him as guilty and repulsive (53:2-3, 7-9) reverse themselves, confessing their own guilt and the servant's innocence (53:5-6, 9-10). Nothing, it seems, is as it first appears.

The narrative dimensions consist primarily in the people's recital of the story of the servant's life. The report begins with an expression of astonishment at what they have seen, indeed, at the power of God that has been revealed to them (53:1) through the life and suffering of the servant. Then they report how he grew up among them, suffered and was despised (53:2-3). They describe in some detail but also through the use of metaphorical language a trial and the subsequent death of the Lord's servant (53:7-9). Legal language and images dominate. He was hauled into court, tried, condemned as guilty, and executed.

In addition to its dramatic and narrative aspects, the passage includes reflection upon and interpretation of the meaning of the servant's life and death. Two points in particular must be noted. First, there is above all the astonishing realization that the death of this one who was despised and rejected is vicarious. It is on behalf of those very ones who had considered him guilty. His suffering is for others, and it is salvific: "He was bruised for our iniquities . . . and with his stripes we are healed" (53:5). Second, the suffering of the servant is seen to bring about a dramatic transformation in those who have witnessed it. The community had considered him repulsive and guilty of some crime. But when they see his trial and death they realize that this one has suffered on their behalf and that it was he who was innocent and they who were guilty. It is not simply that they realized that they were wrong. It was a legal fact that they were the guilty ones. So in one sense the Servant Song becomes a confession of sin on behalf of those who have seen God's suffering servant. That makes it possible to take the next step, to accept the servant's suffering on their behalf, that he "bore the sin of many" (53:12) and that his pain has made them whole (53:5-6). And all of this—the suffering of the servant in order to redeem those who considered him the guilty one—is the will of God. Thus confession of sin leads to the good news that God has chosen this way to make sinners whole.

Psalm 22:1-18

Like Psalm 51, this psalm has become traditional for use during Holy Week and is a lection for Good Friday in all three years (see also Easter 5, year B). The reasons for the association of this psalm with Good Friday are threefold: (1) its content bears striking resemblance to the events of Jesus' trial and crucifixion (so much so that the psalm may be seen as one of the "sources" used by the church in speaking about the crucifixion); (2) according to Mark 15:34, Jesus quoted at least the opening lines of this psalm while hanging upon the cross; and (3) John 19:24 quotes from this psalm to illustrate the belief that actions and events in the life and career of Jesus were to fulfill scripture, in this case Psalm 22:18.

The psalm lection for today does not include the psalm in its entirety. The optimistic, upbeat portion, verses 22-31, is omitted. Thus, the emphasis falls on suffering, not victory.

In verses 1-18, we find an opening address infused with a strong complaint against God for inactivity (verses 1-2), a statement of confidence (verses 3-5), a description of distress (verses 6-8), a second statement of confidence (verses 9-10), a plea for help (verse 11), and a second description of distress (verses 12-18). Thus, in spite of the omission of verses 22-31 with their expressions of hope, trust, and assurance (their Easterlike orientation), the psalm still oozes serenity and optimism in the midst of turmoil.

In the Gospel reading, John places the crucifixion of Jesus prior to Passover (see John 18:28) at about the time the paschal lambs would have been slaughtered in the temple (see John 19:14). The early Christians certainly seem to have combined this psalm, Jesus' death, and the Passover celebration. Given John's Gospel with its particular chronology, it is not out of place to see themes from Passover as providing some perspectives through which to interpret Psalm 22.

The Mishnah, in describing the Passover celebration, noted that in telling the story of the Exodus, the "father" of the household "begins with the disgrace and ends with the glory," that is, begins with the slavery, the servitude, and the suffering and moves to the escape, the freedom, and the joy of the redemption. The Mishnah continues: "In every generation a man must so regard himself as if he came forth himself out of Egypt, for it is written, *And thou shalt tell thy son in that day saying, It is because of that which the Lord did for me when I came forth out of Egypt* (Exod. 13:8). Therefore are we bound to give thanks, to praise, to glorify, to honour, to exalt, to extol, and to bless him who wrought all these wonders for our fathers and for us. He brought us out from bondage to freedom, from sorrow to gladness, and from mourning to a Festival-day, and from darkness to great light, and from servitude to redemption."

In Psalm 22 two themes run through the statements about the person's distress: a sense of alienation from the Deity and hostile opposition from opponents.

The theme of God's distance and correspondingly the person's sense of alienation are sounded in the opening lines. A sense of divine forsakenness pervades the words—God is too far away to hear the sufferer's groanings; day and night move through their ceaseless revolutions, but for the worshiper there is neither answer nor rest from God but only dismay at the divine silence and the loneliness of feeling forsaken.

The theme of human opposition parallels that of divine alienation. If God is too far distant, humans are too near. Human opposition and enmity are described in various ways. People mock, wagging their heads and making faces, ridiculing the person's dependence and seemingly futile reliance on God (verses 7-8). Powers described as bulls, lions, and dogs, and company of evildoers, assail the worshiper (verses 12-13, 16). The depiction might suggest that the speaker was a king and the enemies were foreign powers. In any case, the opponents are portrayed as menacing, life-threatening, and life-destroying. They seize the person's abandonment by God as the occasion for attack.

The consequences of the worshiper's status are described

in terms suggesting low self-esteem, complete despair and disorganization, and overall desperation. The image of a person's self-designation as a worm implies a feeling of utter hopelessness and helplessness, a state of feeling horribly subhuman (verse 6). Fright and incapacitation run through the imagery of verses 14-15 and 17-18 which are extremely graphic. Life seems no longer to have legitimate boundaries and normal structures ("poured out like water"); things do not function as they should ("bones are out of joint"); fear pervades everything ("heart is like wax . . . melted"); strength has ebbed away ("dried up like a potsherd"); speech fails ("tongue cleaves to my jaws"); death seems to be the only foreseeable certainty; and emaciation exposes the body's boney structure ("count all my bones"). The enemies are pictured as already going through the postmortem ritual of dividing up the belongings of the deceased as if death had already occurred. The psalmist speaks of his own demise and the distribution of his goods in a game of fortune and luck. Although not greatly emphasized in the psalm is the fact that God appears as the real enemy of the worshiper. The last line of verse 15 declares that it is God who has already laid the supplicant in the dust of death. Behind the opposition and oppression of the enemy lies the activity of God, so God becomes the real opponent.

In spite of the dismal picture that the descriptions of distress paint, the psalm is shot through with the statements and confessions of great confidence in the Deity. Verses 3-5 affirm that God is holy and that in the past the faith and trust of the fathers were rewarded with divine favor. Such confidence in the worshiper was based on both the nature of God and the experience of the past, that is, the paradigm of the past functions as a source of hope for the future. The confidence in God, expressed in verses 9-10, stresses the prior intimacy that existed between the one praying and God. The psalmist seems to be implying that previously God had been his/her "father," his/her caretaker from the days of birth and youth.

The confidence in God displayed throughout the psalm moves in verses 22-31 to pride of place and suggests that the worshiper received from God some oracle or sign affirming that a reversal of fate was in store, that tears and pains would be replaced by songs and celebration. The lection for Good Friday, however, ends with the pain and tribulation—not with victory and triumph.

Hebrews 4:14-16; 5:7-9

This set of epistolary texts serves as the second lesson for Good Friday in all three years. Additional remarks on the passages may be found in *Lent, Holy Week, Easter* for Years B and C. The first part of today's lection (4:14-16) also serves as the epistolary lection for Proper 24 in Year B, and the reader may wish to consult our remarks in *After Pentecost, Year B.* The second part of today's lection overlaps with the epistolary lesson (5:7-10) for the Fifth Sunday of Lent in Year B, which is also treated in *Lent, Holy Week, Easter, Year B.*

The dominant christological image of these remarks is Christ, the great high priest. It is the major christological theme elaborated in the Epistle to the Hebrews (2:17; 3:1; 5:5, 10; 6:20; 7:26; 8:1; 9:11; 10:21). Great stress is laid on the uniqueness of this role, so much so that Jesus is likened to the enigmatic Old Testament priest Melchizedek (5:10; 7:1-28; cf. Gen. 14:17-20). The metaphor of Jesus as high priest is employed as a way of comparing the work of Jesus with that of Levitical priests. One of its values is that it provides an image with which the readers can identify: the priest was a human figure known in everyday life. It thus serves as an effective image for underscoring the humanity of Jesus. But at the same time, the comparison serves to highlight the differences between Jesus and his priestly counterparts. What emerges is a figure who is incomparably superior.

The context in which today's epistolary text is read is Good Friday. While it is important for the preacher to understand the Levitical priesthood and the elaborate, intricate christological argument unfolded in the Epistle to the Hebrews, we must not get lost in this sacerdotal labyrinth. We must grapple with the essential message of our text within this liturgical setting.

Above all, we should note the way in which our text encapsulates the essential paradox of the Christ-event that we celebrate. There are two strands woven together in our passage. On the one hand, our text speaks of *the* Son of God, the exalted Christ, the great high priest. Unlike the Levitical high priest who annually passed through the outer sanctuary and entered the Most Holy Place, Christ has "passed through" in a more dramatic fashion: he has "passed through the heavens" (verse 14). No longer does this high priest enter the Holy of Holies where God dwells *in absentia*. Instead he presides at the heavenly throne of God. Here we have the heavenly exalted Christ.

But another strand is also woven through today's text. Alongside this image of the exalted Son of God is the high priest who knows human existence as we know it. We are told that "in the days of his earthly life" (5:7, NEB), he besought God to deliver him from death. Here we detect a note of urgency, if not desperation. We are told of "prayers and supplications" uttered "aloud and in silent tears" (5:7, JB). This is not the mood of quiet resignation, of stoic resolve. It is rather the imploring cry of a desperate human being facing death, looking for a way out. This may be a reference to the tradition of Jesus in Gethsemane (cf. Luke 22:32, 39-46; also John 17), or the author may have some other tradition or reminiscence in mind. The particular historical referent is immaterial. What is important is for us to see that it is a kind of fear with which we all can identify.

Our text also insists that in Jesus "we have one who has been tempted in every way that we are" (4:15, JB). This is a claim against which the church has traditionally recoiled. It asserts a level of humanity that we are unable to grant. Naturally this was the central mystery with which the church dealt in the early christological controversies: how the divine Son of God could have been fully human, even to the point of experiencing every kind of temptation that we endure. Even so, we are told that he did, yet was "without sin" (4:15).

As much as Christian faith is anchored in the exalted Christ, so is it tied to the human figure Jesus. Thus we are reminded that "although he was a Son, he learned obedience through what he suffered" (5:8). It is a remarkable claim because we all know that status and privilege often mean exemption from certain experiences. Not so here. Full participation in the human order of things was required for the Son of God to complete his work, that is, to be perfected (5:9). Consequently, he becomes the "source of eternal salvation to all who obey him" (5:9).

Another feature of today's text is that christological reflection is most fully realized in Christian behavior. We are invited to perceive truly who Christ was, but at the same time we are enjoined to "hold fast our confession" (4:14). We are also urged to "draw near to the throne of grace" and to do so "with confidence" (4:16). Christian belief must translate into Christian praxis. Christ's full identification with humanity gave us full access to God, and we are assured that it is possible to "receive mercy and find grace to help in time of need" (4:16).

Our great high priest may be lofty and exalted, but he has succeeded in bridging the gap between us and God. Like the true priest, he lives to assist us in finding God—even more, in being bold in our pursuit.

John 18:1–19:42 *or* John 19:17-30

The reader will recall that on the Sixth Sunday of Lent, when observed as Passion rather than Palm Sunday, the lectionary offered the preacher two avenues in the Gospel texts. One possibility was to read, with or without comments, the Matthean narrative from the conspiracy of Judas (26:14) to the placing of guards at Jesus' tomb (27:66). The other was to develop a message on the crucifixion itself (27:11-54). Those same alternatives lie before the preacher on Good Friday since Passion Sunday and Good Friday carry the same burden and bear the same message. Today, however, the text is John's, recording the story from the events in the garden (18:1) to the burial of Jesus (19:42). If the choice is to speak only of the crucifixion, the text is 19:17-30. Notice that whereas the Synoptics present Jesus moving from the Last Supper to the garden, John separates the two scenes with Jesus' farewell discourses (chapters 14–16) and his farewell prayer (chapter 17). John's time frame, however, seems to be the same as that of the Synoptics.

If it is the tradition of the congregation or choice of the

minister to attend specifically to the crucifixion, two matters will be important in treating 19:17-30. One, let the descriptive element of the message be provided by the text rather than being a composite from all the Gospels. Hence, there will be no crowds at the cross, no taunting passersby, no mocking, no conversation between Jesus and the others being crucified, no earthquake and splitting of the temple veil. The account of the crucifixion is very brief, briefer even than Mark's. Jesus is totally in charge. Jesus himself rather than Simon of Cyrene carries the cross. Jesus speaks and acts not out of need or desperation but to fulfill Scripture. There is no crying out to God as one forsaken. Rather, he commits his mother into the care of the disciple whom he loved (neither of whose names are ever mentioned in this Gospel), says that all is now complete or finished, and gives up his spirit. Unwitting contributions to the event are made by the soldiers who fulfill Scripture (Ps. 22:18) and by Pilate who proclaims in three languages that all may understand, "Jesus of Nazareth, the King of the Jews" (verses 19-20).

The second matter of importance in developing a message on John 19:17-30 is giving attention to Johannine theology of Jesus' death. In the next paragraph (verses 31-37) the Passover lamb interpretation is developed, but in verses 17-30, the image of king is very strong. Earlier, self-serving crowds had tried to make Jesus king (6:15), but Jesus' kingship is not by popular election. Curious crowds had hailed him king (12:13), but they had no idea what the title would mean for Jesus or for themselves. Pilate tossed about the title "king" in his interrogation of Jesus and in talking with the crowds outside the praetorium (18:28–19:16). But in his sarcastic baiting of the religious authorities into confessing, "We have no king but Caesar" (19:15), Pilate has no understanding of Jesus' kingship. He, therefore, says more than he realizes when he proclaims Jesus "King of the Jews" (19:19). And so Jesus is lifted up on the cross, but also lifted up to God, enthroned by his executioners and glorified by those who think they have the power of life and death over Jesus. And through it all Jesus is in charge; even Pilate would have no authority were it not given to him from above (19:11). The final irony is complete:

the violence of an unbelieving world is used of God for the world's salvation.

If choice or tradition determines that the entirety of John 18:1–19:42 be used, perhaps in a three-hour Good Friday service, then perhaps first priority should be given to the public reading of the text. This reading would create its own world in its own way and, therefore, need not be accompanied by comments, especially exhortations. The readings could well be divided into the following units, with music and prayers intervening. If brief comments attend each reading, these would properly precede rather than follow in each case and be descriptive, with such explanations as would serve clarity.

> The arrest (18:1-12)
> Interrogation by religious leaders (18:13-27)
> Interrogation by Pontius Pilate (18:28–19:16)
> The Crucifixion (19:17-30)
> The burial (19:31-42)

Easter Eve, Easter Vigil, or the First Service of Easter

Genesis 1:1–2:2; Psalm 33;
Genesis 7:1-5, 11-18; 8:6-18; 9:8-13; Psalm 46;
Genesis 22:1-18; Psalm 16;
Exodus 14:10–15:1; Exodus 15:1-6, 11-13, 17-18;
Isaiah 54:5-14; Psalm 30;
Isaiah 55:1-11; Isaiah 12:2-6;
Baruch 3:9-15, 32–4:4; Psalm 19;
Ezekiel 36:24-28; Psalm 42;
Ezekiel 37:1-14; Psalm 143;
Zephaniah 3:14-20; Psalm 98;
Romans 6:3-11; Psalm 114;
Matthew 28:1-10
(Easter Vigil is traditionally a service of readings with little or no homily.)

In the ancient church, the tradition of the Easter Vigil played an important role. Catechumens, after remaining awake and watchful throughout Saturday night, were baptized early on Easter morning and then joined the Christian community in Holy Communion. Although this tradition was lost in the later Western church, it has been somewhat restored in churches that hold midnight services. The readings for the Easter Vigil provide a compendium of the sacred past of Israel and of texts seen to foretell and foreshadow the messianic age.

Genesis 1:1–2:2

Ordinarily the Old Testament lessons for the Easter Vigil are simply read, not preached, taking the worshiping community through a summary of ancient Israel's history.

Read in this order and on this occasion, these texts present a history of salvation in preparation for the death and resurrection of Jesus. The story begins with the first chapter of the Bible.

This reading contains all but a verse and a half of the Priestly Writer's account of creation. The mood of the story is solemn and measured; the repetition of phrases lends a liturgical dignity to the recital. If the account was not actually put into this form for worship, it certainly was shaped by persons with a deep interest in liturgy.

In terms of structure, the report consists of two uneven parts, Genesis 1:1-31 and Genesis 2:1-3, that is, the six days of creation and the seventh day of rest. One of the purposes of the story in its present form is to account for the sabbath rest. It was divinely ordained from the very first, and thus is taken by our writer as the most universal of laws.

Creation is not *ex nihilo*, out of nothing, but out of chaos. Before creation there were the primeval waters, within which God established the world. Moreover, as the Priestly account of the flood indicates (Gen. 7:11), the waters of chaos stand as the alternative to creation. If God withdraws his hand, the waters can return. In that sense, then, this chapter actually understands God as both creator and sustainer of the world.

In sharp contrast to the other account of creation which begins in Genesis 2:4b, God is transcendent and distant. The only actor or speaker in this chapter is God, by whose word or act all things that are come into being. Human beings certainly occupy an important place. They are created last of all, and then given stewardship over the creation. If this moving and majestic account can be said to have a major point, it is in the divine pronouncement that recurs throughout: "And God saw that it was good." The natural order is good not only because God created it, but also because God determined that it was so.

Psalm 33

This psalm, as a responsorial reading to the Priestly account of creation, stresses the role of the word of God and especially the creation of the world through the word. The description of God's creating acts are much more poetic and metaphoric in expression in the psalm than in the Genesis account; for example, God is depicted as gathering the sea as in a bottle (verse 7). In addition, the psalm stresses God's continuing interaction with and governance of the world. God's relationship to the world is not a once-for-all creation but a constant guiding and governance.

Genesis 7:1-5, 11-18; 8:6-18; 9:8-13

Like Genesis 1, the account of the flood is part of the primeval history, the story not just of Israel but of the entire human race. Between that initial chapter and Genesis 7 a great deal transpired. There was the second account of creation coupled with story of the fall, ending with the expulsion of the original pair from the garden. Next came the story of Cain and Abel, when a brother kills a brother. Then follow genealogies along with short reports of events in the lives of the earliest generations. The immediate background of the flood story is the little account in Genesis 6:1-4 of how the "sons of God" took the "daughters of men" and gave birth to a race of giants. From the accounts of creation to the time of Noah the story is basically one of human sin and disorder, culminating in God's decision to put an end to the race, with the exception of Noah and his family.

The flood marks an important turning point in biblical history, but as the book of Genesis is organized, it is not the most decisive one. Following the flood, the history of human sinfulness continues, with the story of the tower of Babel. The critical event is reported in Genesis 12:1 ff., the call of Abraham. To be sure, sin continues, but now, with the promise to Abraham, the direction of history is known. It becomes a history of salvation.

The verses for this reading comprise a rather full account of the flood, with the exception of the report of God's decision and his instructions to Noah. The assigned text comes mainly from the Priestly Writer, but some of it is from the Yahwist, whose name for God in most translations is LORD. It is also the Yahwist who reports that seven pairs of clean and one pair of unclean animals went into the ark; P has one pair of every kind. Moreover, in P the water comes when the floodgates of heaven are opened; the Yahwist speaks of rain. But according to both writers, God put an end to all human beings except that one family, and afterward vowed not to do it again. The reading appropriately ends with the good news that the natural order will abide and the rainbow will be a sign of God's promise.

Psalm 46

This psalm praises God for his divine care for his people and especially for Jerusalem, the City of God. With its emphasis on security in the midst of great turmoil and disruptions in the earth, it provides a proper response to the narrative of the flood. The worshipers confess, as Noah and his family may have, that they have nothing to fear should the mountains quake and the whole of the cosmos become chaos again.

Genesis 22:1-18

One must keep in mind the framework in which this reading is placed—both in the Book of Genesis and in the Old Testament—or important aspects of it will be missed. The context is the narrative of the patriarchs, Abraham, Isaac, Jacob, and the sons of Jacob, the leading theme of which is the promise that their descendants will become a great nation, will own their land, and will be a blessing to all the peoples of the earth (Gen. 12:1-3). The fulfillment of those promises comes first with the Exodus and then with the occupation of the land of Canaan as reported in the Book of Joshua.

The immediate prelude to this story is the report in Genesis 22:1-7 of the birth of Isaac. The promise of descendants had been repeated to Abraham and Sarah over and over. Just when it appeared that all hope was lost, they are given a son in their old age. Isaac is not simply symbolic testimony that the divine promise is trustworthy, he is also actually the first step in the fulfillment of that promise.

And then comes the account in Genesis 22:1-18 of God

testing Abraham, by means of a command that threatened to take away the child of the promise. It is certainly one of the most poignant and moving stories in the Bible, and all the more so because of its restraint. Emotions are not described or analyzed, but the reader or hearer can sense the fear and grief. Even though we know how the story comes out, each time we read it we can experience the rising tension, feeling that the results may still be in doubt. Will Abraham go through with the sacrifice of Isaac? Will the angel speak up before it is too late?

The story is so meaningful and fruitful and has been told in so many ways over the centuries that it would be a serious mistake to reduce it to a single point. At one level, in the old oral tradition, it probably dealt with the question of child sacrifice. Being among cultures where child sacrifice was a genuine possibility, some early Israelites could well have asked, "Does our God require that we sacrifice our children?" The answer, through this account, is a resounding no. Our ancestor was willing, but God did not require it. The sacrifice of a ram was sufficient. In the framework of the Easter Vigil one is reminded that God gave his Son.

The leading theme of the story, as recognized through centuries of interpretation, is faith. It is, as the initial verse says, the test of Abraham's faith. What is faith? The biblical tradition answers not with a theological statement, or with a set of propositions, or with admonitions to be faithful, but with a story. It is the story of Abraham, who trusted in God even when God appeared to be acting against his promise. Faith is like that. Faith in this sense is commitment, the directing of one's trust toward God. And it entails great risk, not in the sense of accepting a set of beliefs, but by acting in trust. Did Abraham know that the God he worshiped would not require the life of Isaac? We cannot know. We are told only how the patriarch acted, and how God acted.

Psalm 16

This psalm, probably originally used as a lament by an individual during a time of sickness, contains a strong statement of devotion to God and thus can be read as a theological counterpart to the narrative of Abraham whose faithfulness led him to the point of sacrificing his son Isaac. Like Abraham, the psalmist shows confidence in whatever fate or lot God might assign him. This psalm came to be understood in the early church as a prediction of the resurrection, especially Christ's resurrection, and was quoted in this regard by Peter in his sermon at Pentecost (see Acts 2:22-28).

Exodus 14:10–15:1

With this reading we come close to the heart of the Old Testament story and the Old Testament faith. In ancient Israel's faith no affirmation is more central than the confession that the Lord is the one who brought them out of Egypt. Traditions concerning the Exodus provide the fundamental language by which Israel understood both herself and her God. The basic focus of most of those traditions is upon the saving activity of the Lord; the history is a story of salvation.

The account in Exodus 14 actually follows the Exodus itself. The departure from Egypt had been reported in chapters 12 and 13; the rescue of the people at the sea happens when they are already in the wilderness. The two themes that mark the stories of the wandering in the wilderness are already present in this chapter, namely Israel's complaints against Moses and the Lord (14:10-13), and the Lord's miraculous care (14:13-18, 30-31). The report does mark, however, Israel's final escape from the Egyptian danger, and this relates directly to the theme of the Exodus itself.

This reading, like the flood story, is the combination of at least two of the sources of the Pentateuch, those of the Priestly Writer and of the Yahwist. Two virtually complete accounts have been combined. The writers tell the story differently, with P reporting a dramatic crossing of the sea between walls of water (verse 22), and J speaking of a "strong east wind" (verse 21) and the chariots clogged in the mud as the water returns (verse 25). But a more important implication of the source division for our use of the text in the context of worship is the recognition that the sources place very different theological interpretations upon what happened. For the Priestly Writer, the emphasis is on revelation. The Lord "hardened the heart of Pharaoh" (verses 8, 17) to pursue the Israelites in order to "get glory over Pharaoh and all his host" (verse 17). That is, the Lord's purpose is for the Egyptians to "know that I am the Lord" (verse 18). For the Yahwist, the purpose is the salvation of the people (verse 13), and their consequent faith, not only in the Lord, but also in Moses (verses 30-31). In the combined report, both themes are important. God acts in order to reveal who he is and also to save his people.

Exodus 15:1-6, 11-13, 17-18

The psalm text overlaps with the Old Testament reading and continues where it left off. Moses, having led the Israelites in their escape from the Egyptians at the sea, now leads them in worship. The expression of praise is generally identified as the song of Moses, and much of it is in the first person singular, "I will sing to the Lord." But the introduction points out that it was sung by Moses and the people, and its communal, congregational character is evident throughout. While the song is not in the Psalter, it is a psalm nonetheless and probably was used in worship by faithful Israelites through the centuries. The initial lines are placed in the mouth of Miriam in Exodus 15:21, except that they are in the second person instead of the first; she calls for the people to sing to the Lord.

The song is a hymn of praise, specifically praise of the Lord for saving the people at the sea. The hymn is for the most part narrative in form; that is, it praises God by recounting the story of his mighty deeds. In one sense what emerges is another interpretation of the rescue at the sea, different in some respects from the accounts in Exodus 14. But the language is at points highly metaphorical and rich in imagery which goes beyond the immediate events.

Recollection of the Lord's saving activity at the sea evokes two leading themes in the hymn. The first concerns God's awesome power over events and nature. The specific form of that theme here stresses the image of the Lord as a warrior who triumphs over his enemies. But it also emphasizes that the God praised here is incomparable; there is none like this one (verses 11, 18). The second theme of the hymn concerns God's love and care for the people whom he has redeemed. God is strength, song, salvation (verse 2), the one who cares for his people out of steadfast love (verse 13). Moreover, his past care for the people gives rise to hope that he will continue to act on their behalf in the future (verse 17), and will reign forever (verse 18).

Isaiah 54:5-14

The central message of Second Isaiah (chapters 40–55) is the announcement that the Babylonian Exile is coming to an end; the Lord will bring the people back to Jerusalem. This text incorporates that theme but goes beyond it to proclaim and characterize the new era in Israel's history with her God. In this passage, which actually begins with Isaiah 54:1, the unnamed prophet of the Exile employs a wealth of metaphors to characterize the new relationship between Israel and Yahweh. He is "husband," "Redeemer," the "God of the whole earth" (verse 5). These three expressions remind the hearers that the God who created all that is and acts in historical events to save is also as close to the people as a husband is to a wife.

God speaks (verses 6-10) to assure Israel that he has forsaken her, but only for a moment. He then declares what is in effect a new covenant, like the one sworn in the days of Noah. God now vows not to be angry and establishes a "covenant of peace" (verse 10). Israel has in no sense earned this new covenant; it is simply that the Lord has compassion on those whom he had rejected. The concluding lines (verses 11-14) are addressed to the city of Jerusalem, which will be reestablished in righteousness for an era of peace.

Psalm 30

This psalm was originally a thanksgiving psalm offered by a worshiper who had recovered from sickness. As thanksgiving, it celebrates the transition from a time of sickness and destitution to a time of celebration and joy. Just as Easter marks the transition from death to life so this psalm marks the worshiper's transition from sickness to health. Its two keynote expressions of this transition are: "Weeping may tarry for the night, but joy comes with the morning," and "Thou hast turned for me my mourning into dancing."

Isaiah 55:1-11

Again, as is so often the case in the lectionary as a whole, the words of Second Isaiah come before us. This text from the end of the Babylonian Exile was a call for hope and trust and a promise of salvation to the hearers; it reiterates that same call and promise during the Easter Vigil.

The passage has two distinct parts, verses 1-5 and 6-11, which are similar in both form and content. In the first section God is the speaker throughout, addressing the people of Israel as a whole. He begins with a series of imperatives (verses 1-3a) which resemble on the one hand Lady Wisdom's invitation to a banquet (Prov. 9:5), and on the other hand the calls of street vendors. The invitations to come for what the Lord has to offer are both literal and metaphorical: God offers actual food, and "food" which enables one to live the abundant life ("that your soul may live," verse 3a). What the people are invited to "come, buy and eat" is the proclamation of salvation which follows in verses 3b-5. God announces that the ancient covenant with David (II Sam. 7) now applies to the people as a whole. Again, Israel has in no sense earned this new covenant; it is a free act of God's grace. Moreover, as the Lord made David a witness to the nations, now all nations will come to the people of Israel. The proclamation of salvation, then, is ultimately directed toward all peoples.

The second section (verses 6-11) also begins with imperatives, calls to "seek the Lord" and to "call upon him." The "wicked" and "unrighteous" are invited to change their ways and "return to the Lord." These invitations, while addressed to the human heart, are quite concrete. To "seek" and "call upon" the Lord refer to acts of prayer and worship.

For the wicked to "forsake his way" is to change behavior. The foundation for the imperatives is stated at the end of verse 7, "for he will abundantly pardon." The remainder of the section (verses 8-11) gives the basis for responding to God's call. God's plan for the world ("ways," "thoughts") is in sharp contrast to human designs. That plan is the announcement of salvation which the prophet has presented throughout the book, the redemption and renewal of the people. The will of God is effected by the word of God, another theme found throughout Isaiah 40–55. That word is the one uttered at creation (Gen. 1:3 ff.), and it is the divine announcement of the future through the prophets. In its emphasis on the word of God and its contrast between human and divine wisdom, this concluding section of Second Isaiah alludes to the beginning of the work (Isa. 40:1-11).

Isaiah 12:2-6

Not all Old Testament psalms are found in the Psalter. Isaiah 12 actually includes two, along with traces of the liturgical instructions (verses 1a, 4a). The songs conclude the first section of the Book of Isaiah and suggest that the prophetic book was used in worship even before an official canon of scripture was established. Both psalms are songs of thanksgiving. The first (verses 1-3) celebrates and gives thanks for deliverance from trouble. In verse 2 it echoes the vocabulary of the Song of Moses (Exod. 15:2), moving from thanks for a specific divine act to generalizations about the nature of God as the one who saves and who is the strength, song, and salvation of the worshiper. The second psalm (verses 4-6) consists almost entirely of calls to give thanks and praise (verse 4). God is praised especially for his mighty deeds. Because God, the Holy One of Israel, is great, all the earth should know, and those who live in the shadow of the temple in Zion should sing for joy.

Baruch 3:9-15, 32–4:4

This passage, often characterized as a hymn to wisdom, is not actually a song of praise such as those in the Book of

Psalms. While it does characterize and praise wisdom, it is basically an admonition to the people of Israel to listen to and learn from wisdom.

The book of Baruch is attributed to Jeremiah's scribe and placed in the Babylonian Exile, but it actually stems from a later time. The section from which this reading comes is like other late wisdom literature such as the Wisdom of Solomon. It identifies wisdom with the law of Moses, "the commandments of life" (3:9), and "the way of God" (3:13; see also 4:1). Behind that answer stands a question that became prominent in the so-called intertestamental period, Is there a conflict between the truth that can be discerned by human reflection and that which is revealed in the law?

Our text alludes to the Babylonian Exile (3:10-13), but it is characterized as a spiritual situation of separation from God rather than the actual exile. The verses not included in the reading (3:16-31) also contain somewhat spiritualized allusions to the history of Israel. The reading finds its place in the Easter Vigil, first because of the references to death and its alternative. Israel, growing old in a foreign land, is as good as dead (3:10-11), because the people have forsaken "the fountain of wisdom" (3:12). If they will attend to wisdom they will gain strength, understanding, life, and peace (3:14). All who hold fast to wisdom will live, and those who forsake her will die (4:1). The second reason for the use of this passage in the Easter Vigil is its theme of wisdom as the gift of God which reveals the divine will to human beings. This is quite explicit in 3:37, which is echoed in John 1:14, and has been taken as a reference to the coming of Jesus.

Psalm 19

This psalm of hymnic praise of God declares that God has communicated his will and himself through nature—verses 1-6—and through the law or Torah—verses 7-13. Without speech, God's voice is heard in the world of nature, and his communication, like the light of the sun, falls everywhere and nothing can hide from it. In the Torah, God's will is embodied in commandment and precept and offers its blessings to those whose ways it directs and guards.

Ezekiel 36:24-28

This reading is the central section of a passage in which Ezekiel presents the divine announcement of a new Israel. God, through the prophet (see verses 22, 32), is the speaker. This dramatic announcement of good news presupposes that the people of God are in trouble. The description of that trouble is given in the context (verses 16-21) and alluded to in our reading. Israel is in exile, away from the sacred land, but the trouble is even deeper. Separation from the land corresponds to separation from their God. They are in exile because of their sin, their disobedience which led to uncleanness. Now God is about to act, not because Israel deserves it, but for the sake of his "holy name" (verse 22).

There are two aspects to the coming work of salvation, one external and one internal, corresponding to Israel's present plight. First, the Lord will gather up the people and return them to their land (verse 24). But if they are to remain there (verse 26), a major transformation must occur. That is the second aspect of the good news, the establishment of a new covenant (see Isa. 54:10; 55:3) with a new Israel. This transformation is spelled out in terms of three distinct steps: (1) the Lord will sprinkle (cf. Exod. 24:6) the people with water, purifying them from their uncleanness; (2) he will give them a new heart and a new spirit, replacing their heart of stone with one of flesh (cf. Jer. 31:31); and (3) God will put his own "spirit" within them. "Spirit" here represents both the willingness and the ability to act in obedience. The promise is summarized by the reiteration of the ancient covenant formula, "You shall be my people, and I will be your God" (verse 28). The radical difference between this new covenant and the old one is that the Lord himself will enable the people to be faithful.

Psalm 42

This psalm can be closely associated with the sentiments of Ezekiel 36:24-28, the Old Testament lesson to which it is a response. Ezekiel predicts the coming rescue of God's people from exile and the transformation of the human personality and will. The psalm, originally used as an individual lament, early became associated with the Easter Vigil because it expressed the people's longing for redemption and their lamenting over being absent from the sanctuary. The psalm presupposes that the speaker is living away from the Sacred City. The psalmist's thought about former days when the worshiper went on a pilgrimage to Jerusalem only intensifies the depression and despair that accompany living in a foreign and hostile land and heightens the desire to be at home again in the temple.

Ezekiel 37:1-14

Ezekiel's vision of the valley of dry bones, like so many other Old Testament readings for this season, stems from the era of the Babylonian Exile. That it is a vision report is indicated by the introductory formula, "The hand of the Lord was upon me," which the prophet uses elsewhere to begin reports of ecstatic experiences (Ezek. 3:22). The report is in the first person and, like most prophetic vision reports, consists of two parts, the description of what was revealed (verses 1-10) and the interpretation (verses 11-14). Throughout there is dialogue between Yahweh and Ezekiel.

The message from the Lord communicated through the report is the response to the problem stated in verse 11. The people of Israel are saying, "Our bones are dried up, and our hope is lost; we are clean cut off." Ezekiel sees himself carried by the spirit of Yahweh to a valley full of bones, like the scene of an ancient battle. When the Lord asks if the bones can live again, Ezekiel gives the only possible answer, "O Lord God, thou knowest" (verse 3). While the nuance of the response is not immediately plain, it becomes clear in the context; the God of Israel can indeed bring life in the midst of death. When the prophet obeys the command to prophesy to the bones, a distinct sequence of events transpires: bones to bones, sinews to bones, flesh on the bones, and then skin covering them. The importance of the next step is emphasized by a further divine instruction. The prophet calls for breath to come into the corpses and they live. The view of human life as physical matter animated by the breath that comes from

God is found throughout the Old Testament (cf. Gen. 2:7).

The interpretation (verses 11-14) emphasizes that the vision is a promise of national resurrection addressed to the hopeless exiles. In no sense is the seriousness of their plight denied. They are as good as dead, and death in all possible forms is acknowledged as a reality. But the word of God in the face of and in the midst of death brings to the people of God a new reality, life. It is a free, unconditional, and unmerited gift. When read on the eve of Easter, this text is a strong reminder that God is the Lord of all realms, including that of death. Moreover, the promise of life is addressed to the people of God, and resurrection is a symbol not only for a life beyond the grave but also for the abundant life of the community of faith this side of physical death.

Psalm 143

Originally used as an individual lament by worshipers suffering from illness, this psalm prays for God's intervention and rescue. The condition of the worshiper's distress is described in terms of death, of going down to the pit. Such depictions fit well with the description of the exile as a graveyard in Ezekiel 37. Like those awaiting Easter morning, the psalmist asks to "hear in the morning of [God's] steadfast love."

Zephaniah 3:14-20

The last of the Old Testament readings for the Easter Vigil is a shout of joy and an announcement of salvation to Jerusalem. The passage begins with a series of imperatives addressed to the Holy City, calling for celebration (verse 14). The remainder of the unit in effect gives the reasons for celebration. These reasons include the announcement that the Lord has acted on behalf of the city and is now in its midst as king (verse 15), and a series of promises concerning the renewal of the city and the return of its people (verses 16-20). Both the mood and contents of the text anticipate the celebration of Easter.

Our unit is the fourth and last section in the book of

Zephaniah and stands in sharp contrast to the remainder of the book. The section that immediately precedes this one (Zeph. 3:1-13) had announced a purging punishment upon the city and its people. But now darkness has become light; fear and terror have become hope and celebration.

The prophet Zephaniah was active in the seventh century, not long before 621 B.C. He was concerned with the coming judgment upon his people, particularly because of their pagan religious practices. It is possible that this concluding section of the book was added in a later age, perhaps during the Babylonian Exile (cf. 3:19-20), by those who had actually been through the fires of destruction and who looked forward to celebrating God's forgiveness, which the return from exile represented. But in any case the theological interpretation presented by the structure of the book in its final form is quite clear. The celebration of God's salvation follows the dark night of judgment and suffering.

Psalm 98

Like Zephaniah 3:14-20, this psalm is an exuberant affirmation of divine triumph and success. This affirmation is noted by the word "victory" in each of the first three verses. The psalm proclaims the victory of God and calls upon the whole world to break forth into song and the sound of musical instruments. As part of the Easter Vigil, this psalm contributes its call for a celebration of salvation and for the recognition of God as king.

Romans 6:3-11

This epistolary text is used for all three years in the Easter Vigil service, and the reader may wish to consult our remarks in *Lent, Holy Week, Easter* in Years B and C. It also provides the second lesson for Proper 8 in Year A, which is treated in *After Pentecost, Year A*.

What makes this an appropriate text for the Easter Vigil service is its central emphasis on the death, burial, and resurrection of Christ. Dual themes run through the passage: death and life, old and new, sin and righteousness.

We should note the context in which Paul rehearses these stages of the Christ-event. Unlike the Gospel readings used in each of the three years (Matt. 28:1-10; Mark 16:1-8; Luke 24:1-12), this is not a narrative rehearsal of the Easter story. It is rather intertwined with the initiation rite of baptism. In fact, what we have in this passage is a fairly extensive account of Paul's theology of baptism. It makes sense only if we remember that the early Christian practice was for initiates to be immersed in water. It was only natural to interpret this as a "burial," an act of being submerged underneath the water. Obviously, one did not remain under water, but "arose" from the water to live again. To undergo baptism in this fashion was seen as a reenactment of the death and resurrection of Christ. Indeed, Paul speaks of being baptized *into* Christ (verse 3). Through this act one is actually said to enter Christ.

While this way of understanding baptism may seem logical to us, it was not the only way of understanding this rite. The Fourth Gospel uses an entirely different metaphor: it is a new birth (John 3). Thus baptism is understood as being "born of water and the Spirit" (John 3:5).

But at least from the viewpoint of today's text, baptism is inextricably linked with the death and resurrection of Christ. But how? Merely as a reenactment of a past event? No. If this were the case, the Christ-event and the believer's baptism would be chronologically separated. In one sense, this is true of course. But our text envisions the fusion of these two moments. We see this by the pervasive use of the language of participation. The believer dies *with* Christ, is buried *with* Christ, is raised *with* Christ, and lives *with* Christ. This level of full participation is rendered especially well in NEB: "For if we have become incorporate with him in a death like his . . ." (verse 5). We are also said to be "in union with Christ Jesus" (verse 11).

Such language presupposes that the Christ-event is not bound by time. The Christ with whom we are united is the living Christ. To put it another way: each time a baptism occurs, the Christ-event, in a sense, recurs. We actually become co-participants with Christ in his death, burial, and resurrection. It is not so much that we reenact the event that happened *back there*. It is rather that God's act *back there* becomes unbound by time. It occurs *up here*, now, within us. "In baptism the new world initiated by Christ seizes the life of the individual Christian too, in such a way that the earthly path of the exalted Lord is to be traversed again in this life and Christ thus becomes the destiny of our life. Baptism is projection of the change of aeons into our personal existence, which for its part becomes a constant return to baptism to the extent that here dying with Christ establishes life with him and the dialectic of the two constitutes the signature of being in Christ" (Kasemann).

Our entry into the corporate Christ results in moral transformation (verses 6 and 11). What occurred in the death and resurrection of Christ was more than the expiration of life or the resuscitation of life. In his death, he "died to sin, once for all" (verse 10). Not just to any sin, but to Sin as a universal power. With sin also went death: Christ is no longer "under the dominion of death" (verse 9, NEB). Instead, he "lives to God" (verse 10). What was achieved by God in the Christ-event is appropriated by the believer who is incorporated into Christ. We then are urged to recognize this transformation in our own identity: we must regard ourselves as "dead to sin and alive to God" (verse 11).

Psalm 114

This psalm, read as a response to Paul's discussion of the association of Christian baptism with the death of Jesus, is a celebration of the Exodus from Egyptian bondage and of the entry into the Promised Land. Typologically, one might say that the Exodus, like Christ's death, symbolizes the end of an old state of life and the dawning of a new state. The entry into the Promised Land, like Christian baptism, was a time when the benefits of redemption became real. In this psalm, Exodus from Egypt and entrance into the Promised Land are closely joined so that parallel events are seen as characteristic of the two episodes. At the Exodus, the sea fled and the "mountains skipped like rams"; at the Jordan, the river rolled back and the hills skipped like lambs (verses 3-4). The address to the sea and river, the mountains and hills in verses

5-6, which is continued in the address to the earth in verses 7-8, serves as the means for making contemporary the Exodus and entrance events. Thus the users of the psalm, which was always read at the celebration of Passover, "became" participants in the past events of salvation as the Christian in baptism becomes contemporary with the death of Jesus.

Matthew 28:1-10

Easter Vigil is primarily a service of readings, marked by anticipation of the full Easter service. The preacher will therefore use restraint in sharing the biblical texts because some of them, such as Matthew 28:1-10, offer Easter itself and not the waiting for Easter. In fact, today's reading is the alternate text for the Easter service. If the preacher chooses to comment on Matthew 28:1-10 at the Vigil then it might be best to use the other Gospel reading (John 20:1-18) for the service of Easter.

Matthew's resurrection narrative consists of four units: the empty tomb and the appearance of the angel (verses 1-8); the appearance of Jesus to the women (verses 9-10); the bribing of the guards (verses 11-15); the reunion of Jesus and the disciples in Galilee and the commission to preach to the nations (verses 16-20). This narrative is a revision and an elaboration of Mark 16:1-8. Mark is not, of course, our earliest record of the resurrection tradition. That is to be found in I Corinthians 15:3-8, a summary that makes no reference to an empty tomb or to appearances of the risen Christ to women. Mark tells of the empty tomb, the appearance of a "young man" inside the tomb who tells them to tell the disciples and Peter that Jesus will meet them in Galilee, and the hasty departure of the women in fear and silence. Matthew omits Mark's third woman, Salome, and simply says the two women who had been at the burial (27:61) now go "to see the sepulchre" (verse 1). Matthew omits conversation between them about getting the stone rolled away, adds the earthquake, and describes the descent of the angel and the removal of the stone. The bribing of the guards (verses 11-15) is also Matthew's since only this Evangelist has guards at the tomb (27:65-66; 28:4).

The portion of Matthew's resurrection narrative for this Vigil reading (verses 1-10) underscores two messages. The first consists of the multiple attestations to the resurrection. The earthquake, the descent of an angel who rolls away the stone, the message of the angel to the women, and the appearance of Jesus to the women testify to Matthew's concern to establish the truth of the gospel: Jesus Christ is risen. The two episodes that follow (verses 11-15, 16-20) argue the point even further. Mark's abrupt ending will hardly satisfy Matthew's church.

The second message in verses 1-10 is the promise that Jesus will meet his disciples in Galilee. That this promise repeats a statement of Jesus before his death (26:32) serves to join firmly the risen Christ to the historical Jesus. The one raised is the one crucified; Easter cannot be separated from Good Friday. That the promised reunion in Galilee is stated three times (26:32; 28:7; 28:10) indicates the importance of Galilee for Matthew's church. Jesus' ministry was primarily in Galilee and for both Matthew and Mark (16:7) Galilee was the point of continuing that ministry through the apostles. Luke alters the tradition to say, "Remember how he told you, while he was still in Galilee" (24:6), for in Luke the disciples are to remain in Jerusalem, waiting for the Holy Spirit (24:44-53).

One further note: in Matthew Jesus is worshiped. The women (verse 9) and the disciples (verse 17) worship him, as did the Magi at the beginning of this Gospel (2:2, 11). Apart from Matthew, only at John 9:38 is it said in the Gospels that persons worshiped Jesus. The major impression is that God was worshiped and Jesus was followed as the one who reveals God and speaks of God's kingdom. To speak of Jesus being worshiped reflects the central and elevated place of Jesus in Matthew's church. Such a Christology most likely was hammered out in debate with those who denied the authority (28:18) of Jesus in the community of faith.

Easter Day or the Resurrection of the Lord or the Second Service of Easter

Acts 10:34-43 or Jeremiah 31:1-6; Psalm 118:14-24;
Colossians 3:1-4 or Acts 10:34-43;
John 20:1-18 or Matthew 28:1-10
(If the first lesson is from the Old Testament, the reading from
Acts should be the second lesson.)

The Old Testament selection given for this Sunday is provided for the use of those congregations that wish to retain an Old Testament reading and/or that may not have celebrated an Easter Vigil with its heavy orientation to the Old Testament. The reading from Acts inaugurates the sequential reading of this book throughout the fifty days of Easter.

The Jeremiah text anticipates the coming time when the disruptions and disappointments of Israel's life will be reversed and in their place Israel will experience the redemption of God which will return life to normalcy with its patterns of rest and rejoicing, dancing and adorning, planting and pilgrimages. Psalm 118 is a song of thanksgiving celebrating victory over the enemy and the exaltation of the rejected. Both the Epistle readings celebrate the redemption that has come in Christ and through his resurrection. Both Gospel readings retell the story of the first Easter morning and report on the visits to the tomb.

Acts 10:34-43

Besides serving as the first (or second) reading for Easter Sunday in all three years, this passage also serves as the second reading for the Baptism of the Lord (First Sunday

After Epiphany) in Year A. Accordingly, the reader may wish to consult our remarks in *Lent, Holy Week, Easter,* Years B and C, or *Advent, Christmas, Epiphany, Year A.*

What makes this an appropriate text for the principal Easter service is the compact way in which it summarizes the Gospel story. This brief, but surprisingly comprehensive, resumé of the essential points of the Gospel story has long been regarded as a kerygmatic summary that occurs on the lips of Peter as he addresses the household of Cornelius. It begins with Jesus' baptism by John (verse 37), moves through his ministry in Galilee to his final days in Judea and Jerusalem. There is explicit mention of his "death by hanging on a gibbet" (verse 39, NEB), his resurrection on the third day (verse 40), and his being made manifest to a select group of witnesses (verse 41). Yet this is no new, unanticipated story, but one that continues the prophetic story (verse 43).

It is, of course, a Lukan summary and tells us more about Luke's theology and literary purpose than it does about what Peter is likely to have said on the occasion. The preacher might do well to examine each of the motifs in the sermon summary in light of Luke's Gospel. There are some striking parallels, for example, the stress on Jesus' anointing with the Spirit (verse 38; cf. Luke 3:22; 4:1, 14, 18), his works of healing (verse 38: cf. Luke 4:31-41), and the dawning of the Easter faith in the context of a sacred meal with the risen Lord (verse 41; Luke 24:30-35).

As useful as it might be to examine each of the details of this compact summary and explore the way they are elaborated in the larger work of Luke-Acts, the preacher must finally remember that this text will be read on Easter Day. We should ask, then, what themes are especially heard in this liturgical setting.

First, *the Easter faith.* Perhaps above all, we will hear the proclamation "God raised him to life on the third day, and allowed him to appear" (verse 40, NEB). But even if we hear this note above the rest and read it as the climax of the story, we do well to remember that it is part of a larger, and longer, story. Its roots lie in the Old Testament (verse 43). It was heard first by Israel (verse 36). As climactic as the moment of Easter is, it is not a moment suspended from history but part of a larger drama interwoven with history. The story occurs in places such as Galilee, the country of the Jews, and Jerusalem. It involves human actors such as John the Baptist and those with whom Jesus worked and ministered. It was in ordinary places and among ordinary persons that the Extraordinary was manifested.

Also worth noticing is our text's insistence that the Easter faith was acknowledged by a select group of "witnesses whom God has chosen in advance" (verse 41, NEB). We should also note that the Easter faith was experienced as the disciples ate and drank with the risen Lord (verse 41). This doubtless reflects early Christian reminiscence and practice that the presence of the risen Lord was celebrated and experienced in the Eucharist.

A second theme woven throughout today's text is actually a set of twin themes: *the impartiality of God and the universality of salvation*. The sermon opens on the note that "God does not have favorites" (verse 34, JB). It was an axiom of Jewish thought that God was impartial, which meant that God could not be bought or bribed (Deut. 10:17; cf. Job 34:19; II Chron. 19:7). Among other things, this meant that God was not deaf to the cries of the poor and the disadvantaged, most notably widows and orphans (Sir. 35:12-13). What was axiomatic in Jewish thought also became normative in Christian thought (Rom. 2:11; Gal. 2:6; Eph. 6:9; Col. 3:25; I Pet. 1:17; James 2:19).

The natural corollary to God's impartiality is God's universal concern for all humanity—a recurrent theme of today's text. "Jesus Christ is Lord of *all*" (verse 36, JB, italics added). Jesus went about doing good and healing *all* who were demonically possessed (verse 38). We are assured that *"every one* who believes in him receives forgiveness" (verse 43, italics added). In this context in which the Gospel is being proclaimed to the Gentile Cornelius, the particular force of these claims is to insist that God's salvation no longer rests exclusively with Israel. It now reaches beyond Israel to all nations. To be sure, it includes Israel, but not Israel exclusively. In fact, the reference to God as judge of the "living and the dead" (verse 42) may mean the God who finally judges both Jews, those to whom God has extended life, and Gentiles, those whom Jews normally regard as dead (cf. Eph. 2:1, 12).

What is striking about today's text is the way in which Peter himself comes to believe in God's impartiality and universality. Note the opening line: "The truth I have now come to realize . . ." (verse 34, JB). In fact, one of the unusual features of this sermon is that it is evangelistic in an odd way. It addresses Peter as much as it does Cornelius. It is not so much proclamation as self-confession. What is rehearsed is familiar. The main points of the Gospel story are well known. But it seriously challenges Peter's familiar world.

Perhaps this suggests a clue for homiletical appropriation of this text. It rehearses the main outline of a very familiar story. For many who hear it on Easter Sunday it is a table of contents of a well-known book. Nothing new is being introduced—at least not ostensibly. But a closer look may suggest that some of our most cherished religious convictions are being called into question. Hearing this text may mean that we open ourselves to a gospel in which God does not play favorites—to one race over the other, one sex over the other, even one religion over the other.

Jeremiah 31:1-6

As an alternative first reading for churches that do not celebrate the Easter Vigil, Jeremiah 31:1-6 provides something of a brief summary of the history of salvation given in greater detail in the Old Testament lections for the Vigil. The text does not deal directly with the Easter event, but on the one hand leads up to it with allusions to Israel's history, and on the other hand celebrates God's love manifest in saving actions on behalf of the people of God.

In terms of literary context, this passage is part of a collection of prophetic materials in Jeremiah 30–31, generally called "the Book of Consolation" because most of it is good news. Note, however, that the verses that immediately precede our reading announce the almost apocalyptic judgment by Yahweh because of his "fierce anger" (30:24). The effect of this juxtaposition is to heighten the good news in 30:1 ff. The Book of Consolation itself is quite late, coming from the exilic period, but most of the individual addresses come from Jeremiah. It is generally accepted that Jeremiah 31:2-6 comes from the prophet, but some place it early in his career, during the time of Josiah, and others place it late, during the time of Gedaliah (597 ff.) when Jerusalem had been captured and the capital moved north to Mizpah.

Our passage consists of two distinct parts, verse 1 and verses 2-6, the former in prose and the latter in poetry. Verse 1 is an introduction, not just to verses 2-6, but to the entire chapter that follows, and probably comes from the editor who organized the section. It is a comprehensive statement of the good news of the chapter as a whole, that Yahweh will establish a new covenant with his people (31:31-34). "At that time" is a general reference to an indefinite future. Yahweh's twofold promise is a version of the most basic covenantal formula, "You shall be my people, and I will be your God" (cf. Jer. 30:22; Amos 3:1; Hos. 1:9, 10). The distinctive feature of the announcement here is the reference to "all the families of Israel." That signals a particular concern of the unit before us, and of much of chapter 31, namely, the reunification of the Northern and the Southern Kingdoms, of Israel and Judah.

What follows the introduction, after an appropriate messenger formula, is a prophecy of salvation (verses 2-6). The prophecy has two parts, the affirmation of God's love for his people (verses 2-3) and the promise that this love will be manifest in new saving events (verses 4-6). This word is addressed to a particular context, to a people who had been in trouble and are now seeking "rest." It also assumes some need for renewal and rebuilding (cf. the allusions in verses 4-6). Verses 2b-3a contain allusions to the early history of salvation. "Survived the sword" appears to be an allusion to the escape from Egypt (Exod. 5:21; 15:9; 18:4), and "grace in the wilderness" refers either to the gifts that sustained life (e.g., Exod. 16–17) or to the covenant on Mount Sinai. The first line of verse 3 contains textual and translation problems (read with NEB "long ago the Lord appeared to them"), but certainly refers to the theophany at Sinai. The "rest" that Israel sought included having a place to call one's own, that is, an end to wandering and freedom from threats (Deut. 28:65).

At the center of the prophecy stands God's love. That Israel "found grace" (*hēn*) in the wilderness indicates that God regarded them with favor and affection. Verse 3*b* could be read, "I have loved you with an everlasting love" (RSV), or "I have dearly loved you from of old" (NEB). In either case it stresses the continuity and stability of Yahweh's commitment to Israel. The final line of verse 3 makes the same point. The word used here, *hesed* (RSV "faithfulness"), is common to covenantal relationships, and often is read "steadfast love." At this point Jeremiah clearly is indebted to Hosea (cf. Hos. 11:4).

Just as the Lord's love had been manifest in saving actions, so it will again. The specific good news is the announcement of the rebuilding of Israel (verse 4*a*), the revival of Northern Israel's vineyards (verse 5), and the reunification of the tribes at Mount Zion (verse 6). Thus it includes the reestablishment of physical culture, the renewal of nature, and the proper integration of all the people into worship. There seems to be here a definite allusion to Jeremiah's commission at the time of his call, "to build and to plant" (Jer. 1:10). The prophecy assumes that Israel and Judah are separated from each other, that the Northern Kingdom is in trouble, and that it is God's will to bring all the families together again and to worship in the temple in Jerusalem.

What response is called for to this prophecy of divine love and its manifestation in concrete historical events? The passage gives no instructions, no laws, and does not even call for a renewal of covenant. It limits itself to promises. But two of those promises characterize the response of the people of God to the love of God. First, there is the almost unbounded celebration of this good news, even with dancing and making merry (verse 4*b*). Second, there is the summons to come to Zion to "the Lord our God" (verse 6*b*), presented not as an order but as a promise, a promise that the invitation will be issued. It is an invitation one can only accept.

Psalm 118:14-24

A portion of Psalm 118 is the reading for Palm Sunday in all three years of the lectionary since it is already associated with this occasion in the Gospels. Since the psalm text for today overlaps that of Palm Sunday, the discussion at the latter should be consulted.

Verses 14-24 unfortunately contain only certain elements of the larger thanksgiving composition that is Psalm 118. Specifically these verses contain: (1) a confession by the person previously endangered (verse 14, which form critically and otherwise belongs with the preceding verses); (2) a description of the victory celebrations in the camp following victory that also concludes with confessional assertions (verses 15-18); (3) the spoken elements of a gate liturgy utilized as the triumphant figure enters the sacred temple precincts (verse 19 spoken by the one entering and verse 20 the response given by the priests or the assembled audience); (4) the worshiper's short prayer of thanksgiving to God; and (although this is not completely clear) (5) antiphonal acclamation and praise by the triumphant worshiper and/or the priests/assembled worshipers (verses 22-24).

Characteristic of this psalm is its celebrative tone which, of course, makes it so appropriate for reading on Easter. Further the pattern displayed in the psalm is strikingly parallel to the passion-resurrection of Jesus. The worshiper in Psalm 118 had been placed in a position of danger, apparently a military campaign (see verses 10-13). This danger is depicted in terms of a struggle against death itself (verses 17-18), a struggle in which God protected the threatened and refused to allow his servant to be overcome by death.

In the psalm, of course, the fundamental celebration is carried on and praise offered by the one who has been redeemed. This would be somewhat analogous to hearing the resurrected Christ offer up thanksgiving for the resurrection. In the New Testament, it is, of course, the Christians who offer testimony and thanksgiving. Yet, even in the psalm, the congregation (which may be seen as the ancient counterpart to the early church) joins in the celebration and praise and affirms the corporate benefits of the divine redemption (see verses 23-24 with their plural pronouns).

The litany of entering the temple gates (verses 19-20) can be compared with similar entry liturgies in Psalms 15 and 24.

Inside the temple precincts, the monarch offers thanks (verse 21). Verse 22 may be seen either as part of the king's thanksgiving and thus a continuation of verse 21 or else as part of the community's response and proclamation and thus a link with verses 23-24. At any rate, the theme of verse 22, like the Easter theme, emphasizes the movement from humiliation/rejection to exaltation/glorification. A stone (= the king = Jesus) which has been rejected by the builders (= the nations = the Jews/Romans) as unworthy and a possible structural defect has been elevated to a place of prominence (= the corner of the building = the king's victory in battle = Jesus' resurrection).

The congregation responds to the new reality as "marvelous" and "the Lord's doing" in verses 23-24. Thus the psalm lection closes out with a confessional affirmation.

Colossians 3:1-4

A longer form of today's epistolary reading (3:1-11) also serves as the second lesson for Proper 13 in Year C. For additional comments, see *After Pentecost, Year C.*

It is one thing to believe and confess that Christ has been raised, quite another to be told that *we* have been raised. Yet this is the dramatic step taken in today's second lesson. Whichever Gospel reading is chosen, the focus is the same: the risen Lord on Easter morning. A similar perspective is seen in the kerygmatic summary in Acts 10:34-43: Christ the risen Lord is proclaimed as Lord of all. But the focus shifts in the epistolary reading from Christ's resurrection to our own resurrection.

The text begins with a conditional clause, "If then you have been raised with Christ . . ." (verse 1, RSV), but the form of the sentence in Greek indicates that it is a present reality, not a future possibility. This is captured especially well in JB: "Since you have been brought back to true life with Christ." The New English Bible renders it as a rhetorical question: "Were you not raised to life with Christ?" We may find this unequivocal claim jolting, especially if we recall that Paul ordinarily reserves to the future this level of participation with the risen Lord (cf. Rom. 6:5, 8). It is a form of present realization typical of the post-Pauline letters (cf. Eph. 2:6). Clearly, what is in view here is a form of full sacramental union in which the believer has both died and come to life again. In both instances, this has been achieved *with Christ* (2:20; 3:1). In some definitive sense, we are being told that what Christ experienced on Good Friday and Easter we have already experienced: we are co-participants with him in his death and resurrection.

The effect of such union is to conform our own destiny to that of the exalted Christ who is "seated at the right hand of God" (verse 1; cf. Ps. 110:1). It is transforming in that our perspective is shifted from things below to things above. This well-known spatial distinction between earth and heaven now comes to signify moral choices. The earthly outlook is detailed in the list of vices that follow (verses 5-8), just as the heavenly outlook is profiled with a list of virtues (verses 12-15). We are thus urged to direct our thoughts to the heavenly realm where Christ dwells (cf. Phil. 3:19-20).

This is possible because we have undergone a death: "I repeat, you died" (verse 3, NEB). As a result, our "life lies hidden with Christ in God." We are no longer who we once were. Our identity is explainable only in terms of the risen Christ with whom we have become united (cf. Phil. 1:21). There is a part of us that resides with the risen Lord in the very presence of God.

So close is this union between us and Christ that Christ can be said to be "our life" (verse 4). This is probably true in several senses. Christ is the one through whom the life-giving Spirit is mediated to us and indwells us (I Cor. 15:45; Rom. 8:10-11). He is also the defining norm of our existence (Phil. 1:21). Similar claims are made in the Johannine tradition (I John 5:11-12; John 14:6).

In spite of these claims that we have already been raised with Christ, our text still envisions a future "when Christ is revealed" (verse 4, JB; cf. Luke 17:30). Not everything is experienced yet. Thus at the coming of Christ, the fullness of this union will be manifested (cf. I Cor. 15:43; I John 3:2; I Pet. 5:1).

The word of today's epistolary text, then, is that Easter involves not only celebration, but moral renewal. It calls for reflection that is bifocal: Christ being brought back to life and our own resurrection to "true life with Christ" (verse 1, JB). So celebrated, Easter becomes a fusion of two stories: our own story with the story of Christ. If the two narratives remain separate and fail to intersect and intertwine, Easter may remain as a beautiful story but we are none the better for the telling.

John 20:1-18 *or* Matthew 28:1-10

Since Matthew 28:1-10 was the Gospel of Easter Vigil and commentary was offered there, attention here will be solely on John 20:1-18.

In the Gospels, resurrection narratives are of two kinds: reports about finding the tomb empty and reports of appearances of the risen Christ. The differences in the Gospel records indicate uses of different sources as well as particular emphases by the Evangelists themselves.

In the Gospel of John the resurrection narrative consists of two stories (20:1-18, 19-29). Each containing two parts, the two stories bearing striking similarities. Both are Sunday stories (20:1, 19), perhaps once having existed separately and used in the worship of the church. Each story involves members of the original circle of disciples, then focuses on the faith experience of one individual (Mary Magdalene in the first, Thomas in the second), and concludes with a witness to all believers. In neither story does the writer speak of the resurrection so as to shock or to coerce faith. Some later Christian documents speak of the risen Christ appearing in public places, astounding unbelievers with a faith-overwhelming wonder. In the New Testament, disciples relate the resurrection of Jesus as that of which "*we* all are witnesses" (Acts 2:32, italics added).

As stated earlier, John 20:1-18 is actually the interweaving of two episodes, one involving Mary Magdalene and the other Simon Peter and the beloved disciple. (See comments on John 13:21-30 for Wednesday in Holy Week for a summary statement about this disciple.) As in all their appearances together (for example, see 13:22-25; 18:15-16) the beloved disciple takes the favored position over Simon Peter. Peter comes in second in the race to the tomb (verse 4), and while Peter actually enters the tomb first, there is no evidence that what he saw and did not see generated in him any faith. The beloved disciple, although hesitant to enter at first, did believe once he went into the tomb and saw what Peter saw (verse 8). However, since neither as yet understood the Scriptures that Jesus must rise from the dead, they left the tomb and went home (verses 9-10). Miracles and faith that understands are not as closely joined as some might suppose. What is striking, however, is that the beloved disciple became the first believer in the resurrection, and on the slightest evidence—an empty tomb containing grave cloths.

The major portion of John 20:1-18 focuses on Mary Magdalene. Unlike the Synoptic accounts (see comments on Matt. 28:1-10 for Easter Vigil), John has Mary Magdalene alone at the tomb (verse 1). The empty tomb does not move her to faith; she thinks the body has been removed to another place (verse 13). The appearance of two angels (verse 12; a young man in Mark 16:5; an angel in Matt. 28:2; two men in Luke 24:4) neither allays her grief nor prompts faith in the resurrection. In fact, when Jesus appears she does not recognize him (verse 14). Only when he spoke her name did she believe (verse 16). This fulfills what had been said earlier of Jesus as the shepherd: he knows his own, he calls them by name, and they recognize his voice (10:3-4).

Unlike the beloved disciple, Mary Magdalene comes to faith not by the evidence of an empty tomb and grave cloths, not by the revelation from angels, and not even by the sight of the risen Christ. She came to faith by his word, a word that prompted the memory of a relationship which had already been formed and which, by the resurrection, was vindicated and sealed as an abiding one. Easter alone is a marvel; Easter for those who have followed all the way, even to Golgotha, is a confirmation of trust, a promise kept.

But even for disciples like Mary, Easter does not return her and Jesus to the past; Easter opens up a new future. The earthly ministry is over; now the ministry of the exalted, glorified, ever-abiding Christ begins. "Nevertheless I tell you the truth: it is to your advantage that I go away, for if I do not go away, the Counselor will not come to you" (16:7). In fact, the one who believes will do even greater works than Jesus did, "because I go to the Father" (14:12). Therefore, Jesus says to Mary Magdalene, "Do not hold me" (verse 17). Rather, she is to go and announce his resurrection and his ascension to the presence of God, from whose presence the Holy Spirit will come to lead, comfort, and empower the church.

Easter Evening

Acts 5:29-32 or Daniel 12:1-3; Psalm 150; I Corinthians 5:6-8
or Acts 5:29-32; Luke 24:13-49
(If the first reading is from the Old Testament, the reading
from Acts should be the second.)

In the reading from Acts, we have a brief summary of apostolic witness in which Christ's resurrection is a central theme. The Old Testament reading from Daniel, which is part of the extended apocalyptic vision of the last days, also speaks of resurrection, and is one of the few Old Testament texts to do so. Both readings have this in common: they proclaim faith in resurrection in the face of defiance and trouble. Psalm 150, which concludes the Psalter, is a psalm of repeated praise: Yahweh is praised in every single line. This note of celebration also continues in the epistolary reading where Paul urges his readers to celebrate the Christian Passover. The Gospel reading combines both themes of resurrection and celebration: the risen Lord encounters the two men en route to Emmaus and is revealed to them in the breaking of bread.

Acts 5:29-32

We ordinarily associate Easter with celebration, not conflict. If on Easter evening we are tempted to round off the day in a mood of quiet triumph, even relief, this first lesson will shake us from our lethargy. We have here an instance of preaching under the gun. The church is set against state and refuses to blink.

We should set the context within Acts. It is the second round of apostolic preaching within the temple precincts. The first cycle of such preaching began with a display of prophetic deed (healing the lame man, 3:1-10) and word

161

(Peter's address in the temple, 3:11-26). The gospel is met with resistance as Peter and John are arrested (4:1-31). In the face of opposition, they cannot be quieted (4:19-20). The gospel is vindicated as they are released. The solidarity of the community is seen in its willingness to share their possessions, the avarice of Ananias and Sapphira notwithstanding (4:32–5:11). After this, the gospel makes another prophetic thrust (5:12-16), only to be met with stiffer resistance. This time the apostles are imprisoned, miraculously released, and promptly summoned before the authorities, the Sanhedrin (5:17-26). In this courtroom setting, the high priest reminds Peter and the apostles of his injunction to silence (5:28), and their rejoinder provides us with today's text.

Central to the apostolic witness is *resurrection faith*. Several things are worth noting here. First, the two-stage distinction: "God . . . raised Jesus" (verse 30); "God exalted him" (verse 31). This may be a tradition that distinguished Christ's resurrection on the third day and his ascension forty days later as two separate events (cf. Luke 24 and Acts 1). Or, it may be that the same event is described in two ways. Second, there is an exegetical difficulty the preacher will need to observe. In what sense did God "raise Jesus"? In the sense of "raising up a Messiah" and bringing him into the world (so Calvin; cf. Judg. 2:18; 3:9, 15), or in the sense of raising him from the dead (so Chrysostom, Erasmus; cf. Acts 3:15; 4:10). If the former is in view, we have here a summary of Christ's entire work: God raised up a messiah, Jesus, and brought him into the world (incarnation); you killed him (crucifixion); God exalted him (resurrection).

As important as this text is as an instance of proclaiming the Easter faith, it also serves as an instance of *courageous witness*. Before proclaiming faith in Easter, the apostles proclaim resolute loyalty to God: "We must obey God rather than men" (verse 29). It is an echo of an earlier stand for the faith (4:19), but sharper and more succinct. The stance taken here is reminiscent of other cases where faith requires critical choices. In the biblical tradition, we recall the story of Daniel and the three Hebrew children (Dan. 3:16-18; 6:10-28). Outside the biblical tradition, Socrates poses a similar example. Given the choice between speaking his convictions as a prisoner or biting his lips as a free man, his reply could only be, "Men of Athens, I honour and love you; but I shall obey God rather than you, and while I have life and strength I shall never cease from the practice and teaching of philosophy . . ." (*Apology* 29D).

We should note how sharp-edged these words are. The work of God is placed in polar opposition to those who killed Christ by "hanging him on a tree" (verse 30). Yet this same God has extended to them repentance and forgiveness. Accusation is balanced with invitation, but the contours of the message are clearly etched, so much so that it invites rage, hostility, and the urge to kill (verse 33).

In today's text, we have an instance, as Barth observes, where declaration becomes confession: "A declaration . . . so long as it remains theoretical, entailing no obligation or venture on the part of [the one] who makes it, is not confession and must not be mistaken for it. It becomes confession when the word as such implies an action, making an obvious decision in which its subject is revealed and exposed as a member of the Christian community in the larger or smaller publicity of [one's] surroundings. There are good and perhaps strong Christian words which are not confessions because they are merely spoken among the like-minded where they cost nothing and do not help to make visible the contours of the Christian community. They become confessions when they openly intrude into the sphere of false faith and there bring to light what the Christian community regards as true and untrue, as right and wrong . . . . It is in confessions of this kind, in such words of direct aggression, that the Christian community always was and is built up" (*Church Dogmatics* III, 4, 84-5).

Daniel 12:1-3

This passage is an obvious reading for Easter because it is one of only two or three Old Testament texts that directly express belief in resurrection from the dead. The perspective in Daniel 12, however, is not quite the same as that in the New Testament, and our analysis should take note of the differences. The most important contribution this passage can make to the Christian celebration of Easter is to set the biblical understanding of resurrection into its proper frame of reference. First, however, we should review the passage in its literary and historical context.

Because of the historical allusions and the perspective of the contents, there is general agreement among scholars concerning the date of the final composition of the Book of Daniel and of this section of it in particular. It was written during the Maccabean revolt against the Hellenistic ruler Antiochus Epiphanes IV, after he had taken the Jerusalem Temple in 167 B.C., and before it had been recaptured and rededicated by the Maccabeans in December, 164 B.C. It was a time of military struggle against what appeared to be superior forces, but, equally important, it was a period of religious conflict between faith and culture, between faithful adherence to the ancient traditions on the one hand and acceptance of new Hellenistic customs and practices on the other. Tensions such as these are reflected in sectarian divisions within Judaism during the period. One of the main purposes of the Book of Daniel was to encourage the faithful to resist both the military threat and the temptation to follow foreign practices.

Daniel 12:1-4 is the concluding paragraph of a lengthy apocalyptic vision that begins in Daniel 10:1. Like the other vision reports in the book, this one consists of a revelation of the future to the seer, a future that leads from one kingdom to another to culminate in the final age. History unfolds as a struggle between the righteous Jews and those who oppose them, including both foreign kings and faithless Jews. Through Daniel 11:39, the revelation concerned the past, at least from the actual perspective of the writer. Daniel 11:40-45 is a prophecy of events that will transpire on the plane of history, leading to the death of the evil king that we identify as Antiochus Epiphanes IV. Daniel 12:1-3 gives the vision of the final events, including the historical plane but also transcending it. Daniel 12:4 signals the end of the vision with the instructions to Daniel to seal up the book until the right time for its disclosure, which actually was the time of its composition in the second century B.C.

A great deal is compressed into the three verses before us today. The introductory formula, "At that time," refers to a specific date, but does not say which one. The writer clearly has in view a time in the near future, a time when all things will be transformed. The time has already been characterized as one of serious trouble for the faithful, and now that is stated explicitly (verse 1). The description of what follows is similar in many ways to a judgment scene, with Michael, the patron saint of Israel, standing up as a judge, checking records in "the book," and determining rewards and punishments for those who stand before him. The events include more than a trial, however, for Michael as the agent of the divine will is warrior as well as judge. The events of the end-time transpire in three steps: (1) Michael arises in victory and delivers the nation ("your people," verse 1); (2) there is the resurrection of "many . . . who sleep in the dust of the earth," some to eternal life and some to "everlasting contempt" (verse 2); and (3) there is the exaltation of "those who are wise," "who turn many to righteousness" (verse 3).

Partly because this vision of the end is such a new and bold theological stroke, the meaning of several points is unclear. "The many" who will arise do not include all who have ever died, but who are they? They are not just the faithful Israelites who have fallen in the current war, for some will be raised in order to be punished. The writer seems to have in view those in his time who have not received their just rewards. Who are "those who are wise" (*maskilim*) who "shall shine like the brightness of the firmament"? They probably are not the same as the many who will be raised to eternal life, but some group of leaders within the community. That they have died in the process of turning "many to righteousness" recalls the Suffering Servant of Isaiah 52:12–53:13.

What stands in the center of the proclamation is not the promise of resurrection, but the promise of the deliverance and vindication of the people of God, by God acting through the angel Michael. All of those people will be vindicated, both those living at the time of the divine intervention and those who have already died. Our writer could not believe that God would forget those who had died in the struggle.

Resurrection is part of a larger drama, the triumph of God's justice and righteousness in a transformation of all things.

That, then, is the biblical frame of reference for belief in the resurrection of the dead: the hope for and confidence in the eventual triumph of God's will, even in and through and beyond the most terrible of circumstances. In the biblical view—not only here but in the New Testament as well—resurrection is never a natural phenomenon. Human beings do not live forever because of some innate force or power. However, God may raise even the dead to life, everlasting life. Thus the foundation for the resurrection hope is confidence in God. The specific frame of reference is the apocalyptic view of the world and history. Such a view includes a corporate, communal understanding of the hope; individuals are raised as part of the people of God. To live with that hope is to live in confidence and trust, and also with the urgency that the light of God's kingdom is already shining in the present age.

Psalm 150

This concluding psalm in the Psalter is merely an extended call to praise and adoration of God. It may be viewed as the counterpart to the opening psalm. While Psalm 1 calls the worshiper to study and to a life lived in the light of the divine will (the Torah), so Psalm 150 calls upon all things to join in adoration of God. What begins in the call to joyful service of the law and to the faithful observance of torah leads to the joy of praise.

This final psalm in the Psalter concludes the book with a great and universal call to praise God. As such, it may be seen not only as the fitting conclusion to the book as a whole but also as a statement of faith and confidence in the future. How different the book of Psalms would have been had it concluded with a moaning and depressing lament!

The tenfold repetition of the call to praise in the body of the psalm is its most characteristic feature. Like other examples of the number ten in the Bible, it was probably chosen deliberately both as a memory device (note that we have ten fingers) and as an affirmation of completion or fullness. The two hallelujahs ("Praise the Lord") at the beginning and end are opening and closing liturgical statements which bring the number to twelve.

Three factors in the praise of God are noted: the places of praising (verse 1), the reasons for praising (verse 2), and the means of praise (verses 3-5).

The places of praising are the temple, which was considered the center point of the universe in late Jewish thought, and the firmament, which was considered the dome or heavens encircling the universe. Praise should thus extend from the center outward to the whole of creation and include every living thing (see verse 6).

The reasons for praise are God's "mighty deeds" and "his exceeding greatness." Thus both divine action and divine being are stressed.

The means of praise are multiple musical instruments of all types. This call to orchestrated adulation suggests something of what went on in festive worship services in the temple. The one medium of praising God that is noted, which is not a musical instrument, is the dance. Throughout the Bible, dancing is associated with celebration and joy (see Exod. 15:19-21; Ps. 30:11), and it probably played a significant role in Israelite worship.

The appropriateness of this psalm for the Easter Evening service is based on its call to and emphasis on praise, since Easter is the central day of celebration in the Christian Year.

I Corinthians 5:6-8

This text serves as the first option for the second lesson on Easter evening because it speaks of the sacrifice of Christ "our paschal lamb" (verse 7, RSV; "our passover," JB), and urges us to "celebrate the festival" (verse 8). It creates a mood of festivity that befits the Easter celebration. By connecting the death of Christ with a continuing season of celebration, it serves to remind us that Easter is not merely a day, but a season that extends for seven weeks until Pentecost.

We should note the context in which this graphic image of Christ as the sacrificial Passover lamb occurs. We may be surprised to find that it occurs not in a set of liturgical

167

instructions but as part of moral instruction. At issue is a case of sexual misconduct that Paul had heard about: one of the Corinthian church members was "living with his father's wife" (5:1). From what we can gather, a man was married to his stepmother, a practice forbidden by Jewish law (Lev. 18:8; Deut. 22:30; 27:20). The practice was also unacceptable among Greeks and Romans (cf. Euripides, *Hippolytus;* Cicero, *Pro Cluentio* 14).

What Paul finds shocking is not only that a Christian is engaged in such a practice but that the church blithely accepts it, in fact regards it as something worth boasting about (verse 2). Interestingly, Paul's remarks in the ensuing verses are not directed to the parties involved but to the church and its astonishingly insensitive treatment of the matter. The arrogant attitude displayed here is reflected elsewhere in First Corinthians (cf. 3:18; 4:6-8, 19). Somehow, their new-found freedom in Christ had become translated into a form of unmitigated confidence in themselves. The result was that they had a conspicuously huge sin in their own midst but they were too blind to see it. Thus, our text opens with a word of censure: "your boasting is not good" (verse 6, RSV, NIV), or "the pride that you take in yourselves is hardly to your credit" (JB). To penetrate this barrier of smugness, Paul employs familiar Jewish images and reinterprets them for this situation.

Before doing so, however, he cites a piece of popular wisdom, introduced with the phrase, "Do you not know . . . ?" This formula is commonly employed to confront readers with the familiar, that which they already know, or should know (cf. 3:16). It is an argument from common sense; our own world of experience tells us that "even a small amount of yeast is enough to leaven all the dough" (verse 6, JB; cf. Gal. 5:9). Greco-Roman popular wisdom knows a similar saying: "Yeast is itself also the product of corruption, and produces corruption in the dough with which it is mixed; for the dough becomes flabby and inert, and altogether the process of leavening seems to be one of putrefaction; at any rate, if it goes too far, it completely sours and spoils the flour" (Plutarch, *Quaestiones Romanae* 289F).

This negative connotation attached to leaven is also

reflected in the teachings of Jesus (cf. Matt. 16:6-12; Mark 8:14-21; Luke 12:1; cf. Matt. 13:33; Luke 13:21; also Gospel of Thomas, par. 96).

The point is clear: give sin an inch and it will take a mile. The only proper response is to expunge evil at its first appearance. To make his point, Paul employs imagery drawn from the Jewish practice of observing the Passover and the Feast of Unleavened Bread. According to one biblical tradition (Exod. 12), Passover was celebrated in the spring, in the month of Nisan, as an occasion for remembering God's deliverance of Israel from Egypt. It began on the tenth day of the month when the head of the household selected an unblemished year-old lamb. On the fourteenth of Nisan, the lamb was slaughtered for the celebration of Passover that evening. The Passover evening meal began a seven-day festival during which unleavened bread was eaten, hence its name the Feast of Unleavened Bread (cf. Exod. 23:15; 34:18; Deut. 16:3-4). In preparation for this week, every scrap of leaven had to be removed from the house. Leaven was regarded as ritually unclean because it involved ferment and corruption (cf. Lev. 2:11).

The sequence is clear: first the Passover lamb is slaughtered and the celebration of the Feast of Unleavened Bread immediately ensues. It is a time of ritual purification when all visible signs of evil are removed from sight. Accordingly, it requires moral cleanliness on the part of the participants.

Against this background, Paul insists that Christ is the Passover lamb who has already been slaughtered (verse 7). It is an unusual metaphor for Paul (though cf. Rom. 3:24-26), but one developed elsewhere in the New Testament (cf. I Pet. 1:19; John 1:29, 36; 19:36; Rev. 5:6, 9, 12; 12:11). If Christ is so understood, his death may be seen as the event that begins the celebration of the Feast of Unleavened Bread. By extension, then, we who are in Christ are expected to make ourselves ready for the festival celebration, and this above all requires moral purification (cf. Exod. 12:19; 13:7; Deut. 16:3-4). It means getting rid of "the old leaven, the leaven of malice and evil," and feeding on the "unleavened bread of sincerity and truth" (verse 8).

In the setting of Easter evening, today's epistolary text

serves to link festal celebration with community behavior. What was done in Christ has rippling effects within the community that celebrates his death and resurrection. Above all, the celebrants are expected to adopt a life-style that befits the One whom they worship as the risen Lord. What emerges is a community of faith in which arrogance, pride, and self-satisfaction are alien, but in which sincerity and truth are the native virtues.

Luke 24:13-49

One could hardly imagine a more appropriate text for an Easter evening service than Luke 24:13-49. This passage involves an experience with the risen Christ "toward evening" of the first Easter (verse 29), reflects upon the meaning of the day's events, includes a eucharistic meal, ties the meaning of the resurrection to the ministry of the historical Jesus and to the Hebrew Scriptures, offers the promise of the Holy Spirit, and commissions the disciples to witness to the nations. Easter morning announces; Easter evening interprets.

Luke's resurrection narrative consists of five parts: (1) verses 1-12, the women at the tomb; (2) verses 13-35, the appearance of the risen Christ on the road to Emmaus; (3) verses 36-43, Jesus' appearance to the eleven and to others with them; (4) verses 44-49, instruction and commission; and (5) verses 50-53, the departure of Jesus. Our lection for today consists of parts 2, 3, and 4.

Verses 13-35, the appearance of the risen Christ to two disciples on the road to Emmaus, is a narrative unit, bearing the marks of artistry that we have come to associate with Lukan stories. The preacher may wish to treat this passage as a unit, even though there certainly are distinct accents within it which the sermon can well emphasize. Three will be treated here.

First, verses 13-15 record a resurrection appearance without parallel in the other Gospels and absent from the list in I Corinthians 15:3-8. There are evidences, however, that by the time of Luke's writing, resurrection accounts had begun to influence one another. For example, verse 12 (not found in many of the best manuscripts and omitted in the RSV) reflects John 20:6-10; verse 34 agrees with I Corinthians 15:5; verse 40 (not found in many of the best manuscripts and omitted in the RSV) seems to borrow from John 20:20; and to verse 51 some manuscripts add a line from Acts 1:9-10. It is likely that Genesis 18:1-15 is also influencing Luke since it is his frequent practice to tell his stories so as to echo Old Testament stories. Consistent with the remainder of Luke 24 and with the other Gospels, the resurrection appearance here does not coerce or overwhelm faith. Matthew says some doubted (28:17); Luke has already said the disciples regarded the report of the women at the tomb as an idle tale which they did not believe (24:12); and John records the hesitant faith of both Mary Magdalene (20:11-18) and Thomas (20:24-29). In fact, Luke says of the two disciples on the road, "But their eyes were kept from recognizing him" (verse 16) until they had received the witness of Scripture (verses 25-27) and sacrament (verses 30-35).

The second distinct accent in verses 13-35 is the role of Scripture in generating faith in the disciples (verse 32). Scripture, that is, the Old Testament, is not only central in Luke's portrayal of the life and ministry of Jesus (2:21-39; 4:16-30) but also in Luke's understanding of the formation of faith in the disciples of Jesus (16:31; 24:44-47; Acts 2:14-36). According to Luke, the death and resurrection of Jesus and the preaching of the gospel to the nations is continuous with a proper understanding of the Law, the Prophets, and the Psalms (verses 27, 44-47).

The third distinctive element in verses 13-35 is Christ's self-revelation in the breaking of bread (verses 31, 35). That the meal was a eucharistic meal is evident in the language used to describe it (verse 30). Although a guest, Jesus is host because it is the Lord's Supper. The generation of faith by word (Scripture) and sacrament and the experience of the living Christ in the eucharistic meal not only reflect the theology and practice of the Lukan church but offer to the reader the possibility of faith and the promise of Christ's presence.

The next unit of our lection is verses 36-43. This records the appearance of Jesus to the eleven and to those with them (verse 30) in a scene marked by fear, wonder, and "[disbelieving] for joy" (verse 41). This unit, though much briefer than verses 13-35, is framed on the same pattern: the risen Christ appears, the disciples do not recognize him, they are scolded for doubting, food is shared, Jesus enables them to understand the Scriptures, and they respond in wonder and joy. In this unit, the point is stressed that the risen Christ is not a spirit or phantom; he is the one crucified. The one they followed, believed, and obeyed is the one vindicated by God's raising him from the dead. To be a disciple of one is to be a disciple of the other, for they are one and the same.

The final unit of our lection, verses 44-49, repeats one theme and introduces two others. The theme repeated is that of the continuity of the words of the risen Christ with the words of the historical Jesus and with the words of the Old Testament (verses 44-47). The two new themes are the commission to preach the gospel (for Luke, repentance and forgiveness of sins) to all nations beginning from Jerusalem (verses 47-48; Acts 1:8), and the promise of the power of God (verse 49). This promise of the gift of the Holy Spirit, for which the disciples wait, is fulfilled at Pentecost (Acts 1:4, 8; 2:1-18).

Second Sunday of Easter

Acts 2:14a, 22-32; Psalm 16:5-11; I Peter 1:3-9; John 20:19-31

It is important to note that Easter begins a seven-week period of sustained reflection and celebration. As such, it is the first Sunday of the Easter season. Accordingly, the following Sundays are designated Sundays *of* Easter and not Sundays *after* Easter. At the end of the fifty-day season stands Pentecost, the Eighth Sunday of Easter.

Several themes are prominent during this period. We naturally continue to celebrate the paschal mystery of the suffering, death, and resurrection of Christ. But other themes also emerge: Christ's ascension and the coming of the Spirit. It is quite fitting, then, that the first reading for each of these Sundays is taken from the Acts of the Apostles, which provides a narrative sequel to the death and resurrection of Christ. Prominent among the events it records are Christ's ascension (Acts 1), the coming of the Spirit on Pentecost to mark the beginning of the church (Acts 2), and a succession of events in which the apostles, most notably Peter and Paul, witness to the Gospel.

The second reading during the Easter season is taken from First Peter, First John, and Revelation for Years A, B, and C respectively because "these texts seem most appropriate to the spirit of the Easter season, a spirit of joyful faith and confident hope" (Introduction to the *Lectionary for Mass* [Collegeville, 1970], chapter II, section IV.1, page xxxv, cited in A. Adam, *The Liturgical Year: Its History and Meaning After the Reform of the Liturgy* [New York: Pueblo Publishing Co., 1981], 87).

The Gospel readings for this season focus on the appearances of the risen Lord (Second and Third Sundays) and the farewell discourses and prayers of Jesus from the Gospel of John (Fourth through Seventh Sundays).

Today's texts consist of a portion of Peter's Pentecost sermon (Acts 2), the first main section after the Old Testament quotation from Joel which focuses on Christ's resurrection. Quite appropriately, the psalm reading (16:5-11) encompasses the portion quoted in Peter's sermon (16:8-11). The epistolary reading from First Peter, an opening prayer of blessing that begins with a firm declaration of the resurrection hope, continues the theme of the first lesson. The reading from the Fourth Gospel records the famous episode where Jesus appears first to the disciples, then to Thomas, and concludes with a summary stating the purpose of this Gospel (20:30-31).

Acts 2:14*a*, 22-32

This is the first of several summaries of early Christian preaching found in Acts (cf. 3:12-26; 4:8-12; 5:29-32; 10:34-43; 13:16-41). It occurs here on the lips of Peter as he addresses the crowd of Jews gathered in Jerusalem to celebrate the Feast of Pentecost (2:1; cf. Exod. 23:14-17; Lev. 23:15-21). Today's text consists of the middle portion of this speech. In the preceding section (2:16-21), Peter asserts that the outpouring of the Spirit signifies the arrival of the last days of which Joel had prophesied (Joel 3:1-5).

In this section, Peter turns to the topic at hand: Jesus of Nazareth (verse 22; cf. 3:6; 4:10; 6:14; 22:8; 26:9; also Luke 18:37; 24:19; John 18:5, 7; 19:19). What follows is a brief rehearsal of the main points of the kerygma: (1) his messianic ministry authenticated by displays of divine power (verse 22); (2) his crucifixion (verse 23); and (3) his resurrection (verse 24). Clearly, the accent falls on this last item since it is expounded most thoroughly in the following verses (verses 25-32). Indeed, today's text moves toward this proclamation of Christ's resurrection as its grand climax (verse 32). We can consider each of these items in turn.

1. *Jesus the messianic prophet* (verse 22). Peter begins with what the crowds cannot deny: that a Nazarene named Jesus had recently traveled among them performing signs and wonders. The capsule summary of the Gospel of Luke further connects these authenticating works with his

prophetic role (Luke 24:19; cf. Acts 10:38). It was commonly assumed that such displays of power were signs of divine legitimacy (cf. John 2:18; 3:2). They indicated that God was working through him (verse 22; cf. John 5:36). Nor did the work of God end with Jesus. What began with Jesus continued in the early church (Acts 2:43; 4:30; 6:12; 6:8; 7:36; 8:13; 14:3; 15:12; cf. II Cor. 12:12).

2. *Jesus crucified through divine necessity and human conspiracy* (verse 23). Responsibility for the death of Jesus is dual. The Jews whom Peter addresses are charged with crucifying and killing him (Acts 3:13-17; 4:10; 5:30-31; 7:52; 10:39-40; 13:27-30), but they did not act alone. The actual execution was carried out "by the hands of lawless men," or "by men outside the Law" (verse 23, JB), that is, the Romans. At one level, then, his death was the result of human complicity.

But at another level, his death occurred "according to the definite plan and foreknowledge of God" (verse 23). Early Christians could hardly bring themselves to believe that Christ's death had been a historical accident. As tragic as it was, it could be fitted into God's divine plan. How? It was seen to have unfolded "according to Scripture," which meant in keeping with the divine plan (Luke 24:26-27, 44-47; Acts 3:18; 4:28; 13:29; cf. Luke 22:22). Ultimately, Christ's destiny was seen to have been set "before the foundation of the world" (I Pet. 1:20).

3. *Jesus whom God raised from the dead* (verses 24-32). This is the crux of the matter, the burden on Peter's heart. His main task is to show that the crucified Messiah has been vindicated by God, that human misdeeds have been reversed by divine power.

This Peter proceeds to do from Scripture, specifically Psalm 16:8-11. We read this psalm as an expression of trust on the part of the psalmist who is confident of being delivered by God from peril—nothing more. But early Christians read it differently. They naturally assumed that it was written by David. But if so, it posed a problem. How could David say that God would not abandon his soul to Hades or let his faithful one see the pit, or grave (verse 27 = Ps. 16:10)? The problem was even more sharply focused in the Septuagint, which spoke of God's faithful one seeing "corruption,"

175

which seemed to imply more than mere death. Christian readers of this psalm well knew that David was "dead and buried" (verse 29, JB; cf. I Kings 2:10; cf. Acts 13:36). They logically concluded that it must speak of someone else.

Combined with this was their reading of another psalm which spoke of a scion of David being raised up as his successor sometime in the future (Ps. 132:11-12; also Ps. 89:4). This could only be seen as a prophetic vision on David's part.

Their logic of Scripture interpretation enabled them to see Christ as the one being spoken of in Psalm 16. His resurrection was seen as God's rescuing him from the snares of death (cf. Ps. 18:4-5; 116:3; II Sam. 22:6). Death was unable to keep him in its grip (verse 24, NEB).

In addition to this scriptural proof, the apostles claimed to be witnesses to the risen Lord (verse 32; cf. 1:22; 3:15; 4:33; 5:32; 10:41; 13:31; also I Cor. 15:15). What they had seen and experienced in their encounter with the risen Lord enabled them to make sense of otherwise inexplicable Scriptures. And what they read in Scripture enabled them to make sense of their Easter experience. It was a mutually reinforcing set of interpretations. Scripture illuminated their experience and their experience illuminated Scripture.

Psalm 16:5-11

In his Pentecost sermon, Peter uses Psalm 16 to argue that David had spoken of the resurrection of Jesus (Acts 2:25-28). This example of Christian utilization of the Jewish Scriptures is somewhat typical. Certain allusions and particular terminology in the Hebrew Scriptures were exegeted by the early Christians in terms of beliefs and positions already held by the church.

The ancient rabbis understood this psalm as David writing about himself. In addition they understood the text as speaking about actual death, at least in verse 3a. This text, read as "the holy that are in the earth" (and therefore dead), was said to speak about the deceased since "the Holy One (God) does not call the righteous man holy until he is laid away in the earth. Why not? Because the Inclination-to-evil [the evil *yetzer* of the human personality] keeps pressing him. And so God does not put His trust in him in this world till the day of his death. . . . That the Lord will not call a righteous man holy until he is laid away in the earth is what is meant."

In spite of the translation difficulties found in verses 2-4, where the worshiper appears to refer to the worship of other gods ("the saints" and "the noble" may denote the "holy and mighty [gods]" mentioned in verse 4), the remainder of the text makes reasonably good sense. (In addition to the RSV, one should consult the New Jewish Publication Society Version.)

This lection, verses 5-11, opens with a short confessional statement addressed to a human audience (5*a*) and is immediately followed by a confessional statement of trust addressed to God (5*b*). The terminology of this verse as well as verse 6 speaks of what one has inherited or been given in life—portion, cup, lot, lines, and heritage. The NJPSV translates as:

> The Lord is my allotted share and portion;
> You control my fate.
> Delightful country has fallen to my lot;
> lovely indeed is my estate.

Instead of being guilty of worshiping false gods, the psalmist is depicted as one who constantly thinks of God (verses 7-8). The counsel God gives (7*a*) is matched by that of the person's own conscience (RSV: "heart," although literally "the kidneys," denoting the inner self). The term translated "night" in verse 7*b* is actually the Hebrew plural "nights" (= "watches of the night," "every night," or "the dark night"). The human activity and consistency (verse 8*a*) are matched by God's consistent preservation with the consequence that the psalmist can confess, "I shall not be moved," i.e., threatened or overcome.

The last section (verses 9-11) returns to direct address to God confessing assurance that the request made in verse 1 will be granted, that is, the person will live and not die. It was this section that led to the psalm's usage in early Christian preaching and confession. Again the NJPSV conveys the meaning better than the RSV:

> So my heart rejoices,
>> my whole being exults,
>> and my body rests secure.
> For You will not abandon me to Sheol,
>> or let Your faithful one see the Pit.

Sheol and Pit refer to the realm of the dead and probably the psalm was used originally by persons near death as a result of some sickness. Of course they do not wish to die but wish to remain to enjoy their heritage (verses 5-6 and 11*b*).

I Peter 1:3-9

Today's epistolary text occurs in the form of an opening prayer of blessing addressed to "the God and Father of our Lord Jesus Christ" (verse 3). It conforms to a well-known form of Jewish prayer that opens by addressing God as blessed (Berakah). Along with prayers of thanksgiving, these prayers of praise serve as opening sections of New Testament letters (cf. II Cor. 1:3; Eph. 1:3).

The preacher needs to decide on the limits of the pericope. The suggested division (verses 3-9) conforms to the RSV, JB, and NIV. Another outline is followed in NEB with paragraph divisions occurring at verses 3, 6, and 8. This latter arrangement is similar to that adopted in Nestle 26th ed., in which the prayer includes verses 3-12, with divisions occurring at verses 3, 6, 8, and 12. There is general agreement that a new major section begins with verse 13, as the language shifts to the imperative mood, which is typical of the way moral exhortations begin.

If we adopt the framework of Nestle 26th ed. and NEB, today's text may be divided into three sections.

1. *New birth and living hope* (verses 3-5). In language reminiscent of the Fourth Gospel (1:13; 3:3-5; cf. I John 2:29; 3:9), we are said to have been given a "new birth" (verse 3, JB) as God's children. It is a theme continued in the letter (1:23). Because of this strong baptismal imagery, some scholars have suggested that the Epistle of First Peter at an earlier stage of redaction functioned as a baptismal liturgy. It is a plausible suggestion, for we can envision how the opening

section (verses 3-12) might have been used as a prayer in a baptismal setting and how the following material (1:13–2:10) might have constituted a baptismal sermon in which the newly baptized were exhorted to holy living.

The basis of the new birth is God's "raising Jesus Christ from the dead" (verse 3, JB). Here we have a mixing of the Johannine notion of the baptism as a new birth (John 3:3-5) and the Pauline understanding of baptism as a dying and rising with Christ (Rom. 6:3-4). The new birth imagery is crucial in linking our new status as God's children with the inheritance that is ours (verse 4). Bestowal of this new status as God's children is seen as an act of "great mercy" (verse 3; cf. Eph. 2:4; also Sir. 16:12).

The inheritance is no ordinary legacy, such as land, prosperity, or political security (cf. Gen. 17:1-8). It is rather a heavenly inheritance that "nothing can destroy or spoil or wither" (verse 4, NEB; cf. Eph. 1:18; Col. 1:5, 12; 3:24; Heb. 9:15; also Matt. 6:19-20). Even though it lies in the future as a "salvation ready to be revealed in the last time" (verse 5, RSV; cf. 1:20), it is protected by divine power (cf. I Cor. 2:5). It is reserved for those who live "in faith."

2. *Suffering and the refinement of faith* (verses 6-7). As the prayer unfolds, there is a shift from the lofty language of future salvation and the divine inheritance to the harsher realities of life below. Suffering is hinted at: "for a little while you may have to suffer various trials" (verse 6). Later in the letter, the language becomes more explicit (4:12-13, 19; 5:10).

Suffering is not without value, however. It is like a refining fire (James 1:2; Prov. 17:3; Mal. 3:2-3; I Cor. 3:13; Wisd. of Sol. 3:6; Sir. 2:5). But what emerges from Christian suffering is even more valuable than gold. Though refined, gold is perishable, while Christian faith is not. For this reason, suffering properly experienced can become an occasion for rejoicing (verse 6; cf. Rom. 5:3; I Pet. 5:10).

3. *Loving and believing without seeing* (verses 8-9). As the prayer moves toward its conclusion, it sounds more Johannine in its insistence that we can believe without having actually seen (John 17:20; 20:29; II Cor. 5:7). This becomes reassuring especially for those who were not privy to the words and deeds of the historical Jesus, but who are

not for that reason disadvantaged in the life of faith. Historical and geographical proximity do not ensure faith in the New Testament sense, which involves loving One whom we have not seen with our eyes (cf. Eph. 6:24; II Tim. 4:8).

John 20:19-31

It remains the case experientially if not cognitively that for most congregations Easter is a day and not a season. The lectionary has as one of its benefits as well as its tasks the weekly reminder that today and every Sunday until Pentecost are Sundays *of* Easter and not *after* Easter. Of course, every Sunday, even those during Lent, is an Easter Festival, but human nature being what it is, matters of great importance lose their impact when given only generalized attention. Therefore, for seven Sundays we will be attending to texts that spell out implications of the resurrection of Jesus Christ.

Today's lesson consists of two parts: 20:19-29 and 20:30-31. Verses 19-29 provide the second half of John's resurrection narrative, the first (verses 1-18) having been considered for the Easter Day service. Verses 30-31 constitute a concluding statement by the Evangelist. Chapter 21 is an epilogue and may have been added by the Evangelist or one of his disciples after the Gospel had been formally concluded.

In the comments on John 20:1-18 it was pointed out that both 1-18 and 19-29 involve double stories. In verses 1-18 the resurrection of Jesus touches Mary Magdalene and two of the Twelve, Simon Peter and the beloved disciple. As was stated, faith was generated in the beloved disciple by the sight of an empty tomb and grave cloths and in Mary Magdalene by the word of Jesus. Again now, in verses 19-29 two stories are interwoven with faith being generated in different ways. On Sunday evening of the same day as the events of verses 1-18 (verse 19), Jesus appears to his disciples (except Thomas, verse 24). He bestows on them his peace (verses 19, 21), commissions them to continue the work that God had given him (verse 21), breathes on them, giving the Holy Spirit (verse 22), and grants to them apostolic authority for retaining or forgiving sins (verse 23). Verses 19-23 contain, therefore, not solely an appearance of the risen Christ, the sight of whom generated in the disciples faith and joy (verse 20).

In this brief digest are two additional elements; one is the Johannine Pentecost. Luke, the other recorder of Pentecost, makes the experience a historical narrative consisting of Jesus' forty days of appearances as the risen Christ, his promise of the outpouring of the Holy Spirit, the ascension, ten days of prayer and waiting, and the coming of the Spirit at Pentecost (Acts 1:1–2:42). John has no such chronology or drama, but the promise of the giving of the Spirit as discussed in chapters 14–16 is here fulfilled. A rereading of those chapters will impress again upon the church the life-giving necessity of the Spirit for the life and work of the community.

The other significant event in verses 19-23 is the granting of apostolic authority (verse 23; Matt. 16:19; 18:18). Through the apostles the continuity between Christ and the church is established, and through them the benefits and the work of Christ remain in the world after his ascension. Through the Holy Spirit the departed Christ abides to grant comfort, instruction, and power in the life of the church.

This brings us to Thomas whose absence and hesitation in believing (verses 24-26) has brought upon him the name "Doubting Thomas" and negative attention which forgets his earlier courage (11:16) and theological probing (14:5). However, after his experience with the risen Christ the next Sunday (verse 26), Thomas makes a confession of faith as strong as any in the Gospel: "My Lord and my God!" (verse 28). Whether Thomas actually touched Jesus is not clear (verses 26-27); Jesus simply refers to his having believed because he had seen (verse 29). At this point Jesus pronounces a blessing upon all who have not seen and yet who believe (verse 29); that is, upon all who come to faith through the word of Christ through the apostles and the church (17:20). Nothing could be more encouraging to the Johannine church or to us than the assurance that faith is available to all persons in all places regardless of distance in time or place from Jesus of Nazareth.

The Evangelist's concluding statement (verses 30-31) says three things: the events recorded here are but a selection from many signs that Jesus performed, but these have been related in order to generate faith in Jesus as Christ and Son of God, and the purpose of generating faith is to give life. Saying that these stories are to help the reader believe does not clearly identify the reader. Since the Gospel assumes some familiarity with Jesus and his work, very likely the book is addressing those of weak faith, or misguided faith, or faith that depends too much on signs, or new faith that needs to grow. After all, in this Gospel there is faith seeking, faith confessing, faith faltering, faith questioning, faith praising, and faith deepening. All of us are addressed in these "signs which he did."

Third Sunday of Easter

Acts 2:14a, 36-41; Psalm 116:12-19; I Peter 1:17-23; Luke 24:13-35

The first lesson from Acts consists of the final section of Peter's Pentecost sermon in which he urges his hearers to repent, be baptized, and receive the gift of God's Spirit. If the first lesson sees salvation as a gift extended, the second lesson looks at salvation in retrospect, as something already experienced. It reminds us of what is already ours in Christ and how we should behave accordingly. The Gospel lesson records the familiar episode of Jesus' encounter with the two men en route to Emmaus. Here we see faith in the risen Lord arising from nothing: they first encounter Jesus as one unknown, but eventually their hearts are opened to the true reality of his New Being. The reading from the psalm is the final section of a psalm of thanksgiving in which the psalmist reflects on an experience of divine deliverance and offers himself in thankful praise to the God who delivered him. In one way or another, all four readings today develop the theme of salvation—as something offered, experienced, discovered, and that elicits a response of thanksgiving.

Acts 2:14*a*, 36-41

In today's first lesson, we have the concluding portion of Peter's Pentecost sermon and a description of its impact on the crowd. A few verses intervene between this week's lesson and last week's lesson, but they provide a crucial link in the argument from Scripture and should be read in preparation for this text.

The sermon ends on a note of finality: "The whole House of Israel can be certain that God has made this Jesus whom you crucified both Lord and Christ" (verse 36, JB). These two christological titles are intended to encapsulate the arguments from Scripture that were referred to earlier. Psalm 110:1 has just been cited to show that David envisioned a heavenly Lord other than himself to whom God promised a position of exalted dominion (verses 34-35). Psalm 16:8-11 had been cited to show that God's Holy One, the Messiah, would triumph over the pangs of death. By his resurrection, Christ was seen to have qualified on both scores. He was unable to be bound by death and thus qualified as the Christ. Having been vindicated by God, he now reigned as heavenly Lord.

The crucial link, of course, was that the *crucified Jesus* now bore these titles. More than that, the hearers, some of them at least, had participated in his death. The logic was compelling enough for the hearers to be "cut to the heart" (cf. Ps. 109:16), and they issued the cry of salvation, "What shall we do?" (verse 37). It is the earnest cry of those multitudes who had earlier heard John the Baptist preaching repentance (Luke 3:10). It is echoed later as others are confronted with the challenge of the gospel (Acts 16:30; 22:16).

Peter's response is a call to repentance and baptism. In this instance, repentance involves first the recognition of their mistake in misconstruing the true identity of Jesus and remorse for their misdeeds in putting him to death. Naturally, as it did in the preaching of John the Baptist, it required reorientation of life that was visibly displayed in merciful and just behavior (Luke 3:8, 10-14; cf. Acts 3:19).

Baptism "in the name of Jesus Christ" probably meant baptism in which the name of Jesus was spoken over the initiate (cf. Acts 8:16; 10:48; 19:5). Like John's baptism, it bestowed forgiveness of sins (Luke 3:3; 24:47; cf. Acts 5:31; 10:43; 13:38). But unlike John's baptism, it was accompanied by a bestowal of the Spirit (cf. Acts 19:1-7; also 8:15; 10:47). What is implied here, of course, is that the prophecy of Joel that spoke of an outpouring of the Spirit on all flesh (2:17-21) now becomes a fulfilled promise among these believers. As participants in the events of the "last days," they are now recipients of God's Spirit.

They are assured that God's promise extends to them, their children, and those near and far away. Whether this is to be understood geographically, that is, Jews present in Jerusalem as well as those living in remote regions, or ethnically, that is, Jews (those near) and Gentiles (those afar off), is not certain. Given the prominence of the Gentile mission in the book of Acts, it is likely the latter. Also, similar language is used elsewhere in the New Testament to distinguish Jews and Gentiles (cf. Eph. 2:12-13; also Acts 22:21; Isa. 57:19; Sir. 24:32). In either case, the gospel is understood as a summons by God. The promise is extended to those "whom the Lord our God calls to him" (verse 39; cf. Joel 2:32 = Acts 2:20).

The hearers are urged to deliver themselves from "this crooked generation" (verse 40). The language is supplied by Deuteronomy 32:5 and Psalm 78:8 (cf. Phil. 2:15).

The response was overwhelming. The word reached home and the hearers responded by submitting to baptism (cf. 8:12, 16; 18:8; cf. Matt. 28:19). In one day three thousand persons joined the messianic community, the first of several staggering responses recorded in the book of Acts (cf. 2:47; 5:14; 6:7; 9:31; 11:21, 24). This is Luke's way of showing that the movement was far from negligible. It eventually reaches Rome and en route convinces many that "these things were not done in a corner" (26:26, JB).

The intent of today's text is clear. It seeks to show the impact of the resurrection faith on Jewish hearers. More specifically, it intends to present the crucified Jesus as the most compelling candidate for messiahship and lordship, as the one who most convincingly makes sense of Scriptures such as Psalm 16 and Psalm 110. As such, he is presented as the bringer of the new age of the Spirit in which salvation and forgiveness of sins are extended to the penitent and obedient. What's more, our text wants us to see that proclamation of Jesus as Lord worked its effects on multitudes who were looking for an alternative to a generation of crookedness and an age of brokenness.

Psalm 116:12-19

Verses 1-9 of this psalm were discussed for the Fifth Sunday of Lent, and this text has been treated in the Holy Thursday service.

I Peter 1:17-23

Today's epistolary lesson sounds like instructions given to new converts. In an earlier form it could have been part of a baptismal homily or catechetical instructions for those recently baptized.

The language suggests that the readers are Gentile Christians who have turned from pagan ways. They are reminded of the "desires you cherished in your days of ignorance" (verse 14, NEB) and the "useless way of life your ancestors handed down" (verse 18, JB; cf. 2:10; 4:3). To characterize pagan life as "ignorant" and "useless" ("empty," NIV, NEB; "futile," RSV) reflects the moral superiority Jews, and in this case Jewish Christians, presumed toward Gentiles (cf. Matt. 5:47; I Thess. 4:5). It is, of course, a caricature, for there existed a strong moral tradition in Greek and Roman thought, exemplified in the likes of Epictetus and Plutarch as well as among numerous ordinary citizens. But cases of pagan immorality are well attested too, and there is no reason to deny that some Gentiles who became Christians had left behind a profligate way of life (cf. 4:3-4).

Newly converted Gentiles would find themselves living in a hostile environment, feeling quite alien as "strangers in the world" (1:1, NIV). Their time on earth could well be conceived as a time of exile (verse 17). In this respect, there was a long Jewish legacy of living in the world as sojourners and foreigners (cf. Gen. 23:4; 24:37; Ps. 39:13; cf. Heb. 11:13). For Gentile readers, this could have been true in several senses. They may have been living away from their homeland literally—in scattered regions of Asia Minor (1:1-2). But in another sense Christians saw themselves as exiles on earth whose real hometown was in heaven (cf. Phil. 3:20; Col. 3:1-4; Heb. 13:14). In yet a third sense our readers may have felt like foreigners. They were now part of a new religion and its frame of reference, rituals, and moral expectations was equally new and unfamiliar.

And what is appropriate instruction for persons in this situation? To define the contours of responsibility in light of the change they have recently experienced. This is precisely the move that is made in today's text. It occurs as part of a much larger section of moral instruction (1:13–2:10).

The text betrays two familiar types of material: imperatives that give specific instructions about how to behave and indicatives that describe the basis for such behavior. Thus the readers are charged to be holy in their conduct (verses 15-16), to be "scrupulously careful" in their living (verse 17, JB), and to love one another deeply and sincerely (verse 22). But these moral instructions are grounded in a particular theological understanding, and thus the readers are reminded of certain things about God, the nature of their conversion, and the work of Christ. Let us consider each of these briefly.

1. *The nature of God* (verses 17, 21, 23). In the verses immediately preceding today's text, the readers are reminded of God's holiness (verse 16; Lev. 11:44-45) and the way their own character is expected to participate in and reflect the character of God. But in addition to this, they are reminded of what it means to address God as Father (verse 17). This was a long-standing tradition in Jewish thought, as when David (Ps. 89:26), Isaiah (Isa. 63:16; 64:8), and the Jewish sage (Sir. 23:1-4) address God in this manner, or when Yahweh expects to be addressed in this way (Jer. 3:19). It is a tradition that Jesus appropriates and seems to sharpen even further (Matt. 6:9; cf. 7:11; 23:9). Accordingly, it becomes an appropriate form of address for Christians (Rom. 8:15).

The understanding of God is rendered more specifically, however, as we are told that God renders judgment impartially, which means that God has no favorites (verse 17; cf. Acts 10:34; Rom. 2:11; Gal. 2:6; Eph. 6:9; Col. 3:25; James 2:19; also II Chron. 19:7; Sir. 35:12-13). The basis of God's judgment lies in what we do: we are judged according to our works (Ps. 62:12; Matt. 16:27; II Cor. 11:15; II Tim. 4:14; Rev. 2:23).

2. *The nature of conversion* (verses 18, 22-23). One basis for the moral life is to recall the nature of one's conversion. In this instance, the readers are reminded that they were "ransomed." This metaphor of buying freedom from slavery has Old Testament roots (Isa. 52:3) and becomes a standard way for understanding the Christian experience of deliverance from sin (I Cor. 6:20; 7:23; Gal. 4:5; Titus 2:14). What

makes Christian redemption especially valuable, however, is the purchase price: "the precious blood of Christ . . . a lamb without blemish or spot" (verse 19). The image here is Christ seen as the lamb sacrificed for the sins of the people (Heb. 9:12, 14; Rev. 5:9; also John 1:29).

Conversion is also seen as a purification of the soul (verse 22) that occurs as the result of "obedience to the truth" (cf. Acts 6:7; Rom. 1:5; 15:18; 16:26; Gal. 3:2; II Cor. 10:5). In addition, it is a new birth (verse 23), a metaphor familiar in the Johannine tradition (John 1:13; 3:3-5). The image is taken further here, as we are told that the creative seed responsible for the new birth is the imperishable word of God (cf. Luke 8:11; James 1:18). Unlike grass and flowers, it never fades but abides forever (verses 24-25 = Isa. 40:6-9). Presupposed here is a dynamic understanding of God's creative word (cf. Heb. 4:12; Eph. 6:17; Rev. 1:16; 2:12; also Wisd. of Sol. 7:22-30; Isa. 49:2).

3. *The work of Christ* (verses 19-21). We have already mentioned Christ as the sacrificial lamb whose blood purchases our redemption. New converts need to be reminded that Christ's work is part of an age-old plan that reaches back to the time "before the foundation of the world" (verse 20; cf. Acts 2:23; Eph. 1:14; John 17:24). They are now living in the "end of the times" (verse 20) when God's revelation has been manifested (Rom. 16:25-26; II Tim. 1:9-10). The decisive act was God's raising Christ from the dead (verse 21; cf. Rom. 4:24; 8:11; 10:9; Eph. 1:20), and this provides the basis for Christian confidence and hope (cf. Col. 1:27).

The true test of such theological reflection, however, is the form of life that it produces, what we might call its social implications. Today's text insists that this way of understanding God, Christ, and one's conversion translates into a form of community in which love is deep and genuine (verse 22; cf. I Thess. 4:9; Rom. 12:10; Heb. 13:1; II Pet. 1:7). This is a variation of the Johannine new commandment that was to serve as the guiding principle for Christian community (also 4:8; cf. John 13:34; 15:12-13, 17; I John 2:7-11; II John 5; also cf. Gal. 6:2).

Luke 24:13-35

The reader is referred to the commentary on the Gospel lection for Easter evening. The discussion of Luke 24:13-49 at that point was devoted primarily to verses 13-35.

Fourth Sunday of Easter

Acts 2:42-47; Psalm 23; I Peter 2:19-25; John 10:1-10

Today's first lesson is the first of several Lukan summaries in the narrative of Acts designed to typify life in the earliest Christian community. It reflects the exuberant mood of new movements pulsating with the life of the Spirit. The other three texts, the second lesson, the Gospel lesson, and the psalm, all reflect the common theme of shepherd and shepherding. The famous Twenty-third Psalm depicts Yahweh as the Shepherd of Israel, while the Gospel reading from John applies the shepherd image to Jesus, the "good shepherd [who] lays down his life for the sheep" (John 10:11). The epistolary reading further extends the shepherd imagery to Christ, drawing on Isaiah 53:5-12 and reminds us of our former status as straying sheep who have been rescued by the "Shepherd and Guardian" of our souls (I Pet. 2:25).

Acts 2:42-47

With these remarks at the conclusion of the inaugural sermon on Pentecost, Luke intends to provide us with a sketch of life within the newly formed messianic community, the church. It is clearly an ideal portrait, typical of the way primordial beginnings are sketched. In retrospect, we tend to look at the beginning of a movement, a group, or a nation in romantic, highly idealized terms. This is what Luke does here as he looks back on the beginning of the church perhaps a half-century or so after it began. What emerges is a community of believers solid in their commitment to the apostolic faith that brought them into existence, but equally solid in their commitment to one another in their common life. It bears all the earmarks of a vital religious community.

First, they absorb themselves in the religious teachings to

190

which they are committed (cf. 4:2, 18; 5:21, 25, 28, 42). In this case, they adhered to the "apostles' teaching," which probably refers to instruction designed to fill out the original proclamation (*kerygma*) and explore its implications for Christian living (cf. Heb. 6:1-4). We might regard I Corinthians 7–16 as typical of such instruction. It consists of Paul's detailed instructions on various topics about which Christians at Corinth have written him. In several instances, he cites earlier, foundational preaching and teaching (e.g., I Cor. 11:23-26; 15:3-11), but expands it and explores it more fully as he relates it to concrete questions of Christian practice.

Second, they have fellowship with one another on a regular, everyday basis as well as in sacred settings of worship and eating the sacred meal (Acts 20:7; 27:35). The word for fellowship is *koinonia* and is best rendered in a dynamic, participial form: "sharing." Not surprisingly, it can be used in the New Testament as a synonym for financial contributions (cf. II Cor. 8:4), the act of sharing one's material possessions with another.

In this summary, Luke places great emphasis on this aspect of their common life as he describes their activity of selling "their possessions and goods" and making appropriate distribution to all who had need. Fellowship in this setting means active care for one another. The particular form that it took here was a community of goods in which the members "had all things in common." By mentioning this, Luke manages to portray the church as the embodiment of the common Hellenistic proverb, "for friends all things are common." That this was a sought after ideal is clear from the writings of Plato and Aristotle, among others, who presented the ideal community as one in which the needs of the citizens were cared for by the common efforts of everyone.

Combined with this generous spirit was the spirit of oneness: "all who believed were together." We are later told that they were "of one heart and soul" (4:32). This too is reminiscent of a Hellenistic proverb, "friends are one soul." Generosity and unity are seen to be two sides of the same coin. Willingness to share possessions grows out of a sense of solidarity with one another as well as nourishing and reinforcing it. At this early stage, the church is experiencing unity and harmony (Acts 1:14; 4:24).

Third, they continue steadfastly in prayer. This becomes an earmark of the early Christian community (cf. Acts 1:4; 6:4; Rom. 12:12; Eph. 6:18; Phil. 4:6; Col. 4:2; I Thess. 5:17; I Tim. 2:1). We can surmise that these were prayers of thanksgiving for their experience of divine grace (verse 47; cf. I Pet. 1:3-9), for deliverance from tight circumstances (cf. Acts 4:23-30), as well as petitions in behalf of their own members (cf. Acts 9:32-43). We should also note the correlation between prayer and the spirit of unity (Acts 1:14).

Fourth, they exhibited a proper sense of fear (verse 43, RSV) or awe (NEB, NIV) in the presence of the Divine. This was directly related to the "many wonders and signs" that continued to be done in their midst by the apostles (verse 43). Thus, as the JB puts it, "The many miracles and signs worked through the apostles made a deep impression on everyone" (verse 43). What Luke wants to stress here is that the same power of the Spirit that manifested itself in Jesus' signs and wonders (cf. Luke 4:31-41) continues into the life of the church (cf. 4:30; 6:8; 7:36; 8:13; 14:3; 15:12). The church thus embodies the eschatological vision sketched by Joel (2:28-32; cf. Acts 2:17-21). This respect before the power of the Divine continues to characterize the community (cf. 5:5, 11; Acts 19:17).

Fifth, they flourished (verse 47). To the original three thousand (verse 41), the Lord adds members daily. As Luke unfolds the story of the church, it is a story punctuated by numerical growth (cf. 6:7; 9:31; 11:21; 12:24; 14:1; 16:5; 19:20). This is Luke's way of showing that the movement has God's approval. It also attests the power of the word to convict.

How should this text inform preaching? As a blueprint against which to measure performance? As an ideal toward which we should aspire? As primitive vision to which the church should be recalled? Perhaps all, perhaps none. We all know that churches at every level—local congregations, denominations, and the church universal—are more fractured than this portrait allows. Nor should we assume that community of goods is the only, or even the best, form of responsible sharing—certainly not in every time, place, or situation. Even Luke-Acts allows other forms of fellowship, such as almsgiving and showing hospitality. We also know that fidelity may not translate into growth. For whatever reason, churches can teach, pray, worship, and share and not grow numerically. Should we use this text to flail them? Maybe. Maybe not. Certainly we should not bow before the idol of numerical growth and assume that if the numbers are there, we are therefore faithful. They may be high for the wrong reasons.

So we best use this text as Luke intended it: as a broad stroke sketch of the church at its beginning—faithful in teaching, active in sharing, devoted to eating, praying, and worshiping together, fearful before the Divine, exuberant in its praise of God. It is a picture of the church on its best behavior.

Psalm 23

This psalm was discussed for the Fourth Sunday of Lent on pages 54–56.

I Peter 2:19-25

The preacher will first have to decide where to begin this passage. The compilers of the *Common Lectionary* have decided to include verse 19, instead of beginning with verse 20 or 20*b*, since it helps provide the context. But the exact context is obscured by omitting verse 18, which specifies that the remarks are addressed to servants. To modern ears, verse 18 will sound anachronistic if not offensive as it charges slaves to be docile in their obedience.

This set of instructions to servants (verses 18-25) occurs as part of a longer set of exhortations that are intended to be comprehensive in dealing with various relationships in which ancient persons might find themselves. It is an abbreviated form of the "household code," a form of Greco-Roman moral instruction adopted by Christian writers to enumerate the duties of various members of a household: masters and servants, husbands and wives, parents and children (cf. Col. 3:18–4:1; Eph. 5:22–6:9). In First Peter, the author intends to instruct his readers in their political (2:13-17), social (2:18-25), domestic (3:1-7), and ecclesiastical (3:8-12) responsibilities.

The specific problem with which today's text deals is this—how should we behave when we are treated unjustly? In the setting of our text, the question was, What should a slave do when mistreated by a harsh, unjust master? It requires little imagination to think of the abuses that must have occurred in this social situation. Our knowledge of a more recent era in which slavery was the norm in American life may supply ample illustrations. In particular, our text may envision a situation in which a slave has become a Christian, thus creating special tension within the household. Old allegiances were perhaps being threatened by new allegiances to another Lord and Master, Jesus.

In any case, our text instructs slaves to be obedient and respectful to masters of every stripe, whether kind and gentle or overbearing (verse 18). We are informed that suffering pain unjustly has "some merit . . . if it is done for the sake of God" (verse 19, JB). If we are beaten because we have done wrong, so be it. There is no merit in this. We are getting what we deserve. But what if we are beaten when we have not done wrong? We are urged to bear such maltreatment patiently, assured that such fortitude commends us to God (verse 20).

As an incentive to bear up under unjust suffering, the readers are presented with the example of Christ (verses 21-25). He is presented as the one who suffered for us, and in doing so he set an example for all who suffer unjustly to follow (cf. Matt. 16:24). What emerges is an image of Christ as the Suffering Servant. Various echoes from Isaiah 53 inform our passage: he did not perjure himself (verse 22 = Isa. 53:9); "he . . . bore our sins" (verse 24 = Isa. 53:12); "through his wounds you have been healed" (verse 24, JB, = Isa. 53:6).

One of the distinctive features of this passage is how Jesus' conduct at his trial becomes exemplary for Christians. Elsewhere in the New Testament, other aspects of his life and teaching serve as examples, but rarely events from his trial. We are assured that "he committed no sin" (verse 22), which may be rendered in a softer form as "he had not done anything wrong" (JB). Legally this may have meant that he was not guilty as charged, but in Christian teaching his innocence came to mean his sinlessness in the broadest sense (3:18; cf. John 8:46; II Cor. 5:21; Heb. 4:15; 7:26; I John 3:5; also John 7:18).

One of the elements preserved in the story of the trial was his non-retaliation: he did not return insult for injury, threats for torture (verse 23; cf. Matt. 26:14, 26 and parallels). This was in keeping with his teaching of non-retaliation (cf. Matt. 5:39), which became a standard element of Christian teaching (Rom. 12:19, 21; I Thess. 5:15).

What was especially exemplary was the level and quality of trust Jesus displayed in the trial: he committed his cause to the One who judges justly (cf. Jer. 11:20). God is finally the one who vindicates the cause of the elect (Rom. 12:19; Deut. 32:35).

Not only is the death of Christ exemplary; it is redemptive as well. His sacrificial death is seen as the act through which our own cause is vindicated before God (cf. Col. 1:22; Heb. 10:10; also John 1:29; Rev. 5:6, 12). In language strikingly Pauline in tone, we are reminded that Christ's death makes it possible for us to "die to sin and live to righteousness" (verse 24; cf. Rom. 6:11, 18).

At this point, another christological image emerges: Christ the shepherd (verse 25). This is, of course, also suggested by Isaiah 53, where the Suffering Servant is pictured as a lamb led to the slaughter (53:7), as is the reference to us as those who have "gone astray like sheep" (53:6; cf. Matt. 9:36; also Ezek. 34:5, 16). It is an image more fully expanded in the Gospel reading for today (John 10), and also resonant with the image of Yahweh as shepherd in today's psalm (Psalm 23). The image of "Guardian" (*episkopos*) is a natural extension of the same image.

The preacher may wish to connect this christological image of Jesus as shepherd with the Gospel reading and the psalm and explore the ways in which Christ serves as our example. The first part of the text will be more problematic homiletically, because it rubs against the grain of the modern conscience, which is less willing to yield in docile submission to oppressive forces and masters. The issue remains perennially current, for in every age there are instances when people suffer unjustly. The difficult task is to frame a response that is appropriate to our calling (verse 21) and that is properly "mindful of God" (verse 19).

John 10:1-10

The language and imagery of John 10:1-10 are so stirring and homiletically suggestive the preacher may prefer not to wrestle with the literary problems related to this text. However, the problems are there, and knowing what they are, even when not satisfactorily resolved, is a requirement of honest study and undergirds preaching with confidence.

The problems are three. The first has to do with ascertaining the context for 10:1-10. These verses are a portion of the larger unit, 10:1-21, but does 10:1-21 continue chapter 9 or does it belong with what follows, 10:22-42? In subject matter, 10:1 seems to continue 9:35-41 which deals with leadership of the people of God. If this is the position taken, then the preacher may locate the teaching of Jesus in 10:1-10 in Jerusalem at the Feast of Tabernacles, since the last time reference (7:2) was that feast. On the other hand, 10:22 states, "It was the feast of the Dedication at Jerusalem." Does that reference apply only to what follows or to the entirety of chapter 10? The preacher may decide the uncertainties are greater than any value to be gained by indicating when and where John 10:1-10 can be placed. Historical curiosity may have to give way to the conclusion that our text has its own integrity and does not depend for its meaning on geographical or chronological context.

The second problem has to do with the writer's introduction at 10:6 of the word "figure," sometimes translated image, analogy, or even parable. This Gospel contains no parables of the kinds we meet in the Synoptics, but Jesus does speak "in figures" (16:25, 29) which refers to language that is not plain. Note two statements that make this clear: "I have said this to you in figures; the hour is coming when I shall no longer speak to you in figures but tell you plainly, not in any figure" (16:29). As with the parables in Mark (4:10-11), Jesus' language in this Gospel is not such as to make the truth of the kingdom immediately obvious to any and all within earshot, whether they are committed or not. Understanding Jesus is more a matter of faith and character than it is of intellectual ability. As stated in 7:17, whoever wills to do God's will shall know whether the teaching is of God.

The third problem related to our lesson has to do with its internal unity. This is not simply an academic problem. Within 10:1-10 and extending to verse 16 there are so many rich images that no one sermon can clearly embrace all of them. Even a casual reading raises questions prompted by confusion, Is Jesus the shepherd who enters the door while others steal their way in or is Jesus the door by which all must enter? Perhaps clarity will be served by regarding verses 1-6 as one unit and verses 7-10 another (some commentators further divide 1-6 into 1-3*a* and 3*bc*, and 7-10 into 7-8 and 9-10). Verses 7-10 seem to offer commentary on verses 1-5.

The governing thought in verses 1-6 deals with leadership of God's people, the shepherd being one type, thieves and robbers the other. The shepherd comes naturally to the flock, acting in trust and loving care. The relationship between the shepherd and the sheep was a familiar one and of such special favor as to provide both Old and New Testaments with images of divine caring (Isa. 40:11; Ps. 23; Mark 6:34; Luke 15:3-7). But who were the thieves and bandits? It seems insufficient to identify them totally with uncaring leaders among the Jews; throughout the New Testament, warnings about false church leaders make it evident that from the beginning the Christian communities were plagued by those whose concerns were pride, power, and purse (Matt. 7:15-23; Acts 20:29-35; Phil. 3:18-19; I Pet. 5:1-5). Despite twenty centuries of warning, the church continues to have difficulty discerning a thief in the sheepfold.

In verses 7-10 the governing image is that of Christ as the door. This is to say, Christ, both doctrinally and pastorally, both in word and in example, is the canon by which to measure and evaluate Christian leadership. The Shepherd is the door to shepherding; the flock that knows the Shepherd can recognize his voice in the teaching, preaching, and pastoring of those who are his shepherds. And not only to the leaders but also to the whole membership, Christ as door is the promise of both security ("will be saved") and freedom ("will go in and out and find pasture," verse 9). In the background of these statements is the description of Joshua as shepherd of Israel (Num. 27:15-17). In the foreground lie those guarantees of the continued relationship between Christ and the church: the word of Christ, the apostles, and the Holy Spirit.

Fifth Sunday of Easter

Acts 7:55-60; Psalm 31:1-8; I Peter 2:2-10; John 14:1-14

The first lesson from Acts reports the final scene of the death of Stephen. It comes at the end of his highly provocative sermon in which he rehearses Israel's history from Abraham forward. The reading from the Psalter is a lament in which the Psalmist prays for deliverance from his enemies. It provides one of the most well-known last sayings of Jesus: "Into thy hands I commit my spirit" (Ps. 31:5 = Luke 23:46). The second lesson provides another selection from First Peter with a clear christological focus on Christ as the rejected stone. Like other passages from First Peter, christological reflection is combined with moral exhortation. The Gospel lesson is taken from John 14, the well-known passage in which Jesus declares himself to be the way, truth, and life, and thus the only true access to God.

Acts 7:55-60

In this passage, we have recorded the death of Stephen. It comes at the end of a sermon in which he rehearses Israel's history from the call of Abraham down to the time of Solomon's temple, but treating mainly the lives of Joseph and Moses. It is a highly provocative sermon, to say the least, especially in its concluding remarks in which Stephen launches a penetrating criticism of the Jerusalem temple. He regards Solomon's decison to build a temple for God as a major step backward, siding instead with the prophetic sentiment that God's presence cannot be confined to sacred buildings (verses 47-50; cf. Isa. 66:1-2). The language becomes ever sharper as he accuses his audience of hardhearted resistance to the will of God and a consistent

199

history of destroying those messengers whom God sent, the last of which was Christ (verses 51-53).

Apart from these concluding sentiments, which were bound to be received unfavorably before an audience of Jewish temple loyalists gathered in Jerusalem, other themes in the sermon could be read as direct challenges to the established order. One common theme that links his treatment of Abraham, Joseph, and Moses is locating the primary sphere of their dealing with God in Egypt, and thus outside Palestine. Read one way, this would be seen as a direct affront since it could imply that God has had some of the most decisive encounters with the patriarchs *outside* the land. The Gospel will pose a similar challenge to the entrenched values of Jews bent on resisting the mission to the Gentiles.

In any event, the audience is enraged to the point of gritting their teeth against Stephen (verse 54; cf. Ps. 35:16; 37:12; 112:10; Job 16:9; Lam. 2:16). Their anger forces them to cast him out of the city (verse 58), a move reminiscent of Jesus' eviction from Nazareth after his inaugural sermon (Luke 4:29). The form of death was stoning, which was prescribed in the Old Testament for certain serious offenses (cf. Lev. 24:14; Num. 15:35-36; Deut. 17:7).

Here we see a man die, but from the way his death is recorded it is clearly a triumphant death, the death of a martyr vindicated by God. We are assured that it is the death of another of God's prophets who is "full of the Holy Spirit" (verse 55). Earlier, Stephen's character is attested in this way (Acts 6:3, 5), and he belongs with others in the narrative of Acts so designated, including Barnabas (11:24) and the disciples (13:52). But most notably, he stands in the succession of Jesus himself (Luke 4:1, 14, 18, 21). Since Stephen is described in this way, the actions of the crowds against him are fully in character: another of God's prophets has fallen in Jerusalem (cf. Luke 13:33).

He not only dies as a prophet, but as a prophet vindicated by God. The heavens are opened, as they were at the baptism and confirmation of Jesus (cf. Luke 3:21 and parallels), which is typical of revelatory moments (cf. Acts 10:11; John 1:51; Rev. 19:11). As he gazes into the heavens, like the psalmist

(Ps. 63:2) and Isaiah (6:1; cf. John 12:41), he beholds "the glory of God" (verse 55). He also sees the exalted "Son of man standing at the right hand of God," as he had promised (verse 56; cf. Luke 22:69; also Matt. 26:64 and parallels).

But above all Luke wants us to see the death of Stephen in terms reminiscent of the death of Jesus. Thus his last words recall the last words of Jesus. There is first the prayer, "Lord Jesus, receive my spirit" (verse 59; cf. Luke 23:45), and finally the prayer of forgiveness, "Lord, do not hold this sin against them" (verse 60; cf. Luke 23:34). His death is one of confident expectation that his cause has been vindicated. It is a death experienced in a mood of forgiveness. Like God's own Son, Stephen is vindicated by God even in death.

This text portrays the death of a martyr. It is in no sense tragic, but triumphant. Stephen's cause is clearly aligned with the cause of God and the exalted Son of man. A host of similar martyrdoms will be described in subsequent Christian history, such as those of Polycarp, Ignatius, and many others.

There are many possibilities here homiletically. The preacher may wish to play out the similarity between the death of Stephen and Christ and explore the ways in which Luke depicts God's messengers, such as Peter, Stephen, and Paul carrying out the work of Christ in word, deed, and life. There is also the triumphant tone of the episode that fits well with the overall tone of Luke-Acts. The persistent danger, however, is that triumph can easily shade off into triumphalism, and its bedfellow imperialism. The preacher needs to be cautious in this respect. But there are many appropriate ways to expound the Easter faith as it leads to forms of daring, prophetic witness. One such way may be to interpret the death of Stephen as the result of posing a serious challenge to the established religious order.

Psalm 31:1-8

Verses 9-16 of this psalm were the lection for Passion Sunday, which should be consulted (see pages 76–79).

I Peter 2:2-10

Like the other readings from First Peter on the previous Sundays, today's text resembles baptismal catechesis. It appears to give instructions to recent converts. In doing so, today's text employs a series of images with which new Christians could define themselves. Seen in another sense, today's text provides us several images for the church.

First, *newborn babies* (verses 2-3). It was natural enough to liken the beginning of the religious life to the birth and growth of an infant. Thinking of baptism as a new birth (1:3; John 1:13; 3:3-5) was the logical launching point for this metaphor. Consequently, Christian instruction comes to distinguish between elementary and more advanced instruction in terms of milk and meat (Heb. 5:12-14; I Cor. 3:1-3). It could even affect liturgical practice, as was the case in the second century A.D. when Christian initiates were fed milk and honey after their baptism.

It was also a truism that for milk to be truly nourishing, it should be pure (verse 2). Informing the author at this point is Psalm 34:8, "O taste and see that the Lord is good!"

Second, a *living temple* (verse 5). For Christians to be likened to "living stones" grows out of their christological understanding in which Christ is seen as the rejected stone who has become the cornerstone of the building. Certain Old Testament passages were crucial in this development. Psalm 118:22, which is cited in verse 7, "The stone which the builders rejected has become the head of the corner." Early Christians used this to interpret the death and resurrection of Jesus. On the one hand, he was rejected, but through his resurrection he has been exalted to a position of prominence, like the capstone in an arch or the cornerstone in a building.

Two other passages also employed the stone imagery: Isaiah 28:16 and 8:14. The former envisions God's "laying in Zion a stone, a cornerstone chosen and precious" (verse 6), while the latter speaks of a "stone that will make men stumble, a rock that will make them fall" (verse 8). In the one instance, those who believe in God's promise are pictured as resting their faith on a solid, rock foundation. In the other instance, the stone becomes a stumbling block for those who disbelieve and disobey.

With Christ viewed as the stone that God lays in Zion, the readers are urged to come to "that living stone" that was rejected by humans but regarded as precious by God (verse 4). By extension, followers of Christ are said to be "living stones." This is logical enough considering that believers were understood to be incorporated with Christ in a close, even mystical union. They partook of the nature of the one with and to whom they were joined. Accordingly, they are pictured as a "spiritual house," or temple. This same image can be used as a way of visualizing the Christian body or the Christian church as the dwelling place of the Spirit, much as the temple was the place where the Shekinah was located (I Cor. 3:16-17; 6:19-20).

Third, *holy priesthood* (verses 5 and 9). If Christians are understood as a temple, it is not a long step to extend the metaphor and compare them with the priests who officiate in the temple. It is common for Christians to be compared with priests who offer sacrifices, either their own lives as spiritual sacrifices (Rom. 12:1) or appropriate forms of worship as fitting sacrifice (Heb. 13:15-16). Paul can think of his apostolic service in similar terms (Rom. 15:16). The usage is also informed by the Old Testament notion of Israel as a "holy priesthood" (Exod. 19:16; cf. Rev. 1:6).

Fourth, the elect people of God (verses 9-10). Election actually encompasses several images: "chosen race . . . holy nation, God's own people" (verse 9). As Israel had been regarded as God's Elect, the chosen people (Isa. 43:20), so does the church come to be understood in similar terms (Col. 3:12). The relationship is one of close identity, even possession, so much so that Yahweh lays claim to Israel as "the people whom I formed for myself" (Isa. 43:21; cf. Mal. 3:17).

As the elect people of God, Israel lives to give glory to God (Isa. 43:12). Similarly, the church sees itself as basking in God's glory, and hence as having moved from darkness into light (verse 9; cf. Acts 26:18; II Cor. 4:6; Eph. 5:8; I Thess. 5:4-5).

The transition can be stated even more sharply, drawing

on language from the prophet Hosea. It will be remembered that two of the children born to Hosea and Gomer were given names to symbolize the status of Israel's broken covenant with Yahweh: a daughter "Not pitied" (Lo-ruhamah) and a son "Not my people" (Lo-ammi). Today's text seizes on these two names to signify the status of Gentiles prior to their conversion, but asserts that those who were "no people" have now become "God's people," and those who "were without mercy" have now "received mercy" (verse 10; Eph. 2:4).

The preacher will find here numerous suggestive images for defining the nature of the church and our commitment as those who have embarked on the life of faith. If nothing else, the text sharply etches the contours of life as it "once was" over against life as it "now is." This contrast, if properly drawn, can provide powerful incentive to those who have committed themselves to that living stone.

John 14:1-14

The Gospel reading for today falls within a larger body of material extending from 13:31 to 17:26. This large section, usually referred to as the farewell discourse and prayer of Jesus, is set in Jerusalem, following Jesus' last meal with his disciples (13:1-30) and ending with the group's movement to the garden where Jesus was arrested (18:1). The Synoptics have nothing comparable. The entire section consists of Jesus' words to his disciples (except for the prayer in 17:1-26), broken only now and then by a question or a comment by one of the disciples (14:5, 8, 22). The material is marked by a great deal of repetition which quite possibly could be the result of drawing from several sources. Imbedded within the discourses are smaller units that have their own integrity and that may have existed previously in other contexts, similar to sayings in the Synoptics that occur in various literary settings with almost no change in form. Notice, for example, 14:1-3 or 14:6. On the whole, however, natural breaks such as change of time or place or audience are missing, and the preacher will be hard pressed to determine where a unit begins and ends.

The themes developed in the farewell materials are not for the public but for the disciples; that is, for the church. The primary concern is not what events will soon befall Christ, but rather what will happen to his disciples after he is gone. The reader will, therefore, find here an interweaving of promises and commands. While the textures of these two kinds of statements from Jesus may seem at first very different, it gradually becomes clear that Jesus' promises carry a commission and his commissions imply a promise. He who sends also goes with those whom he sends, and he who commands to love empowers to love. And the reverse is equally true; he who loves expects the loved to love others and he who abides with his followers expects them to go just as the Father sent him.

Because 14:1-14 comes early in the farewell material it is not surprising that the primary thrust of this unit is to soften with assurance the blow of Jesus' announcement of his departure. It requires only minimal reflection to realize that the departure of Jesus, leaving behind a group of followers to continue faithfully in an indifferent and sometimes hostile world, was the first major crisis of the church. The assurance to the church takes the form of three promises.

First, there is the promise of an abiding place with God. The image here is of the future even though the principal eschatological accent of this Gospel is on the present; that is, on a realized eschatology (3:36; 5:24; 11:25-26). The word translated "rooms" (RSV), "dwelling-places" (NEB), or "mansions" (KJV) is the noun form of the verb "to abide." This is a key term throughout this Gospel (see 15:1-11, for example) and represents a relationship characterized by trusting and knowing, such as exists between Christ and God. Christ's death and departure will not sever but will rather fulfill that relationship between the disciples and Christ.

The second promise is that of a sure and clear way to God (verses 5-7). For this Evangelist the way to the God whom no one has ever seen is Jesus Christ, for "the only Son, who is in the bosom of the Father, he has made him known" (1:18). While this is clear to the Johannine church, what is not clear to the reader is whether "no one comes to the Father, but by me" (verse 6) is a polemic and, if so, against whom. The writer is very much aware of the John the Baptist sect and the Jewish synagogue. However, given the strong and repeated words about the Holy Spirit (14:15–16:15), the statement could be addressed to pneumatics who discounted the historical Jesus in favor of new experiences in the Spirit.

The third promise in 14:1-14 is that of a power not only to sustain the believing community in the world but also to enable it to do even greater works than Jesus did (verse 12). Next Sunday our lesson will deal with the promise of the Holy Spirit (verses 15-21). However, here it is important to notice that the promise is to those who believe in Christ and pray in his name (verses 13-14). Two comments are in order: (1) the "you" in verses 13-14 is plural, implying a promise to the community and not a private one; and (2) praying in Jesus' name is not simply a formula for closing a prayer. To use Jesus' name as authorization for one's petitions to God implies that those who do so know Christ, abide in Christ, and make their requests from that relationship rather than making selfish requests imported from another value system. To pray in Christ's name means, among other things, to be thoughtful about one's prayers, and to pray about what to pray.

Sixth Sunday of Easter

Acts 17:22-31; Psalm 66:8-20; I Peter 3:13-22; John 14:15-21

The readings for today announce the meaning of the resurrection of Jesus Christ to persons who live in a variety of difficult circumstances. In John 14:15-21 Jesus says farewell to his disciples, soon to feel alone and abandoned in a hostile world. He charges them to continue in obedient love and promises the comfort of the Spirit. Similarly, I Peter 3:13-22 speaks to suffering Christians, recalling Christ's suffering, death, and triumph in which they participate. In Acts 17:22-31, Paul announces the resurrection as God's call to those trapped in idolatry with its attendant ignorance and sin. Even Psalm 66 calls the suffering to worship and praise the God who sustains life and answers prayer.

Acts 17:22-31

The book of Acts is distinguished by the amount of space (approximately 20 percent) it devotes to speeches. Today's text consists of one of those speeches, Paul's sermon at Athens. Unlike some of the readings from Acts during the previous Sundays, which gave only portions of lengthy sermons, today we have the complete sermon. When we say "sermon," naturally we mean sermon summary, because it is generally understood that Luke, at best, gives us in Acts abstracts rather than verbatim accounts of early Christian sermons. What we have today, then, is a resumé of early Christian preaching as it is likely to have sounded when addressed to a sophisticated pagan audience. It should be compared with the rather brief summary in Acts 14:15-17, which gives an idea of the Christian kerygma addressed to a less sophisticated, popular audience.

207

The sermon is set in Athens during Paul's mission in the Aegean area. Previously, Luke has given rather extended treatment to Paul's stay in Philippi (Acts 16:11-40) and shown us a typical day in the life of Paul the missionary to the Gentiles. In Philippi, the gospel effectively reaches every social stratum. After rehearsing Paul's movements through Thessalonica and Beroea (Acts 17:1-15), Luke pauses to give a more detailed account of his stay in Athens. The audience he addresses is populated with Epicurean and Stoic philosophers, representatives of Greco-Roman popular philosophy (verse 18). The situation is described as one in which intellectual inquiry and debate is the norm, and thus Paul is portrayed "standing in the middle of the Areopagus" (verse 22), that is, positioned as a Greek orator, and addressing this learned audience.

The tone and substance of the sermon is unlike every other extended kerygmatic summary in Acts. It is of course missionary preaching, as many of the other sermons are, but most of them occur in synagogue settings. Consequently, they often rehearse Israel's history and link Christ with that history. In this sermon, however, we have no such rehearsal of Israelite history, although there are numerous echoes from the Old Testament. Rather, the sermon attempts to establish common ground between Paul and his non-Jewish hearers.

Paul begins by acknowledging that the Athenians are "very religious" (verse 22), or as the NEB says, "I see that in everything that concerns religion you are uncommonly scrupulous." This observation is reinforced by Luke's graphic description of the numerous idols that decorated the city (verse 16), one of which had the inscription, "To an unknown god" (verse 23). This Luke intends as an indication of their genuine religious thirst for knowledge of the Divine. Accordingly, it serves as an invitation for Paul to "make known" his God (verse 23).

Fundamentally, Paul's sermon is about God, although at the end he finally gets around to mentioning Christ (verse 31). The Christian understanding of God is presented in stark opposition to the pagan understanding of God. For one thing, it was a difference between polytheism and monotheism, and thus this episode serves as a critique of pagan polytheism. In this respect, Christian preaching was heavily indebted to the Jewish critique of pagan religion begun in the Old Testament and continued in the Hellenistic-Roman period (cf. Isa. 40:18-20; 42:17; 44:9-20; 45:16-20; Jer. 10:1-6; Wisd. of Sol. 13:1–15:17). But what is absent in Paul's sermon at Athens is the supercilious, satirical streak that characterizes much of the earlier Jewish, and even pagan critique of idolatry. He gives his hearers the benefit of the doubt, pictures them as earnest seekers of God and sees their previous, misguided attempts as forgivable instances of ignorance (verse 30; cf. 3:17; 13:27).

Positively, we have God presented in two ways: as Creator and Preserver of life.

1. *God as Creator* (verses 24, 26). In language reminiscent of the Old Testament, the Lukan Paul proclaims, "The God who made the world and everything in it" (verse 24; cf. Exod. 20:11; II Kings 19:15 [= Isa. 38:16]; Neh. 9:6; Ps. 146:6; Isa. 42:5; Wisd. of Sol. 9:1, 9; also Acts 4:24; 14:15; Rev. 10:6; 14:7). The corollary is that God is consequently "Lord of heaven and earth" (Tob. 7:17; Matt. 11:25).

Not only has God created the whole universe as we know it, heavenly and earthly, inanimate and animate, but human life as well: "from one single stock [God] . . . created the whole human race" (verse 26, JB). This reflects the theology of the Genesis creation story (Gen. 1:28) as well as the later narrative that sees God scattering the various nations throughout the earth (Gen. 10). Not that it was random scattering; instead God "fixed the epochs of their history and the limits of their territory" (verse 26, NEB; cf. Ps. 74:17; Deut. 32:8).

In proclaiming God as Creator, Paul would have been on common ground with much Greco-Roman philosophy. In the well-known Stoic hymn of Cleanthes, Zeus is praised above all other gods with the opening declaration: "The beginning of the world was from thee."

2. *God as Preserver* (verses 25, 28). God not only creates, but sustains life. It is God "who gives everything—including life and breath—to everyone" (verse 25, JB; cf. Isa. 42:5; 57:15-16; Wisd. of Sol. 9:1). Earlier, in the sermon at Lystra, Paul provides a variation on this theme as he proclaims God

as the one who gives "rains and fruitful seasons" (Acts 14:17; cf. Jer. 5:24; Ps. 147:8; Lev. 26:4).

But God is more than provider in the active sense of giving us what we need. As the Greek poet Epimenides observed, God is the one "In whom we live and move and have our being" (verse 28). It was common Stoic theology to say that God lives in us, indeed in everything. It was less common, if not unusual, to claim the reverse: that we live *in God*. This may be a way of saying that *through God* we are sustained, or it may suggest that God is the sphere of life in which our own life is sustained. A modern way of putting it would be to say that God is the oxygen tent in whom we live. To live, move, and have being suggests life in its most comprehensive sense—every fabric of our being is sustained by our life in God.

If life as we know it and life as we ourselves experience it is traceable to God who creates and sustains it, two things follow.

First, as the Greek poet Aratus observed in his *Phaenomena*, we are God's "offspring" (verse 28; also Gen. 1:27). In our very being we are like God because we owe our existence to God.

Second, we should acknowledge our dependence on God in appropriate forms of worship. As aesthetically pleasing as portraits and images of God might be, they can only be inadequate representations of God, since they by definition impose limits on the Unlimited. They also lead to misplaced emphasis—on the house in which God lives rather than on the God who lives there (verse 24), on the service that worshipers can render to God rather than on God's sovereignty (verse 25), on human imagination rather than on divine nearness (verse 29). What Paul calls for is a form of worship that captures the essence of God as Creator and Preserver of life. The worship of idols fails essentially in this respect: it neither reveals to us who God is nor does it reveal to God who we are.

Toward the end of the sermon, Paul moves the readers' attention into the future, to a time when God the Creator and Preserver becomes Judge (verse 31; cf. 10:42; Rom. 2:16; 14:9-10; II Tim. 4:1; I Pet. 4:5). We are assured that God does not judge capriciously (as many of the pagan gods were observed to do), but righteously (verse 31; cf. Ps. 9:8; 96:13; 98:9). Testimony to this is provided by his raising Jesus from the dead (verse 31; cf. Acts 2:24, 32; 4:10; 5:30; 10:40; 13:36-37; also I Thess. 1:10).

At this point, the sermon stops rather abruptly. The response was mockery combined with delay (verse 32). Converts were few (verse 33-34). The gospel does not win every time, even when dressed in sophisticated clothing. But Luke remains convinced that the God presented here is the One whom we all seek, indeed grope after (verse 27; cf. Deut. 4:29; Isa. 55:6; Wisd. of Sol. 13:6), and the irony is that this God is not that far away (verse 27; cf. Ps. 145:18; Jer. 23:23).

Psalm 66:8-20

Few psalms fall into the category of community or communal thanksgiving. As a rule, ancient Jewish worship probably utilized general hymns of praise to express thanks rather than psalms of thanksgiving which focused specifically on the particular reason for thanksgiving. (At least, this is one explanation for the almost total absence of psalms of community thanksgiving.) Even in Psalm 66, one of the best candidates for a community thanksgiving, the focus shifts in verses 13-20 to individual speech (note the "I" throughout this section), perhaps suggesting that a community leader or the king representing the community is the speaker.

The psalm appeals to the people (the nations, the earth) to participate in the praise and to behold the works of God (verses 1, 5, 8, and 16; the opening verbs in these verses are all plural imperatives). The reasons for praise and observance are given in verses 3-4, 5b-7, 9, and 17-19. These include God's awesome deeds (verse 3), his mighty works (verse 5), his sustenance of life (verse 9), and his response to prayerful requests (verse 18).

Different audiences are addressed in the psalm: verses 1-9 call upon the peoples of the world; verses 10-11 are communal speech to God (note the plural pronouns); verses 13-15 are addressed to God (note the singular first person pronouns); and verses 16-20 are individual speech addressed to a plural human audience.

Although not included in this particular lection, verses 1-7 emphasize Yahweh's triumph over his enemies and his parting of the Red Sea and the Jordan River (see Exod. 14; Josh. 3; and Ps. 114:5-6).

Verses 8-9 praise God for having kept the people alive and for protecting their way, suggesting that this psalm may have been employed in some annual thanksgiving ritual.

God as the tester and protector appears in verses 10-12. The NJPSV translates these verses as follows:

> You have tried us, O God,
>   refining us, as one refines silver.
> You have caught us in a net,
>   caught us in trammels.
> You have let men ride over us;
>   we have endured fire and water,
>   and You have brought us through to prosperity.

Neither the nature of the trouble, in spite of the various images (being refined, being caught like a bird or wild animal, being overrun by horsemen, and being forced to endure extremes), nor the goal of such calamities is discussed. The troubles are there as divinely sent phenomena but as phenomena through which divine guidance has carried the community, carried it to prosperity (the harvests of another year?).

Verses 13-15 have a worshiper (the king?) speak of fulfilling the vows made earlier in a time of trouble. Note the extravagance as a token of thanksgiving.

Finally, the psalmist invites people to hear the testimony, the witness offered about what God has done (verses 16-20).

I Peter 3:13-22

The latter portion of today's text (3:18-22) serves as the epistolary lesson for the First Sunday of Lent in Year B. The reader may wish to consult our remarks in *Lent, Holy Week, Easter, Year B*.

This passage, like the rest of First Peter, confronts the reality of Christian suffering (cf. 1:6; 2:20-21; 4:12-19; 5:9-10). It envisions just people being dealt with unjustly. It echoes the sentiments of the Matthean beatitude that followers of Jesus would be persecuted for righteousness' sake (verse 14; Matt. 5:10). In the words of a recent popular book, our text recognizes that bad things happen to good people.

What should be the Christian's response in this situation? Several suggestions are offered in today's text.

First, we should be assured that ours is a just cause and that we are in the right (verses 13-14, 17). Earlier, we are cautioned against doing wrong (2:20). The New Testament is consistent in urging good, responsible conduct as the norm (Rom. 13:3; Titus 2:14). It is this that enables us to live with a good conscience (verse 16). Luke draws a consistent image of Paul as one who pursued his work with a clear conscience (Acts 23:1; 24:16; cf. II Cor. 1:12). A clear conscience is also important enough to become a prerequisite for service as a deacon (I Tim. 3:9). Later in today's text, we are assured that the central motivation for Christian baptism is "an appeal to God for a clear conscience" (verse 21).

Suffering is made more bearable, then, when our minds are cleared of the cobwebs of evil, mixed motives, and injustice. If we are "zealous for what is right" (verse 13), we have already eliminated a number of false adversaries (cf. Isa. 50:9; Job 34:29; Rom. 8:34).

Second, we are not to be fearful (verse 14). It is advice drawn from Isaiah, who urges his hearers not to be intimidated by the leaders who act out of fear: "Do not fear what they fear, nor be in dread" (Isa. 8:12). Rather, be committed to the Lord of hosts: "Let him be your fear, and let him be your dread" (Isa. 8:13). In our text, Christ now replaces Yahweh as the ground of our confidence: in our hearts we are to "reverence Christ as Lord" (verse 15). If early readers were being threatened because of their fidelity to Christ as opposed to state rulers, this injunction would remind them of their sole allegiance to Christ. In a later setting, the Johannine apocalypse calls for facing suffering without being fearful (Rev. 2:10).

Third, we should stand ready to make our defense (verse 15). The word for defense is *apologia,* which by the second century A.D. had become a technical term to describe the case Christians made for themselves against their detractors. Today's text may not envision such protracted apologies as those of Justin Martyr, Athenagoras, and other early Christian apologists, but it does call for the ability to articulate our faith in ways that are both intelligible and responsible to the faith. The New Testament, in various ways, speaks of giving responsible account. At the final judgment, we will be held accountable for what we have said (Matt. 12:36; cf. Rom. 14:12). Christian leaders will have to give account for the quality of their leadership (Heb. 13:17; cf. 4:13).

There is the suggestion here that such occasions may take us by surprise and that we will be called on to state the case for our belief on the spot. We are thus urged to "always be prepared." Along with this constant readiness, we are instructed to do so in the proper spirit: "with gentleness and reverence" (verse 15; cf. Col. 4:6).

Fourth, we are to relate our suffering to that of Christ (verses 18-19). Somehow, the suffering of Christ is intended to be definitive for us, especially when we suffer unjustly. It is likely that at this point in our text, the author quotes an early Christian hymn. It is printed strophically in Nestle, 26th ed., but not in RSV, NEB, JB, or NIV. In any case, these verses direct our attention to Christ's suffering, especially because it was a case of the "righteous [dying] for the unrighteous" (verse 18). His was a clear case of a just person suffering unjustly (cf. Acts 3:14; 7:52; 22:14; Matt. 27:19; Luke 23:47).

In addition, the death of Christ served a purpose beyond himself. It was a death for sins, thus a vicarious death (verse 18; cf. 2:21-24; Heb. 9:26-28; 10:12, 14). His death is instructive in showing us how suffering can become an occasion for transcending our own self-interest and acting in behalf of others.

At this point, our text moves in another direction. The end of the Christ hymn referred to Christ's enigmatic preaching mission to the "spirits in prison" (verse 19). These mysterious figures are said to have been disobedient in the days of Noah, and this prompts the author to compare the salvation of Noah and his household with Christian salvation. Both were achieved through water, although in one instance water destroyed, whereas in the other instance it saves. This baptismal theme reflects a recurrent concern of the letter.

The text concludes with a reference to the ascension of Christ, which foreshadows our next liturgical event, Ascension Day.

John 14:15-21

The introductory comments on verses 1-14 for last Sunday set the context for today's lection and need not be repeated here. A word does need to be said about the parameters of the text before us. Very likely verses 15 through 24 would be a more natural unit than verses 15 through 21. While the question of Judas in verse 22 seems to provide a break, in fact that question simply calls for an elaboration of verse 21. Actually verse 24 ends the unit as it began in verse 15 with the statement about love which keeps God's commands. A literary unit that ends as it begins is called an inclusion, a way of framing a body of material. Knowing this, the preacher may wish to treat the whole unit (verses 15-24). However, since verses 22-24 elaborate on verse 21 at the request of Judas, we can safely assume that the central thought had already been stated in verses 15-21 even if not fully comprehended by the disciples.

In order to understand this and other passages in this Gospel that join love and obedience, the reader must think of love as other than feeling. Feelings are not commanded but love can be, for to love is to be for another person, to act for another's good, to do that which brings benefit to the other. This is much more than liking a person or having a particular set of feelings that may be contingent on a variety of factors. To love obediently is to submit to God's own precedent (3:16) and call, even if loving costs dearly, as God's love did. By placing love and obedience at the beginning (verse 15), middle (verse 21), and end (verse 24) of this unit it is clear that the promises offered are not for any and all who may be passing by, but for those who love obediently.

The promises in our text are two, one a Johannine form of Pentecost and the other a Johannine form of the Parousia (the coming of Christ). In the sense that Pentecost has come to represent the giving of the Holy Spirit to the disciples (Acts 2:1-13), verses 16-17 may be called the promise of Pentecost. This is the first of five passages in the farewell discourses that present the Holy Spirit's work in the church (14:15-16, 26; 15:26; 16:7-11, 12-14), all of which make it clear that Easter is completed in the coming of the Spirit. The meaning of the Holy Spirit for the church according to verses 16-17 is as follows: (1) the Spirit will come from God at the request of Jesus; (2) the Spirit will replace Jesus as "another Counselor," being to the church the helper, comforter, companion that Jesus had been; (3) the Spirit, unlike Jesus, will never go away but will be with the church forever; (4) the Spirit will be with and in the church forever; (5) the Spirit will be with and in the church in ways distinct from any functioning of the Spirit in the world; and (6) the Spirit will be for the church a source and a confirmation of truth.

The second promise of verses 15-21 is a Johannine form of Parousia; that is, of the coming of Christ (verses 18-21). "I will not leave you desolate" (the word from which we get orphan); "I will come to you" (verse 18). One should not attempt to make in this Gospel too sharp a distinction between the coming of the Spirit and the coming of Christ. The presence of the Spirit and the presence of the Christ in the church are not clearly differentiated. In fact, verse 23 includes also the promise of the presence of God: "We [Father and Son] will come to him and make our home with him." Whatever the distinctions that must be honored by one's theology, the fact remains that experientially "God with us," "Christ with us," or "the Spirit with us" are for the church one promise of power, guidance, and comfort without which the church cannot live faithfully.

Ascension Day

Acts 1:1-11; Psalm 47; Ephesians 1:15-23; Luke 24:46-53 or
Mark 16:9-16, 19-20

The Ascension Day service is set by Luke's calendar: forty days after Easter and ten days before Pentecost. While Luke in Acts 1:1-11 provides the basic narrative, both Gospel readings offer an appearance of the risen Christ to his followers to answer them, to promise his continued presence, and to commission them to a worldwide mission. Ephesians 1:15-23 grounds that mission in the universal lordship of Christ risen and seated at God's right hand. Psalm 47 likewise praises God as sovereign over all nations of the earth.

Acts 1:1-11

Since the same texts are used for Ascension Day in all three years, the reader may wish to consult our remarks on this passage in *Lent, Holy Week, Easter* in Years B and C. Also, this text overlaps with the first lesson (Acts 1:6-14) for the Seventh Sunday of Easter in Year A, the additional portion of which is treated later in this volume.

Today's first lesson is Luke's account of the ascension of Christ forty days after his resurrection (verse 3). To be more accurate, we should say that one portion of today's text describes the ascension (verses 6-11). The first part of the passage consists of a preface to Acts (verses 1-2) and a brief summary of the tradition relating to the appearances of the risen Lord to his disciples (verses 3-5).

We may fail to appreciate this Lukan account of Christ's ascension unless we realize how unusual it is in the New Testament. It is by far the most detailed narrative account of this event in the New Testament. We might say that Luke is the only New Testament writer for whom the event has appreciable significance, at least as a separate event in the life of the Lord. To understand this better, let us examine some of the other traditions in the New Testament relating to the ascension.

Among the Synoptic Gospels, Matthew knows of no ascension tradition in its original form, nor does Mark. In the much disputed "longer ending" of Mark, it is reported that "the Lord Jesus, after he had spoken to them, was taken up into heaven, and sat down at the right hand of God" (Mark 16:19). This is rightly regarded as a later tradition and is probably dependent on Luke's account of this event.

The Gospel of Luke concludes with Jesus leading the disciples out to Bethany, where he lifts his hands and blesses them. Then we are told, "While he blessed them, he parted from them" (24:51). One textual tradition adds to verse 51 the following phrase, "and was carried up into heaven." If this was an original part of the Gospel of Luke, it stands in tension with Luke's account in Acts 1. In the first place, it suggests that Christ's ascension occurred on Easter Day, as do all the other events recorded in Luke 24, whereas Acts 1 places it forty days later (Acts 1:3). In the second place, it locates the ascension in Bethany, whereas Acts 1:12 implies that it occurred on Mt. Olivet, "a sabbath day's journey away."

In the Gospel of John, the risen Lord forbids Mary to touch him, claiming, "I have not yet ascended to the Father" (John 20:17). She is instructed to tell the brethren that he is ascending to the Father (verse 17). There are other allusions to the Son of Man's ascending to the Father (John 6:62; cf. 3:13). It is more usual for John to speak of "going to the Father" or "returning to the Father" (cf. 7:33; 14:12, 28; 16:5, 10, 28). For John, Christ's ascension is to be understood as part of the glorification that occurs after his resurrection. It signifies the return of Jesus to the presence of the Father, his original and natural abode. It does not function as an explanation of how various post-Easter appearances came to an end.

In the Pauline tradition, there is no real place for Christ's ascension as an event separable from his resurrection. Paul seems to regard Christ's resurrection as equivalent to his exaltation (Rom. 8:34; cf. Eph. 1:20). In the well-known Christ hymn in Philippians 2:5-11, which is probably pre-Pauline, the work of Christ unfolds in a "V-shaped" fashion, descent to the earth to take on human form (verses 7-8) and ascent, or exaltation by God, to heavenly status (verses 9-11). Other references are more cryptic (cf. Rom. 10:6). At a later stage in the Pauline tradition, we find a more fully elaborated notion of ascension, but not distinguishable from resurrection (cf. especially Eph. 4:8-10). What appears to be an early christological creedal statement is preserved in I Timothy 3:16, which concludes with the phrase "[he was] taken up in glory." This too sounds like ascension language but there is no separate mention of Christ's resurrection.

The Epistle to the Hebrews ordinarily speaks of Christ's exaltation, not his resurrection per se. Thus we find that Christ "has passed through the heavens" (4:14), is "exalted above the heavens" (7:26), has entered the heavenly sanctuary (9:24).

In I Peter 3:21-22, mention of "the resurrection of Jesus Christ" prompts the description of Christ as one who "has gone into heaven and is at the right hand of God." This may very well be an allusion to a tradition that approximates Luke's account: resurrection, ascension, and exaltation.

Against this background of various New Testament witnesses, which reflect a variety of understandings of Christ's return to God, Luke's narrative account in Acts 1:6-11 is set in sharper relief. Its literary function appears to be a way of terminating the post-Easter appearances of Christ, Luke's way of saying that henceforth Christ's presence will be experienced by the church in a different way. Moreover, since Luke stresses that the risen Lord had instructed the disciples concerning the kingdom of God during this forty-day interval (Acts 1:3), the ascension marks the transition to the period when the apostles, as Christ's witnesses, function as preachers and teachers in his behalf. It has a legitimating function. After Christ is gone, the apostles serve as the legitimating link between Christ and the church. Their task is to wait for the outpouring of the Spirit (verse 8), after which they will serve as harbingers of the new age.

Luke, then, has sensed the theological problem posed by the physical absence of Christ. With Christ gone, how does the church function? It listens to the apostolic witness, assured that in and through it Christ is speaking. It also waits in expectation for the return of Christ (verse 11). But it does so with a new realization that the focus of the kingdom of God is not on liberating Israel from Roman rule but on witnessing to the presence of the Spirit in the world.

Psalm 47

Like a number of other psalms (Pss. 93, 95–100), Psalm 47 seems to have been employed in ancient Israel during the annual celebration of God's kingship. According to such an interpretation, the kingship of God was celebrated in the cult just as was the kingship of the ruling earthly monarch. The emphasis on the kingship of God can be seen in Isaiah's temple vision (Isa. 6) in which he says he saw Yahweh the king sitting upon his throne, high and lifted up.

The center of this psalm is verse 5, which proclaims that "God has gone up with a shout, Yahweh with the sound of a trumpet." (The NJPSV translates this verse: "God ascends amidst acclamation; the Lord, to the blasts of the horn.") Parallels to this can be seen in the accounts of the anointment and acclamation of Solomon and David's successor: "Zadok the priest took the horn of oil from the tent, and anointed Solomon. Then they blew the trumpet; and all the people said, 'Long live King Solomon!' And all the people went up after him, playing on pipes, and rejoicing with great joy, so that the earth was split by their noise" (I Kings 1:39-40; see also II Kings 11:12-14). The texts from Kings reflect several features in the king's coronation that are also found in Psalm 47: (1) the king (God) goes up to the place of enthronement; (2) the people engage in vocal and joyous celebration; and (3) the sound of the trumpets plays an important role.

Ephesians 1:15-23

The popularity of this text is seen in the frequency of its use in the *Common Lectionary*. It serves as the second lesson for

Ascension Day in all three years. A longer form (1:11-23) provides the second lesson for All Saints Day in Year C. It overlaps with the epistolary lection (1:3-6, 15-18) for the Second Sunday After Christmas in all three years. Additional comments on this text are provided in each of these settings, and the preacher may wish to consult the appropriate volumes for more information.

The setting for today is the celebration of Christ's ascension into heaven. The practice of remembering this event in the life of Christ as a special day dates to the late fourth century.

In celebrating Christ's ascension, we do more than ponder the historical question, What actually occurred when Christ finally departed from the disciples? Luke's narrative account in today's first lesson supplies one answer. The epistolary lection offers a different perspective. It is not concerned with any particular moment when the risen Lord took leave of the disciples. It rather views Christ's exaltation to the presence of God in much broader, grander terms.

Two Old Testament texts are formative influences on today's text. Psalm 110:1 underlies the statement in verse 20, "[God] made him sit at his right hand in the heavenly places." Psalm 8:6 supplies the image in verse 22, God "has put all things under his feet." In both instances, we see a clear formulation of the early Christian conviction that Christ embodies the messianic hope as no one else had done. He had died, but more than that, God had "raised him from the dead" (verse 20).

Early Christians well knew what a staggering claim this was. They could conceive of it in no other terms than as an event in which God demonstrated, and unleashed, incredible power. Indeed, it was seen as an instance of "the immeasurable greatness of his power" (verse 19). But power in what sense? In the sense that God had reversed the course of nature by bringing Christ through death to a form of life that was unprecedented, and therefore new. This resurrectional life is thus called "new life."

In today's text, there is the recognition that the vistas of our thinking will have to be stretched to grasp the full implication of this faith in Christ's resurrection. Our tendency will be to think of Christ's departure from the earth in terms too small, too constricted, too limited for the event as it was. At work may have been a form of gnostic thinking comparable to what we find combated in Colossians, in which Christ is viewed as a heavenly figure to be sure, but as one among many figures in the angelic hierarchy. He could be seen as high and exalted in this hierarchy, but not necessarily at the pinnacle of the heavenly order.

Whether our text is directed against such a Christology that is too low, too tentative, it nevertheless succeeds in pulling out all stops as it depicts the heavenly status of Christ. The claims are unqualified: "far above *all* rule and authority and power and dominion, and above *every* name that is named" (verse 21, italics added). Christ breaks every spatial barrier that we can imagine and every temporal barrier as well: "not only in this age but also in that which is to come" (verse 21). The boundaries of time are unable to contain Christ, for he has transcended "this age" in a way that qualifies him to dominate "the age to come." Like the victor in battle, he can stand with one foot on the vanquished enemy. The enemy may be death (cf. I Cor. 15:51-57), but now he is seen as having subjected "all things."

Even though he may be seen as having cosmic dominion, his exalted Lordship is most properly defined and experienced with reference to the church, here conceived as "his body" (verse 23). Once again, our minds are being stretched to think of the "body of Christ" in terms greater than his physical body, his crucified body, even his resurrected body. He now is seen to have a corporate existence large enough, expansive enough, to incorporate the existence and identity of hosts of others, those "in Christ." Obviously, the church is being conceived here in terms larger than the congregation, but also larger than the "church universal" in the sense that the latter represents the sum of all living communities of faith on earth. It is rather a reality that extends into "the heavenly places" (verse 20), where Christ is.

We are being summoned to think of Christ in the most comprehensive sense possible, as the One who encompasses all reality as we know it, as the One who brooks no rivals, as the One who has transcended both space and time and in doing so has redefined both.

We begin to see that Ascension Day challenges our limited views of Christ. It recognizes, to paraphrase J. B. Phillips, that our Christ may be too small. It is for this reason that these exalted reflections on Christ's heavenly status are prefaced with the prayer for enlightenment (verses 17-18). To grasp the full significance of Christ will require an uncommon measure of wisdom, revelation, and knowledge (verse 17). It will require an increase in wattage within our hearts so that we can see our hope more brightly. It will require a fuller appraisal of the true value of our inheritance, which may entail using a different currency (verse 18). But, above all, we must understand that achieving this level of understanding is a gift of God (verse 17). Our text speaks of enlightenment, to be sure, but not in the ordinary sense. It is rather receiving light from above, where Christ is, "at the right hand of God."

Luke 24:46-53

That Jesus Christ is Lord, seated at the right hand of God, is an affirmation found frequently in the New Testament, often framed on the declaration of Psalm 110:1: "The Lord says to my Lord: 'Sit at my right hand, till I make your enemies your footstool.'" Less frequent, however, is the expression of the lordship of Christ in the form of an ascension story. The narrative in Acts 1:1-11 is the most complete, but in the two Gospel lections for today references to Christ's ascension are made.

Luke 24:46-53 continues two portions of the Lukan resurrection narrative (24:1-53). The comments on Luke 24:13-49 for Easter evening will set our verses for today in that context. The two portions of that narrative in verses 46-53 are instruction, commission, and promise (verses 46-49), and blessing, departure, and waiting (verses 50-53). In verses 46-49 several Lukan themes are stated and are central to the entire Luke-Acts presentation of Christ and the church. One such theme is the continuity of Jesus' mission with that of Israel. Luke has repeatedly stressed this point

(2:21-40; 4:16-30; 24:25-27; 24:44-45). The death and resurrection of Jesus and the proclamation of the gospel to all peoples were in the plan of God revealed in the Hebrew Scriptures and do not constitute a new departure following the failure of previous efforts. A second theme is the universality of God's offer of repentance and forgiveness of sins (verse 47). Luke made this point as early as the presentation of the infant Jesus in the temple (2:29-32), and Jesus placed it on his agenda at the opening of his ministry in Nazareth (4:16-30). Of course, both the commission (Acts 1:8) and its fulfillment in the proclamation to the nations (Acts 2:1-36) are central to Luke's second volume.

A fourth and fifth theme in verses 46-49 lie in the command to the disciples to stay in Jerusalem until they receive "power from on high" (verse 49). Jerusalem is the center from which the word of the Lord is to go to the nations (Isa. 2:3), while Mark 16:1-18 and Matthew 28:10, 16-20 focus upon Galilee as the place of the risen Christ's reunion with the disciples. For Luke here and throughout Acts, Jerusalem is the center of Christian mission. However, that activity has to wait on the outpouring of the Holy Spirit (verse 49; Acts 1:4-8).

The second portion of our lection, verses 50-53, relates very briefly the departure of Jesus from the disciples on whom he has pronounced his blessing. The manuscript evidence for the phrase "and was carried up into heaven" (verse 51) is mixed and debated, but if it is absent here, the account appears quite fully in Acts 1:9-11. The disciples return to Jerusalem and to the temple in particular. For Luke's story both of Jesus and of the church the temple in Jerusalem is important (Luke 2:22-38, 41-51; Acts 2:46–3:1; 22:17). The disciples' waiting for the Holy Spirit was in joy, praise (verses 52-53), and constant prayer (Acts 1:14).

Mark 16:9-16, 19-20

Mark 16:9-16, 19-20 is the alternate reading for today. If this lection is used, the preacher will want to study to a point of clarity about this longer ending of Mark (verses 9-20). The various English translations handle it differently. The editors of the RSV have reversed their position, omitting verses 9-20 in 1946, but including them in 1971. Because the listeners use a number of different translations, the use of this lection almost demands some opening remarks of clarification. It should be pointed out, however, that the issue is not uncertainty about the truth contained in these verses. In fact, the material in Mark 16:9-20, with the exception of verses 17-18, is found in the closing paragraphs of Matthew, Luke, and John. In this writer's judgment, the longer ending of Mark is, in fact, a composition of lines from the other Gospels.

This lection is composed of four elements: (1) appearances to Mary Magdalene, to the two walking in the country, and to the Eleven (for these appearances recorded elsewhere, see John 20:1-18; Luke 24:13-35, 36-43); (2) the commission to evangelize the world (a variation of Matt. 28:18-20 but with the addition of supporting signs); (3) the declaration of Christ's ascension and enthronement; and (4) a summary of the disciples' missionary activity. With the closing summary, this Gospel has more of a conclusion, a finish, than the other Gospels. With the others the reader is left with "to be continued" and a sense of an assignment. Mark closes more like a history than a sermon.

However, in using this alternate reading the preacher will want to keep ascension before the listeners. The special nature of the day provides the focus for sharing the text. This means concentrating on verse 19: "The Lord Jesus, after he had spoken to them, was taken up into heaven, and sat down at the right hand of God."

Seventh Sunday of Easter

Acts 1:6-14; Psalm 68:1-10; I Peter 4:12-14; 5:6-11; John 17:1-11

All the biblical texts for today, although expectedly different from one another in many ways, have in common two emphases: the world contains much evil and violence, some of it directed against the faithful; and those who trust in God recall the former deliverance by the Lord who rides upon the clouds and comes in the mysterious power of wind and fire. Acts 1:6-14; Psalm 68:1-10; and I Peter 4:12-14 employ such imagery to encourage the believers to be strong (I Pet. 5:6-11) and to be in prayer (Acts 1:6-14). In John 17:1-11 it is Christ who prays that his followers will remain true and faithful in an unfaithful world.

Acts 1:6-14

The first part of Acts 1 (verses 1-11) has been treated under Ascension Day. We will concentrate our remarks here on the second section of the chapter (verses 12-14).

After Christ's ascension into heaven, the disciples return to Jerusalem from Mt. Olivet (verse 12). Luke notes that it was only "a sabbath day's journey away," a half mile or so. This incidental note about distance serves to keep events located in and around Jerusalem. A similar preoccupation is seen in Luke 24, where all the events recorded occur within close range of Jerusalem. For Luke, Jerusalem is more than a geographical location. It has great theological significance, for there is where God's prophet was destined to meet his death (Luke 13:33). Jerusalem was also to be the gathering place for the newly established messianic community. The disciples are thus urged by the risen Lord to stay close by and await the promise of the Spirit (Acts 1:4). From here, the kingdom of God would emanate to the ends of the earth (Acts 1:8).

Luke takes time to record the names of the eleven apostles. They are to form the nucleus of the messianic community, but not before the Eleven are restored to the original Twelve. The replacement of Judas by Matthias serves to reconstitute the full apostolic circle (Acts 1:15-26). The number is important for Luke, for the Twelve serve to represent the tribes of Israel, and they are now to function as God's representatives in the newly established kingdom of God (cf. Luke 22:29-30).

This list takes its place alongside other such lists of the apostles (Matt. 10:2-4; Mark 3:16-19; Luke 6:13-16; cf. John 1:40-49). It is remarkable in several respects. For instance, it is unusual in naming Peter and John first, instead of the usual grouping together of brothers. This is probably because they emerge in the later narrative as apostolic colleagues (cf. 3:1, 3, 4, 11; 4:13, 19; 8:14). James is in the prominent third position, likely because his death is recorded later in the narrative (Acts 12:1-2). The others fade from the story, except in those various references to the apostles as a group (cf. 2:14, 37, 42, 43; 4:35; 5:12; *passim*).

Luke stresses the solidarity among the group: "All these with one accord devoted themselves to prayer" (verse 14). As the apostolic circle expands to include other members of the messianic community, a similar spirit of unity and harmony prevails (2:46; 4:24; 5:12).

In addition to the Apostles, the nucleus of the faithful include "the women and Mary the mother of Jesus, and . . . his brothers" (verse 14). Earlier in the Gospel of Luke, women played a prominent role as close associates of Jesus in his ministry (Luke 8:2) and were among those who observed his crucifixion (Luke 23:49). Members of his family as well were counted among his close followers (Luke 8:19-21; cf. Mark 3:31-35; Matt. 12:46-50; cf. Matt. 13:55; John 2:1, 12; 6:42; 7:3; 19:25).

With this description, we are pointed toward Pentecost. By this time, the company of believers numbered some one hundred and twenty (1:15). After the selection of Judas' successor, the stage is set for the dramatic outpouring of the Spirit (2:1-4).

Psalm 68:1-10

Like Psalm 47, this psalm is built around the imagery of a grand procession. The procession is, on the one hand, that of God's worshipers (verse 27) and, on the other hand, that of God himself (verse 24). Again we should probably think of this psalm as used originally in an annual celebration that commemorated the kingship of God and his victory over his and the nation's enemies.

Some general features of the psalm should be noted as backdrop for verses 1-10.

1. Military imagery—battles, victories, the gore of battle, the distribution of war spoils—abounds throughout the psalm. This would suggest the psalm's usage in victory celebrations following warfare or that the psalm was used in the fall New Year festival when God's triumph over his enemies was celebrated.

2. The procession of God depicts him as coming from Mt. Sinai to take up his residence in Zion or on his sacred mountain (verses 7-8, 15-17). The procession is pictured as a journey through the wilderness accompanied by rainstorms and earthquakes.

3. The description of the procession of the people blends into the description of the procession of God (see verses 24-27). The people accompanying God (see Ps. 24:7-10) participate in music-making, dancing, and singing (see II Sam. 6:12-15).

The first ten verses of this psalm are comprised of human to human address (verses 1-6) and human to divine address (verses 7-10). Verses 1-3 are what might be called an indirect request; it asks that God do something but does not ask God directly. The request takes the form of a double wish: destroy the enemies (verses 1-2) and bless the righteous (verse 3). Obviously the righteous are those singing the psalm.

In the call to praise God, in verse 4, we find probably an ancient but infrequently used designation for the Divine— "him who rides upon the clouds." Even this translation is somewhat uncertain as the RSV marginal note indicates. The imagery elsewhere in the psalm, however, suggests a close association between God and storms and thus the correctness of this translation.

The description of God in verses 5-6 emphasizes his support, care, and responsibility for the powerless and dispossessed in Israel: the fatherless (perhaps illegitimate and abandoned children rather than orphans), the widows (who had no male to defend them in a patriarchal culture), the desolate (perhaps those without either social support in the form of families or clans or the economically uprooted), and the captives. The final line of verse 6 provides a summarizing statement on the wicked in general. God's work is not just positive and protective; it is also negative and destructive.

An epiphany of God is the subject of verses 7-10. Perhaps the description of God's appearance here has a thunderstorm as the background for the imagery. Several features of this description are noteworthy: (1) God marches at the head of his people, probably as they process to the sanctuary; (2) God comes from, or at least is associated with, Mt. Sinai, the old traditional mountain of God; (3) thunderstorm and rainfall accompany his appearance; such imagery and interests would have been right at home in the fall festival which celebrated the close of the old year and the beginning of the rainy season inaugurating a new agricultural year; and (4) God's coming restores and rejuvenates the people and offers them new hope for the time ahead.

I Peter 4:12-14; 5:6-11

With this reading from First Peter, we come to the end of selections from this epistle that began on the Second Sunday of Easter. The passage actually has two parts, but they are linked by the common theme of suffering, which, as we have seen, is a constant concern addressed in First Peter. The second part of today's passage is especially appropriate for this day because it provides a powerful ending to the season of Easter celebration. We are confronted with the God who calls us, who also restores, establishes, and strengthens us (5:10). To this God belongs everlasting dominion (5:11).

Once again, suffering is spoken of in stark, realistic terms, here as "the fiery ordeal which comes upon you" (4:12). The image of fire recalls the earlier reference to gold that is tested and refined by fire (1:7). This may be an allusion to the celebrated burning of Rome in A.D. 64 and Nero's blaming the Roman Christians for arson.

The text also speaks of suffering reproach "for the name of Christ" (4:14), and the possibility is later allowed that one may "suffer as a Christian" (4:16). This is an unusual reference because it is one of the rare instances in the New Testament where the word "Christian" occurs (cf. Acts 11:26; 26:28). It suggests a time when followers of Christ were already distinguishable as a separate religious group in the Roman world. It may suggest that they had no legitimate legal status and that simply bearing the name "Christian" was a criminal offense.

That this was the case in the second century is clear. Justin Martyr wrote his "Second Apology" protesting the execution of three persons merely because they bore the name Christian rather than because of any illegal or immoral conduct. In the late second century, Athenagoras wrote an apology addressed to Marcus Aurelius, asking, "Why is a mere name odious to you? Names are not deserving of hatred; it is the unjust act that calls for penalty and punishment." Tertullian made a similar protest in his typically memorable fashion, "No name of a crime stands against us, but only the crime of a name." He went on to ask, "What crime, what offence, what fault is there in a name?"

Several responses to suffering are suggested in today's text.

First, suffering should not take us by surprise (4:12). When Christians are forced to endure pain for the sake of Christ, we should not act as if "something strange were happening" (4:12). Suffering is part and parcel of the Christian experience. It should not be considered exceptional. Yet it is not as if this were a uniquely Christian approach. Traditionally, it is expected that the righteous will be tested through suffering (cf. Wisd. of Sol. 3:4-5; Sir. 2:1).

Second, suffering should be an occasion for rejoicing (4:13). This is not an unqualified remark, however. It is not as if we should find some twisted delight in having to undergo pain. It is rather that, given the choice between grinning and grimacing in the face of suffering, we should find it within ourselves to view it positively rather than negatively. Meeting various trials should be done in a way that produces steadfastness and a refined will (James 1:2; Matt. 5:11-12). There are, however, occasions when it should be a source of pride to endure rather than cave in under pressure (cf. Acts 5:41; II Thess. 1:4). Some things are more important even than life itself.

There is also a future dimension. How we respond to suffering here helps shape our future responses and finally our participation with Christ when he is revealed in glory (4:13; cf. I Cor. 1:7; Phil. 3:20; II Thess. 1:7; also Rom. 8:17).

Third, our suffering should link us to the suffering of Christ (4:13). The condition for being joyful in suffering is that we "share Christ's sufferings" (4:13). The word for share is *koinoneo*, which suggests full participation. In another context, Paul speaks of completing "what is lacking in Christ's afflictions" (Col. 1:24). Both passages suggest that we should not think of Christ's suffering merely in terms of the historical event of the cross, as if when he finally died his suffering ended. It is rather that his suffering on the cross symbolized a much larger, more enduring part of his experience that continues on into the life of the church.

Fourth, we should view our suffering in solidarity with others who suffer (5:9). We all know the relief and strength we gain when we find others who have experienced pain in ways that we have. We discover that our form of suffering is not unique to us. We also learn from one another ways of coping effectively. We also come to realize that suffering is larger than any one of us and that we stand linked with the rest of humanity in our frailty and limitations.

Fifth, instead of detaching us from God, suffering connects us with God (4:14; 5:10-11). We are assured that the "spirit of glory and of God" will rest on us (4:14; cf. Isa. 11:2). Also, we are promised that the God who has called us (I Thess. 2:12; 5:24; II Pet. 1:3) will also "restore, establish and strengthen" us (5:10; II Thess. 3:3). This is a worthwhile reminder, because the common assumption is that where pain and suffering are present, God is absent. Our text assures us that this is precisely where God is present.

It is in this overall context that we should read the general exhortations in 5:6-8. We are called on to define ourselves properly before God in humility (5:6; cf. James 4:10). Anxieties are bound to come, but they should be entrusted to the God who cares (5:7; cf. Ps. 55:22; also Matt. 6:25-34; Luke 12:22-32; Phil. 4:6; I Tim. 6:6, 8; also Wisd. of Sol. 12:13). We are to be alert in the presence of evil: "be sober, be watchful" (Mark 13:37; Matt. 24:42; Acts 20:31; I Cor. 16:13; I Thess. 5:6, 8, 10; II Tim. 4:5). We should not face the world naïvely as if good can overcome evil without a struggle (5:8; James 4:7; Eph. 6:11-13, 16).

John 17:1-11

The Gospel for today is a portion of Jesus' farewell prayer for his disciples. This prayer follows the discourses of chapters 14–16 and immediately precedes the arrest in the garden (18:1-12). While the prayer is set within the ministry of the historical Jesus, the perspective of the prayer is also that of the glorified Christ looking pastorally on his church in the world. Notice: "And now I am no more in the world" (verse 11); "While I was with them" (verse 12); and "But now I am coming to thee" (verse 13). The prayer seems, then, to hang between heaven and earth, between the historical and the glorified Christ. But this characteristic is not confined to this prayer; this Evangelist unites the two, often indistinguishably, throughout the Gospel.

Those who speak of John 17 as more a sermon than a prayer properly identify the homiletical quality of Jesus' prayers in this Gospel (11:42; 12:30). However, two comments are in order: First, the Bible words addressed to the people and words addressed to God are often interwoven. Psalm 23 and Moses' farewell speech (Deut. 32–33) are two examples. Sermons are prayerful and prayers are sermonic. Second, the reader can best experience John 17 as a parishioner listening to a pastoral prayer. Such a listener overhears, is involved, and is represented in the prayer but not, of course, addressed by it.

The prayer in John 17 consists of three movements: Jesus' own return to glory (verses 1-5); intercession for the disciples (verses 6-19); and intercession for the readers who are disciples at least once removed (verses 20-26). Our lection includes the first movement and part of the second. The first movement (verses 1-5) gathers up in summary fashion several major themes of this Gospel. One has to do with Jesus' "hour." Jesus' ministry unfolded according to his hour (2:4; 7:6), and his death likewise (7:30; 12:23; 13:1). This Evangelist is persistent in his view that the life and death of Jesus were not contingent on circumstances, family, friends, or enemies, but on the will of God. The Christ of this Gospel came from God, knows God, and returns to God (13:3). This perspective provides a second major theme: God's purpose extends beyond Jesus to the church as those whom God has given to Jesus (6:36-40, 65; 17:2). This "all things are from God" viewpoint does not rob us of responsibility, but it gives encouragement to those so overwhelmed as a minority group in a hostile world that they can easily nurse a victim mentality. To say God's will prevails not only supports the believers but also reminds them of the radical grace that has taken initiative in Christ for our salvation. That initiative cannot be finally countered by any force that seeks to destroy. This thought introduces a third theme; God's offer is eternal life (verse 3; 3:16, 36; 5:24; 11:25-26). And finally, this life eternal is a relationship with God, here called "knowing God," which is possible through faith in Jesus Christ. This, says John, was the purpose of Christ's coming, to reveal the God whom no one has ever seen (1:18).

The second movement of the prayer (verses 6-19; our lection ends at verse 11) concerns the apostles, the original band of disciples. One might wonder why include intercessions for a group who were probably deceased at the time of the writing of this Gospel. One answer lies within the petitions themselves: the apostles were given of God to Jesus (verse 6); Jesus gave to them the word of God (verses 6-8); they had received, believed, and kept that word (verses 6-8); they had not been corrupted by the unbelieving world in which they had to live and work (verses 9-11). All of this is to assure the church of the clear and authoritative continuity between Jesus and the church. In chapters 14–16, the tie between Jesus and the church was presented in terms of the Holy Spirit; here that tie is the apostles. The Evangelist leaves no one in doubt: the church is not an orphan in the world, an accident of history, a thing dislodged, the frightened child of huddled rumors and superstitions. The pedigree of truth is established and unbroken: from God, to Christ, to the apostles, to the church.

Pentecost

Acts 2:1-21 or *Isaiah 44:1-8; Psalm 104:24-34; I Corinthians 12:3b-13* or *Acts 2:1-21; John 20:19-23* or *John 7:37-39*

Pentecost concludes the Easter season because the resurrection of Christ has its promise fulfilled in the giving of the Holy Spirit to the church. The name of the day itself and the powerful image of the coming of the Holy Spirit like the sound of rushing wind and as the appearance of tongues like fire are given to us in the account of Acts 2:1-21 (which may function either as the Old Testament lesson or the epistle). However, the other readings provide rich and meaningful expressions of the giving of the Spirit of God: "poured" (Isa. 44:1-8); "sendest forth" (Ps. 104:24-34); "varieties of gifts, but the same Spirit" (I Cor. 12:3b-13); "breathed on" (John 20:19-23); and "rivers of living water" (John 7:37-39).

Acts 2:1-21

The celebration of Pentecost as a Christian feast day is linked directly with this first lesson from Acts, in which Luke gives his account of the church's beginning. The place is Jerusalem within the temple precincts and the time is the day of Pentecost.

This is only one of three references in the New Testament to the Jewish feast of Pentecost (cf. Acts 20:16; I Cor. 16:8). It was one of the three most important Jewish festivals, along with Passover (the Feast of Unleavened Bread) and the Feast of Tabernacles, or the Feast of Booths. It was also known as the Feast of Weeks (Exod. 23:16; 34:22; Num. 28:2), because it was observed seven weeks after Passover (Lev. 23:15-21). Accordingly, it came to be designated Pentecost ("fiftieth") since it was celebrated on the fiftieth day after the sabbath on which Passover began.

In Christian practice, it occurred fifty days after Easter, although the entire season from Easter to Whitsunday, or Pentecost, was observed as a time of festivity and joy. No fasts were observed during this period, and it was the practice to pray in a standing position to symbolize the resurrection of Christ.

In today's text, we have the first portion of Acts 2, which includes an opening description of the day's events (verses 1-4), a detailed roster of those in attendance (verses 5-11), their response to these events (verses 12-13), and the first section of Peter's sermon (verses 15-21), the major part of which is a quotation from the prophet Joel (verses 17-21). Let us consider the text in these three sections.

1. *The coming of the Spirit* (verses 1-4). As the band of faithful followers of Jesus, who are described earlier (1:12-14), are gathered in one place, they experience a shattering noise that is accompanied by a spectacular vision. It should be noted that by this time in Jewish history, Pentecost had come to be observed as the anniversary for the giving of the Law at Sinai (cf. Jubilees 1:1; 6:17). The Old Testament describes this event as accompanied by deafening sounds and dazzling sights (Exod. 19:16-24). Such imagery is typically used to dramatize moments of divine revelation (cf. Judg. 5:4-5; Ps. 18:8-16; 29:4-9; I Kings 19:11-13).

It is against this background that we should understand Luke's account. It is an equally dramatic moment in that God is now being manifested through the Spirit. Something as significant, indeed more significant than, the giving of the Law is occurring.

2. *The universal audience* (verses 5-11). Luke takes the trouble to itemize all the nations represented at this event. As an annual feast of great importance, Pentecost became an occasion for pilgrims to come to Jerusalem. Those who would make the trek would be "devout [Jews] from every nation under heaven" (verse 5). The nations are doubtless mentioned because of the common conception that the final messianic ingathering would be a time when Jews from every part of the earth would stream to Jerusalem to participate in God's restoration of Israel (Isa. 2:2-4; Mic. 4:1-4). This vision became translated into eschatological hopes, and thus

described what the New Age would be. Against this background, Peter claims these to be the events of "the last days" (verse 17).

3. *The response of the audience and Peter's sermon* (verses 12-21). The effect of various people's speaking in other tongues was dumbfounding and perplexing. The apostles are accused of being drunk, which Peter denies (verse 15). Instead, these marvelous signs point to this event as the fulfillment of Joel's eschatological vision (Joel 2:28-32*a*).

The quotation from Joel has several prominent features: (1) God's Spirit would be poured out on all flesh, Jews and Gentiles alike; (2) a variety of persons, male and female, young and old, would become spokespersons for the Spirit and would prophesy; (3) the inbreaking of the New Age would be accompanied by a host of signs both visible and audible; and (4) the universal quest for salvation would be answered.

This quotation becomes programmatic for the rest of Acts. We see the people of God come to include Gentiles as well as Jews. Various prophetic figures emerge through whom God's message is spoken. At every turn, as the Spirit impels the church to new action, there is a visible display of signs and wonders to attest the presence of God. In case after case, individuals and groups of individuals are confronted with the Word of God, they ask what they must do, and they are extended God's invitation to call on the name of the Lord.

The mood of today's text fits the spirit of Pentecost. Festive it is, even rollicking. Luke wants us to see that a New Age has broken in, that the people of God are being reconstituted. The work of Christ begun at Easter is coming to fruition as the people of Christ become empowered with the Spirit.

Isaiah 44:1-8

This passage has been assigned, originally for reading during the Pentecost Vigil and then as a lection for Pentecost, primarily because it contains the promise that God will pour out his Spirit and the people of God will be transformed. In addition to that particular contribution to the occasion, Isaiah 44:1-8 assists us in two other ways. It furthers our theological reflection on the Spirit of God and it supports the mood of joyous celebration appropriate for the day.

The mood of enthusiastic and animated gladness is typical of the speeches of this prophet, Second Isaiah. His proclamations both express the joy of the good news he brings and mean to evoke happiness in his audience. That audience would have consisted of the Babylonian exiles from Judah, ca. 539 B.C., just before the end of the Exile. Obviously a great many of them had lost all hope of returning to their homeland, the land promised to the patriarchs and given to them in the time of Joshua. Their hopelessness was one of the impediments to the actualization of the good news that the prophet proclaimed. So one of the tasks Second Isaiah faced was that of kindling expectations that God would act to save them.

Today's reading is a prophetic address that begins with a traditional call to attention that identifies the addressees: "But now hear, O Jacob my servant, Israel whom I have chosen" (verse 1; cf. Amos 3:1; 4:1; 5:1; Isa. 1:2, 10). It contains messenger formulas ("Thus says the Lord," verses 2, 6) that indicate the prophet is not speaking for himself; the speaker clearly is God. In terms of both form and contents, the passage contains two distinct units. The first, verses 1-5, is a proclamation or announcement of salvation, concerning the immediate future. The second, verses 6-8, is a divine disputation in which God speaks to argue that there is no other god. The larger section of which our text is a part (Isa. 43:8–44:8) is a poetic imitation of a legal process in which the question of who is God is argued. Verses 6-8 conclude that all others are pretenders, beyond comparison with God, and insist that the people of Israel can testify as witnesses to this fact. They know that God announced events before they happened and then they came to pass. What ties the two units together is a phrase they have in common, "Fear not" (verses 2, 8). The expression is a salvation oracle, long known in Israelite worship and prayer, a formula pronounced by priests or prophets to people in trouble who petitioned God. It means what it says—the people should no longer fear—but it also conveys the sense that God has heard the people's deepest prayers and means to act on their behalf.

These eight verses contain the basic message of Second Isaiah. Above all, Yahweh is about to intervene to save Israel, his chosen and beloved people (verses 1-2), from their distress. Their problems are "spiritual," but they are also concrete and physical. Thus the Lord will bring them back to their land, giving them their freedom. Here that promise is stated somewhat metaphorically in the allusions to "water on the thirsty land" (verse 3a), suggesting the return to Israel through the desert (cf. Isa. 40:3, 17-20). The foundation for that message of good news is the affirmation that Israel's God is in fact God, the only one. This confession insists that God is both powerful ("king") and loving ("redeemer," verse 6a).

The distinctive motif in this passage is the announcement of the gift of the Spirit of God, and its effects (verses 3-5). The pouring out of the Spirit upon the people of God is compared to pouring "water on the thirsty land" and is parallel to the granting of divine blessing. The Spirit of God is an extension of God's will, God active in and through human beings, and it brings dramatic transformations of the people to whom it is given. Two transformations are described, one metaphorically and the other quite directly. First, the people will grow and thrive "like grass amid waters, like willows by flowing streams" (verse 4); they and their descendants will receive new life with the gift of the Spirit (cf. Ezek. 37:1-14). Second, they will know and affirm who they are, saying and writing on their hands that they belong to the Lord and calling themselves by the name of Jacob or Israel (verse 6). In view of the opening lines of the address (verses 1-2), it appears that to identify with Jacob or Israel is to acknowledge that one is God's chosen servant. It is entirely possible that the gift of the Spirit is not limited to the people of Israel, but that others will now choose to identify themselves with the chosen people of God.

Thus, the outpouring of the Spirit is a gift from the one who alone is God (verses 6-8); it is given not fundamentally to individuals but to the people of God; it brings those people to life; and it enables them to know who and whose they are.

Psalm 104:24-34

An ancient Egyptian pharaoh, Akhenaton (ca. 1380–1363 B.C.), composed or had composed a hymn to the sun god Aten, which praised Aten as the only god (other than the pharaoh who claimed divinity). This ancient hymn has many parallels to Psalm 104. Whether the Hebrews copied this text from the Egyptians or not cannot be known. Perhaps the contemplation of aspects of creation in both cultures led to similar perspectives and parallel descriptions.

The selection of this lection for Pentecost Sunday is based on its emphasis on the role of God's Spirit in creation (see verse 30) and the psalm's universal perspectives. Verses 24-34, however, should be seen within the overall structure of the psalm.

The various stanzas in the psalm, excluding the summarizing depiction and the conclusion in verses 27-35, focus on the various wonders of creation: the sky (2-4), the earth (5-9), the water (10-13), the vegetation (14-18), the moon and sun (19-23), and the sea (24-26). (It is instructive to compare these with the structure and characterization of the six days of creation in Gen. 1).

The selection for the lectionary picks up with the depiction of the sixth wonder. Verses 24-34 may be divided into three units: verses 24-26 center on the sea in the world of creation, verses 27-30 offer a reflection on creation's dependence upon God, and verses 31-35 (which are no longer addressed to the Deity) marvel at the grandeur and awesomeness of the Lord of creation.

For the psalmist, the sea (verses 24-26) is God's pond, not some murky, mysterious, monster-laden source of chaos. From the ships and Leviathans (see Ps. 74:14; Job 41:1; Isa. 27:1) that ply its waves to the innumerable creatures small and great that scurry through its waters, they all have been made in the wisdom of God.

Verses 27-30 speak of what might be called "vertical universality." All living things are seen as dependent upon God—for food that fuels and sustains the living and for the breath of life that creates new being. That is, every part of life from top to bottom is the gift of God, not the possessor of that life. When God turns away, the creatures (including humans; note verse 23) become dismayed; when God withdraws his life spirit, the creatures succumb and return to dust. For all the world's greatness, for all its wonder and amazement, for the psalmist, the world is no independent entity. Without divine sustenance it would not survive. Creation is depicted so that, in the words of the Heidelberg Catechism, God "rules in such a way that waves and grass, rain and drought, fruitful and unfruitful years, food and drink, death and sickness, riches and poverty and everything else come to us not by chance, but by his fatherly hand."

The psalm concludes with a confessional statement addressed to a human audience (verses 31-35). These verses affirm gratitude and praise for the grandeur of the cosmos and its creatures and above all for the God who creates and cares.

I Corinthians 12:3b-13

This text overlaps the epistolary lection (12:1-11) for the Second Sunday After Epiphany in Year C. It also slightly overlaps the epistolary lection (12:12-30) for the Third Sunday After Epiphany in Year C. The reader may wish to consult our remarks in connection with these two settings in *Advent, Christmas, Epiphany, Year C.*

It is slightly awkward to begin the lection with the second half of verse 3, which claims that no one can confess Jesus as Lord except when motivated by the Spirit. Because the first half of the verse speaks of cursing Jesus, it is understandable why it might be thought an offensive opening for a public reading. In any case, the lection has been defined as beginning with verse 3b to highlight the role of the Spirit in the Christian confession.

The context in which today's lection occurs is Paul's discussion of spiritual gifts in I Corinthians 12–14. His remarks are given in response to a question sent him by the Corinthian church (cf. 12:1). The question had to do with either "spiritual gifts" or "spiritual persons," depending on how one renders *pneumatikoi* in 12:1. The overall issue being dealt with is Christian enthusiasm that manifests itself chiefly through glossolalia, the gift of speaking in tongues. In chapter 14, Paul provides an extensive comparison of tongues and prophecy, arguing for the superiority of the latter over the former, at least in this particular situation. As often happens, those who specialized in speaking in tongues apparently came to assume that their gift was of paramount importance, and that every member should aspire to this as the highest manifestation of spirituality. For them, it would be better for every one to have the same gift (assuming that it is the chief gift) than for there to be a plurality of gifts.

It is in response to this theology of uniformity that Paul crafts his remarks in today's text. Throughout his remarks, he underscores the preeminent importance of the Spirit, and perhaps this is what we should see especially in the context of Pentecost. Several observations are worth making.

First, the Spirit provides the primary impulse for making the Christian confession (verse 3*b*). The New Testament recognizes that there are various ways in which people can say, "Lord." But the mere utterance of the word is not self-authenticating; confession must be embodied in appropriate forms of obedience (Matt. 7:21; Luke 6:46). The name that is confessed should appropriately correspond to the One confessed (John 13:13). The heart of the Christian confession is that "*Jesus* is Lord" (italics added, Rom. 10:9; II Cor. 4:5; Phil. 2:11; Col. 2:6; I John 5:1), and this, Paul contends, can only be done "in the Spirit," or "under the influence of the Holy Spirit" (NEB, JB).

Second, the Spirit is the source of the various gifts in the church (verses 4-11). Paul insists that diversity is axiomatic in the life of the church. In the church there are "varieties of gifts . . . varieties of service . . . varieties of working" (verses 4-5). Whether one thinks in terms of personal gifts, ministerial functions, or forms of activity, diversity is the norm, not the exception.

It is perhaps with a slight bit of irony that Paul makes this point in trinitarian terms: the same Spirit, the same Lord, the same God. Even God can be spoken of in terms of diversity! But even with this division of labor, the accent lies on the Spirit, which is singled out as the common source in his exposition of the various gifts. The sheer repetition of the phrase "the same Spirit" (verses 4, 8, 9, and 11) would have a hammering effect. He intends his readers to see that the Spirit cannot be straitjacketed. The one Spirit "distributes different gifts to different people" at will (verse 11, JB; cf. Rom. 12:6; Heb. 2:4).

Third, the Spirit is the unifying force within the body of Christ (verses 12-13). Paul reminds us that Christ himself is multi-membered (verse 12). We should note the line of his argument: just as the human body is one yet has many parts, *so it is with Christ.* Apparently this was not self-evident to some of the Corinthians. There is one Christ, Paul insists, but our participation in the one Christ must be conceived in diverse terms.

Naturally the danger in a theology of pluriformity is that the church will lose its organizing center and be flung apart. But the cohesive force within the church, Paul insists, is the Spirit. The Spirit is both the agent and medium in which we were baptized. In one sense, it is the Spirit who baptized us, and it is also the Spirit who is the sphere in which we have our existence in Christ. Regardless of our ethnic or social status, we all drank from the common source of the Spirit (verse 13; cf. Gal. 3:28).

Fourth, the Spirit works for the common good (verse 7). A theology of pluriformity works as long as the various gifts are deployed for a common purpose: the upbuilding of the whole church. One of the consistent tests that Paul applies in his churches is to ask whether a certain attitude or activity "edifies" (I Cor. 6:12; 10:23; 14:26). Similarly, here he insists that diversity only becomes productive when we each exercise our gift(s) in the interest of others (cf. 10:33).

In the context of Pentecost, Paul's words in today's text point the way toward a vital theology of the Spirit that energizes rather than enervates the church.

John 20:19-23

Pentecost completes Easter. Without Pentecost, Easter must carry all the pathos of saying farewell to a Christ who rises to return to glory. Without Pentecost, Easter reminds the church that Jesus has now gone to be with God and his followers are left alone in the world. Without Pentecost, Easter offers us a risen Christ whose return to glory leaves the church to face the world armed with nothing but fond memories of how it once was when Jesus was here. But with Pentecost, Easter's Christ promises to return and has returned in the Holy Spirit as comforter, guide, teacher, reminder, and power. With Pentecost, the church does not simply celebrate but participates in Easter. With Pentecost, the risen Christ says hello and not good-bye to the church.

Because Luke has elaborated on Pentecost in a dramatic and powerful narrative, his account (Acts 2:1-21) has tended to govern the thoughts and images spawned by the firm and central Christian belief that the Holy Spirit was and is a gift of God to the church. However, the Gospel of John makes the same affirmation; concise to be sure, but it contains the basic elements of the conviction: the Holy Spirit is from God through the crucified and risen Christ; the Holy Spirit is associated with the commission of Christ to the church to continue his mission in the world; and the Holy Spirit empowers the apostles to give authoritative leadership to the church. This, in essence, is the content of John 20:19-23. This text received our attention as the Gospel lesson for the Second Sunday of Easter and further comments on it can be found there. We will here devote the remainder of our commentary to the alternate Gospel lection.

John 7:37-39

The major portion of the discussion of the Holy Spirit in the Fourth Gospel is confined to the farewell section; that is, to chapters 14–20. That location of the discussion is appropriate because the coming of the Holy Spirit is consistently presented as subsequent to the resurrection and exaltation of Jesus. "If I do not go away, the Counselor will not come to you; but if I go, I will send him to you" (16:7). The brief account of the giving of the Spirit to the disciples (20:19-23) involves the post-resurrection Christ. Given this scheme—Jesus is raised, receives the Spirit from God, and gives it to the disciples—any mention of the Holy Spirit earlier in the Gospel would have to be anticipatory; that is, in the framework of Jesus' earthly ministry, an offer of the Holy Spirit would be a future promise.

This is precisely the case in 7:37-39. Earlier, in the conversation between Jesus and Nicodemus (3:1-15), the Holy Spirit is referred to as essential to the birth from above, and that birth is of both water and Spirit. Close examination of that conversation, however, reveals that its perspective is post-resurrection, but set within the framework of Jesus' earthly ministry. For example, verse 13 states, "No one has ascended into heaven but he who descended from heaven, the Son of man." Statements about the Spirit are offered by Jesus who, from the writer's angle of vision, "has ascended into heaven." Likewise, in 7:37-39 the Spirit is associated with water (verse 38) and is promised subsequent to Jesus' ascension in glory (verse 39). The promise of living water is reminiscent of the conversation between Jesus and the Samaritan woman (4:4-26) and of Isaiah 44:1-5. Apparently the association of the Spirit with water in baptism was rather widespread in the early church (Mark 1:9-11 and parallels; Acts 2:38; I Cor. 12:13). The union of the Spirit with the image of drinking (verse 37) may be an association of the gift of the Spirit with the Eucharist. This seems to be the case in I Corinthians 12:13: "and all were made to drink of one Spirit."

But regardless of whether the gift of the Spirit was and is joined to baptism or the Eucharist or both, the promise itself is repeatedly and consistently made. Jesus crucified, dead, and buried, who sits in glory at the right hand of God, sent and sends the Holy Spirit to sustain and to nourish the church in its life together and in its mission to the world.

Annunciation, March 25

Isaiah 7:10-14; Psalm 45 or 40:6-10; Hebrews 10:4-10;
Luke 1:26-38

March 25, exactly nine months prior to the date for celebrating Jesus' birth, is observed in some traditions as the day of the Annunciation. Central to the observance is Luke's story of the visit of the angel Gabriel to Mary in Nazareth of Galilee (1:26-38). However, the other readings gather around Luke 1 in strong support and in meaningful elaboration. Isaiah 7:10-14 prophesies the birth of a child to be called Immanuel. Hebrews draws on both Psalm 40:6-10 (10:4-10), and Psalm 45 (1:8-9) for its portrait of the preexistent Son, crowned, sceptered, and anointed, coming from his eternal home into the world to become as we are that we might become as he is. Needless to say, even though March 25 comes during Lent it is a day of joyful anticipation.

Isaiah 7:10-14

This passage from the Book of Isaiah provides important background for the Lucan account of the Annunciation. Central here is the prophecy of a birth as a sign of God's intentions toward his people. Moreover, the name of that child, "Immanuel," which means "God is with us," is an interpretation of the Lord's will. Although we now recognize that Isaiah had in view a particular woman and child in his own time, and not Mary and her son Jesus, the ancient promise still has its contribution to make to Christian worship.

Some of the literary and historical questions concerning our passage can be answered with relative certainty. It is one of a number of reports of encounters in Jerusalem between Isaiah and King Ahaz at a particularly critical moment in the

246

history of Judah. The historical situation is summarized in Isaiah 7:1-2 and spelled out further in II Kings 16:1-20. When the Assyrian king, Tiglath-pileser III, started to move against the small states of Syria and Palestine, the leaders of those states began to form a coalition to oppose him. Apparently because Ahaz of Judah refused to join them, the kings in Damascus and Samaria moved against Jerusalem (ca. 734 B.C.), to topple Ahaz and replace him with someone more favorable to their policies. In the passage (7:1-9) that immediately precedes our reading, Isaiah counseled nonresistence based on faith in the ancient promise to David that one of his sons would always occupy the throne in Jerusalem. The fact that our unit begins with the expression, "Again the Lord spoke to Ahaz" (verse 10), indicates that it is a continuation of the prophet's actions in the same situation.

Isaiah 7:10-14 is good news in the form of a prophetic symbolic action, especially to the king but also to the people as a whole. Note that the entire section is presented as if the Lord himself is speaking directly to King Ahaz, but it would have been the prophet who conveyed the message. In the previous unit Ahaz had been afraid. Here he refuses even to inquire of the Lord, even when Isaiah instructs him to do so (verses 11-12). It was common for kings or other leaders to inquire of the Lord, often through prophets, before deciding to go to battle (see II Kings 13:14-19). When Ahaz refuses to ask for a sign, the prophet becomes impatient and says that the Lord himself will give a sign: "Behold, a young woman shall conceive and bear a son, and shall call his name Immanuel" (verse 14). He goes on to interpret the sign, promising that before the child knows how to "refuse the evil and choose the good," that is within a short time, the present military threat will have ended. Although the means are not stated, the prophet promises that God will intervene to save his people.

Few textual and translation problems in the Old Testament have generated more controversy than those of Isaiah 7:14. However, there can be little doubt about the meaning or translation of the crucial word. The Hebrew word *'almah* is correctly rendered by the RSV and almost all other modern translations "young woman." The term is neutral with regard to her marital status. It was the Greek translation of the Book of Isaiah, the Septuagint, that read "virgin" (Greek *parthenos*), thus setting the stage for the particular messianic interpretation of the passage expressed in the New Testament. The bridge between the eighth century and the early church is thus yet another historical and theological context, the translation of the Hebrew scriptures for Jews in a Hellenistic, pre-Christian culture. It is equally clear that the Book of Isaiah originally read here "young woman" and that the Evangelists inherited a translation of Isaiah that read "virgin."

As in most other prophetic announcements or symbolic actions, Isaiah has the immediate future in view, and thus the woman and child are his contemporaries. In fact, verse 14 probably is best translated, "Look, a young woman is pregnant and will bear a son" (cf. NEB and RSV footnote). But the identity of the woman is difficult if not impossible to establish. In view of a context that stresses the significance of the Davidic dynasty, many commentators have taken the child to be the crown prince, and the woman as the wife of Ahaz. Others, seeing the passage in some ways parallel to Isaiah 8:1-4, have argued that the woman was the wife of the prophet and the child his son. It is quite likely, however, that the "young woman" was simply a pregnant woman whom Isaiah saw as he was addressing the king.

One of the keys to the meaning of this passage is the word "sign" (Hebrew *'oth*). It is the same word used in the tradition about the "signs and wonders" performed in Egypt before the Exodus, and thus has come to be associated in our minds with the so-called miraculous. However, it may refer to ordinary events as well as extraordinary ones. The decisive point in the Old Testament view is that a "sign" is revelatory, that it communicates God's word, will, or nature. Thus, it is not remarkable that in Isaiah 7 something as common as the birth of a baby boy is a message from God, and concerns the future. The name embodies the promise of God's saving presence.

To be sure, it is hardly possible for Christians to hear this passage and not think of the coming of Jesus. But in addition to directing our attention to the Incarnation, Isaiah 7:10-14 has its own good news. It is a message that sees pregnancy and birth—even when not understood as miraculous—as signs of God's concern for his people. Furthermore, this message is directed to a people living in chaos and fear, faced with such specific problems as international politics and the threat of destruction. Even in such a situation, the word of God offers hope.

Psalm 45

Tradition has long associated this psalm with Christ and the Incarnation. No doubt written by some court composer—a poet laureate at the Jerusalem court—the psalm is addressed to humans, to the reigning king and his bride-to-be. After an opening introduction (verse 1), the king (verses 2-9) and the bride (verses 10-15) are addressed in order before the king is extolled in the concluding words (verses 16-17).

In associating this wedding song with the Annunciation to Mary and the Incarnation, the early church took certain liberties with the "original" meaning of the text. Hebrews 1:8-9 connects this psalm with Jesus and uses it to argue that Jesus "the son of God" is superior to angels. That the psalm had been understood to refer to the Messiah in pre-Christian Judaism helps explain its utilization by the early church.

References to the king and the bride in the text have been generally approached in one of four ways.

1. One line of interpretation is what might be called the metaphorical approach. This assumes that the marriage described is simply a conventional wedding. The normal, everyday groom is described in metaphorical language as a "king" and the bride as a "princess."

2. A second approach can be called the mythological. This assumes that the wedding partners are actually the male deity, played by the king, and the female goddess, played by the queen.

3. A third approach is the allegorical. The king in the text stands for Yahweh and the bride is his chosen people. What is said in the text is not to be taken literally but allegorically.

249

4. A fourth interpretation is the historical. This assumes that the text was composed for an actual wedding for an actual ancient Israelite or Judean king. Since the text refers to Tyre, it has sometimes been assumed that the psalm was composed for the marriage of King Ahab of Israel to the Phoenician princess Jezebel who hailed from the city of Tyre.

The association of this text with the Annunciation strains any reading of the text unless one wants to understand the king in the text as God and the bride as the Virgin Mary. The more common Christian interpretation is to relate the figure of the king to that of Jesus as is already done in Hebrews 1:8-9. If Jesus is identified with the groom, the bride is best understood as the church, not as Mary. At any rate, any exegesis of the text that Christianizes the interpretation forces the imagery considerably.

Four features in the psalm can be easily interpreted in commemoration of the Annunciation. (1) The theme of the psalm, even if only implied, is the theme of love. The opening heading to the psalm alerts the reader to its theme: "a love song." Divine love for the human condition undergirds the Incarnation. (2) Another theme is that of union, in this psalm, the union of man and woman, groom and bride. In the allegory of Christian theology, the union is between the divine and human, the impregnation of Mary by the Holy Spirit. (3) A third theme is royalty. The king is described as one who rules in righteousness. The Incarnation celebrates the coming of the royal one to whom God has assigned authority and royalty. (4) Finally, the psalm allows the bride to fade into the background and emphasizes her offspring instead. In the offspring, the name of the father lives on and the memory of the mother is held dear (verses 16-17). As a Davidide, Jesus, the offspring, ensured forever the line of the son of Jesse from Bethlehem.

Psalm 40:6-10

This lection is excerpted from the thanksgiving portion of a psalm probably originally used by the king. Verses 5-10 comprise the worshiper's thanksgiving spoken directly to the Deity in response to having been redeemed from some great distress (described in verses 1-3). The association of this text with and its appropriateness for the Annunciation are its emphasis on a person willingly submitting to the divine will (see especially verse 8), as was the case with Mary.

Several statements in the text require explanation. Verse 6 declares that God does not desire sacrifice. Four different types of sacrifice are referred to, some of the free-will type and others mandatory. What the verse intends to emphasize, however, is that what God really requires is a faithful, hearing attitude. The expression, "ears thou hast dug for me," probably was a proverbial way of saying, "I am really hearing you." For the worshiper, what God desires is a faithful hearing, a receptive response.

The hearing response leads to voluntary obedience (verses 7-8). In terms somewhat reminiscent of the prophet Isaiah (see Isa. 6), the person volunteers—"I come" ("Here am I"). The second half of verse 7 with its reference to the book could denote that (1) in the book of his life it is written (and preordained) that the psalmist will make the will of God the delight of living, (2) the record of the person's life kept in the divine world demonstrates that the psalmist is one delighting in obedience, or (3) the book of the law, the Torah (the Pentateuch?) was written as if speaking of the psalmist. However one understands the particulars, the affirmation is clear. The psalmist claims a complete submission to and obedience to God. "Thy law is within my inward parts" is an affirmation of the internalization of the law—inward being, the conscience, the heart, the ultimate commitments are devoted to the will of God.

Verses 9-10 affirm the public testimony of the commitment. This affirmation is stated twice positively and three times negatively. "I have told," "I have spoken," "I have not restrained my lips," "I have not hid," and "I have not concealed."

The psalmist thus delineates an action sequence pattern—sincere hearing leads to responsive commitment which leads to public exuberance, the testimony in the congregation.

Hebrews 10:4-10

What qualifies this epistolary lection as a suitable text for Annunciation is the phrase in verse 5, "when Christ came into the world . . .". This is a remarkable text within the Epistle to the Hebrews in which the stress lies less on his incarnation than on his exaltation to the heavenly sanctuary where he officiates as our great high priest. There are, however, some allusions to his "coming," e.g., 9:11, "when Christ appeared as a high priest of the good things that have come."

But our text is concerned with more than the fact of Christ's coming into the world. It intends to explain for us the motive for his coming as well as expose the interior of that motive. To achieve this, the author makes an unusual move. He attributes the words of Psalm 40:6-8 to Christ himself. We have no indication in the Gospel tradition that Christ actually quoted this psalm or that the church interpreted him in light of it. Certainly, some of the sentiments of the psalm are expressive of Christ's teachings, most notably the denigration of sacrificial offerings as the way to God's heart (cf. Matt. 9:13; 12:7). Another motif that seems to echo sentiments of Jesus as known through the Gospel tradition is the statement in verse 7, "Lo, I have come to do thy will, O God." To be sure, in this form the phrase sounds Johannine (cf. John 4:34; 5:30; 6:38-39). There is also some correspondence with the words attributed to Jesus in the tradition relating to the Gethsemane experience (cf. Mark 14:36).

But what especially intrigues the author of our text is the relationship between these two sentiments: the inefficacy of sacrifice and the primacy of obedience. The conclusion that is drawn is: "He abolishes the first in order to establish the second" (verse 9). Christ's coming is thus interpreted as a critique of the sacrificial system that results in its abolition. In its stead, he establishes the obedient will as that which pleases God. It is for this reason that our passage opens with the outright assertion, "For it is impossible that the blood of bulls and goats should take away sins" (verse 4). Why? Because they represent a form of worship that is intrinsically displeasing to God. Not only are animal sacrifices ineffective in doing what they are intended to do—take away sin—they are fundamentally the wrong kind of response to a God who is more interested in obedience than sacrifice.

It is finally the obedient will of Christ that results in his self-sacrifice, the offering of his own body "once for all" (verse 10; cf. 9:26; 10:14). This is the event in which our own purification, or sanctification, has been achieved (10:29; 13:12; cf. I Thess. 4:3; Eph. 5:2).

As we can see, today's epistolary lection takes us well beyond reflection on the single event of Christ's birth, or of its Annunciation. But it does direct our attention to the central purpose of his coming into the world. It was a mission of one who came to do the will of God. So motivated, he was not concerned with the proper protocol of making sacrificial offerings. Instead, he himself became the preeminent sacrificial offering.

Luke 1:26-38

It would be a mistake to think that the early church's sole interest in the calendar was in various attempts to ascertain the time of the end and the return of Christ. While such calculations have waxed and waned throughout the life of the church, the calendar has held other interests for Christians. Quite early there was a desire to structure the disciplines of worship and prayer on the significant hours and days in the life of Christ. Christian calendars were developed and framed primarily around the seasons of central importance, Easter and Christmas. Once a date was set for the celebration of Jesus' birth, it was only a matter of time until the day nine months earlier would be observed as the Annunciation, the day of Gabriel's visit to Mary. By thus observing March 25, the church was able to focus upon the beautiful text of Luke 1:26-38 outside the already rich and full season of Advent.

Luke says that Mary received the word of God's favor from the messenger (the meaning of the word "angel") Gabriel. In later Judaism, angels, both in the service of God and in the service of Satan, came to figure prominently in theology and in popular religion. Such beings were common in religions of

Persia and may have found a welcome in Jewish thought in a time when the distance between a transcendent God and human beings required mediators. Angels carried messages and performed other functions in God's dealings with creation. In some literature important angels were given names, Gabriel being one of the most familiar (Dan. 9:21). In the New Testament, Luke's stories are the most populated with angels, with the obvious exception of the heavenly scenes in the Apocalypse. Christians have differed in their ways of appropriating the conversation between Mary and an angel: some literally, others by means of literary, psychological, or sociological categories. The story has survived all interpretations.

Luke apparently has no need to speculate on the choice of Mary as the mother of the Christ. The point is, God has chosen her, and as in any act of divine grace, the reasons are enfolded in God's purposes and not in the recipient. The angel's message that Mary's child will be son of God and son of David is a composite of phrases and lines from Isaiah, Genesis, Second Samuel, Micah, Hosea, and Daniel. It is possible that this hymnlike expression of praise (verses 32-33) came to Luke from an early Christian liturgy. Many scholars believe that the church quite early put together Old Testament verses that were useful in worship, preaching, and teaching new members.

Mary wonders, quite naturally, how she, without a husband, can conceive and bear a son. She is given no answer that approaches biology. Rather she is given an announcement and a bit of information which functioned as a sign of the truth of the promise. The announcement was that the birth would be the work of the Holy Spirit and the power of the Most High (verse 35). In other words, Jesus of Nazareth is God's act of grace and power. The information that encourages Mary's faith is that her kinswoman Elizabeth, old and barren, is in her sixth month of pregnancy. Echoed in the Elizabeth story is that of Abraham and Sarah (Gen. 18:14). But behind the stories of Mary's, Elizabeth's, and Sarah's conceptions is the creed beneath and behind all other creeds: "For with God nothing will be impossible" (verse 37). It is to this word that Mary responds in trust and in obedience.

Scripture Reading Index